Efficiency and Competitiveness of International Airlines

Almas Heshmati · Jungsuk Kim

Efficiency and Competitiveness of International Airlines

 Springer

Almas Heshmati
Jönköping International Business School
Jönköping
Sweden

Jungsuk Kim
Sogang University
Seoul
Korea, Republic of (South Korea)

ISBN 978-981-10-1015-6   ISBN 978-981-10-1017-0   (eBook)
DOI 10.1007/978-981-10-1017-0

Library of Congress Control Number: 2016938667

Printed on acid-free paper

This Springer imprint is published by Springer Nature
The registered company is Springer Science+Business Media Singapore Pte Ltd.

Preface

This manuscript compares efficiency and competitiveness of world's major 39 airlines over the 1998–2012 period. We analyzed airlines' production and cost efficiency using stochastic frontier function methodology and investigated which factors account for differences in level and variations in technical efficiency of airlines. The results suggest that our approach which looked at cost and production efficiency seems to have an advantage over the commonly used approach of estimating efficiency using only one of the two aspects. An estimation of efficiency from both perspectives better captures the factors affecting the efficiency and more accurately reflects the reality of the ongoing process of airline mergers and exits from the market. The mean and the distribution of both production and cost efficiency among airlines differ according to geographical areas of operation, which may be a result of different market structure and de-regulation processes, and of specific competitive conditions such as resource availability and strategic cooperation with competitors.

The empirical results from rigorous analysis of the unique and up-to-date data confirmed that the sample airlines displayed a reasonable level of production efficiency during 1998–2012, but they were much less successful in achieving cost efficiency. Airlines with a higher market share achieved a relatively better production efficiency. Airlines' operation performance measured in terms of stage, flying hours, and frequency showed a positive correlation with the production efficiency and their statistical significance were very robust. The effect of airline alliances was, however, not progressive. Airline size showed a progressive effect on the level of output efficiency, but larger airlines were not more competent than their smaller counterparts with respect to cost efficiency.

Our main findings show that carriers based in the Asia region are in general more capable of achieving production efficiency than carriers based in Europe and North America, but as regards cost efficiency, we could not establish the transcendence of the Asian carriers. Airlines in Asia region including People's Republic of China attained a remarkable gain in efficiency over time. The high performance and growth achievers include CA (Air China), CZ (China Southern Airlines), and MU

(China Eastern Airlines)—in the case of production efficiency and GA (Garuda Airlines) and SU (Aeroflot Russian Airlines)—in the case of cost efficiency.

Considering that the quality of human capital and level of education are relatively high among the service staff of the airlines in this region, Asian carriers are suggested to concentrate on enhancing the software with the maximum utilization of skilled manpower, which will help airlines to attain premium brand value while still keeping prices reasonably low. Asia, especially East Asia, now has a well-developed, globally competitive manufacturing sector, but its service sector still lags far behind that of the advanced economies. As such, competitiveness analysis of the airline industry, one of the most important service industries, can help Asian policymakers to better prepare for the liberalization of the service sector, which is expected to gain momentum in the coming years.

Acknowledgements

In the process of completing this book manuscript we have benefited from several individuals support. In particular, the authors express their gratitude to two anonymous referees and Mr. William Achauer, Editor at Springer for their constructive comments and suggestions which have improved the manuscript significantly.

Dr. Jungsuk Kim's heart is filled with gratitude for all the support that she has received in the process of writing her Ph.D. thesis and this book. She offers her sincerest gratitude to Profs. Se-Young Ahn and Yoon Heo for their encouragement and help in completing this book. She wishes to give a very exceptional thanks to Prof. Insik Min and Dr. Donghyun Park who helped her with their unsurpassed knowledge of economic theory and econometrics and Prof. Jacob Wood who shaped this book with his excellent and meticulous correction of the language. She is also especially grateful for the excellent support from Yangho Cho and Heather Cho at Korean Air, who have, as always, given Dr. Jungsuk Kim a great deal of support throughout, for which her mere expression of thanks would not be enough.

Last but not least, she would like to extend her utmost thanks and gratitude to her late sister, Jaehee Kim, for her support and encouragement throughout the process before she deceased on 2015. She is very much missed by the family. This book is dedicated to her and her memory.

Almas Heshmati
Jungsuk Kim

Contents

About the Authors

Almas Heshmati is Professor of Economics at Sogang University. He held similar positions at the Korea University, the Seoul National University, the University of Kurdistan Hawler, RATIO Institute (Sweden), and the MTT Agrifood Research (Finland). He was Research Fellow at the World Institute for Development Economics Research (WIDER), the United Nations University during 2001–2004. From 1998 to 2001, he was Associate Professor of Economics at the Stockholm School of Economics. He has a Ph.D. degree from the University of Gothenburg (1994), where he held a Senior Researcher position until 1998. His research interests include applied microeconomics, globalization, development strategy, efficiency, productivity, and growth with application to manufacturing and services. In addition to more than 150 scientific journal articles, he has published books on EU Lisbon Process, global inequality, East Asian manufacturing, Chinese economy, technology transfer, information technology, water resources, landmines, power generation, development economics, economic growth, world values, and renewable energy.

Jungsuk Kim is currently Researcher at Institute of International and Areas Studies of Sogang University in Korea and teaches data analysis and economics at Sogang University and Kyung-Hee University in Korea. Dr. Kim has worked in airline industry including Korean Air, Cathay pacific Airways, and Asiana airlines for more than 25 years before she got Ph.D. in International Trade from Sogang University. Her main fields of research are international trade, microeconomics, and fiscal policy.

Abbreviations

Carrier	Carriers Name
AA	American Airlines Inc.
CL	Capitol International Inc.
CO	Continental Air Lines Inc.
DL	Delta Air Lines Inc.
E0	EOS Airlines, Inc.
E8	US Africa Airways Inc.
EA	Eastern Air Lines Inc.
ER	Astar Air Cargo Inc.
ER	Astar USA, LLC
ER	DHL Airways
FF	Tower Air Inc.
FM	Federal Express Corporation
FT	Flying Tiger Line Inc.
FX	Federal Express Corporation
MY	MAXjet
NW	Northwest Airlines Inc.
PA	Pan American World Airways
PE	People Express Airlines Inc.
PI	Piedmont Aviation Inc.
PO	Polar Air Cargo Airways
QH	Air Florida Inc.
RP	Chautauqua Airlines Inc.
TW	Trans World Airlines Inc.
TW	Trans World Airways LLC
TZ	American Trans Air Inc.
TZ	ATA Airlines d/b/a ATA
UA	United Air Lines Inc.
US	US Airways Inc.

US	USAir
WO	World Airways Inc.
YX	Republic Airlines

2DED	Two-Dimensional Efficiency Decomposition
2SLS	Two-Stage Least Squares
AC	Aircrafts
AGE	Age of aircrafts
AIDS	Acquired Immune Deficiency Syndrome
ALI	Air Liberalization Index
ASA	Air Services Agreements
ASAP	Air Service Agreement Projector
ASIA	Asian region
ASK	Available Seat Kilometers
ASM	Available Seat Miles
ATKC	Available Ton Kilometers of Cargo
ATKP	Available Ton Kilometers of Passenger
AVIANCA	AVIANCA airline
AWAs	Airlines-Within-Airlines
BASA	Bilateral Air Service Agreements
BRICS	Brazil, Russia, India, China, and South Africa
CASM	Cost Per Available Seat Mile
CD	Cobb–Douglas functional form
CES	Constant Elasticity of Substitution
COLS	Corrected Ordinary Least Squares
CPI	Consumer Price Index
CRS	Constant Return to Scale
DEA	Data Envelopment Analysis
DFP	Davidon–Fletcher–Powell algorithm
DOM	Domestic
EBIT	Earnings Before Interest and Taxes
EC	Error Component Model
EE	Efficiency Effects Model
EFF	Efficiency
EMP	Employment
ENERGY	Energy consumption
EU	European Union
EXPN	Expenditure
FDI	Foreign Direct Investment
FFA	Five Freedoms Agreement
FHRS	Flying Hours
FOPM	First-Order Profit Maximizing conditions
FREQ	Flight Frequency

FTE	Full Time Equivalent
GATT	General Agreement on Tariffs And Trade
GDP	Gross Domestic Product
GLS	Generalized Least Squares
GMM	Generalized Method of Moments
GPE	Ground Property and Equipment
HHI	Herfindahl–Hirschman Index
IATA	International Air Transport Association
ICAO	International Civil Aviation Organization
IMF	International Monetary Fund
INTL	International
LCC	Low-Cost Carriers
LF	DOM Load Factor Domestic
LF	INTL Load Factor International
LR	Likelihood Ratio test
LRT	Generalized Likelihood Ratio Tests
LSDV	Least Squares Dummy Variable
MCDM	Multivariate Statistical Analysis and Multiple Criteria Decision Making
MERS	Middle East Respiratory Syndrome
MLE	Maximum Likelihood Estimation
MOP	Mean of Platt's Singapore
MS	Market Share
O&D	Origin & Destination
OECD	Organization for Economic Co-operation and Development
OLS	Ordinary Least Squares
PAX	Passenger
PPP	Purchasing Power Parity
PRC	People's Republic of China
PRICE	Average Service Price
PSO	Public Service Obligations
RPK	Revenue Passenger Kilometers
RPM	Revenue Passenger Miles
RPTK	Revenue Passenger Ton Kilometers
RTK	Revenue Ton Kilometers of cargo
SARS	Severe Acute Respiratory Syndrome
SEM	Structural Equation Models
SFA	Stochastic Frontier Analysis
SFP	Single Factor Productivity
STAGE	Stage length
STATA	STATA statistical package
TFP	Total Factor Productivity
TREND	Time Trend
TS-DEA	Two-Stage Data Envelopment Analysis
UK	United Kingdom

UN	United Nations
UNDP	United Nations Development Program
UNWTO	United Nations World Tour Organization
USA	United States of America
USD	United States of Americas Dollar
VC-DRSA	Variable Consistency Dominance-based Rough Set Approach
VECM	Vector Error Correction Model
VRS	Variable Returns to Scale
WASA	World Air Services Agreements database
WTO	World Trade Organization

List of Figures

List of Tables

Chapter 1
Introduction to Efficiency and Competitiveness of International Airlines

Abstract This chapter provides the background on the significance of an efficiency analysis of airline industry in terms of its performance, motivation, and main objectives. This introductory chapter reviews the market size and economic contributions of the aviation industry to the global economy and briefly discusses the key issues in the industry in recent decades. It also provides an outline of the research questions, methodologies used, and the structure of the chapters in this volume.

Keywords Stochastic frontier functions · Cost efficiency · Production efficiency · Panel data · Airlines

1.1 Overview of the Airline Industry

Aviation is one of the major global industries, creating more than 8.7 million jobs within the industry and contributing to 2.4 trillion USD in revenues, which is around 3.4 % of the global GDP,[1] to the world economy. Since its first operation with passenger and mail services in 1903, the airline industry has undergone wide-ranging changes, keeping with the fast development of technology and the evolution of the world economy. Despite the industry's technological, economic, managerial, and social impacts, it has become a major challenge from an environmental perspective. Table 1.1 shows the recent developments in the industry in terms of various standard performance indicators. These include revenues, expenses, operating profit, net profit, profit margin, and returns on investment for the period 2004–2015.

---

[1]IATA (2014b), "Aviation benefits beyond borders" page 2–8.

A. Heshmati and J. Kim, *Efficiency and Competitiveness
of International Airlines*, DOI 10.1007/978-981-10-1017-0_1

Table 1.1 Airline industry's financial statistics, 2004–2015. (*Unit* USD billion)

Category	2004	2005	2006	2007	2008	2009	2010	2011	2012	2013	2014	2015F[b]
Revenue	379	413	465	510	570	476	564	642	706	717	733	727
Expenses	376	409	450	490	571	474	536	623	687	692	699	677
Operating profit	3.3	4.4	15.0	19.9	−1.1	1.9	27.6	19.8	18.4	25.3	33.9	50.1
Net profit	−5.6	−4.1	5.0	14.7	−26.1	−4.6	17.3	8.3	6.1	10.6	16.4	29.3
% margin	−1.5	−1.0	1.1	2.9	−4.6	−1.0	3.1	1.3	0.9	1.5	2.2	4.0
ROI[a] capital (%)	2.9	3.0	4.6	5.5	1.4	2.0	6.3	4.7	4.3	4.9	5.7	7.5

[a]Return of invested
[b]Forecasted
Source IATA (2014a) fact sheet
Note The statistics is for worldwide commercial airlines

According to the World Bank's estimates, the services sector GDP—which includes value added in wholesale and retail trade (including hotels and restaurants); transport; and government, financial, professional, and personal services such as education, health care, and real estate services[2]—accounted for 63.3 % of the world GDP in 2013, with air transportation revenue alone contributing to 1.49 % of the world's service sector GDP.[3] If we compare the economic contribution of aviation with that of other industries, the global air transport sector is bigger than pharmaceuticals ($451 billion), textiles ($223 billion), and automotive industries ($555 billion), and it is roughly half as big as the global chemical ($1282 billion) and food and beverage ($984 billion) sectors (IATA 2014b). In other words, "if air transport were a country, its GDP would rank as 21st in the world, roughly equal to that of Switzerland and more than twice as large as that of Chile or Singapore" (IATA 2014b). Table 1.2 provides some basic statistics on the air transportation industry, including the number of airlines, airports, and aircrafts; employment; and handling volume.

According to the studies conducted by the International Air Transport Association (IATA 2011) on air travel trends over the last 40 years, the volume of air travel worldwide, measured with aggregated revenue passenger kilometers (RPKs), has expanded more than tenfold and the total cargo volume has grown 14-fold (IATA 2011) despite repeated disruptions, including recessions and various global problems such as epidemics (e.g., AIDS, SARS, Avian Flu, Ebola Virus, and MERS), environmental degradation, natural catastrophes, and terrorism (Pearce 2012).

---

[2]The aggregate world GDP in 2013 was 74,909,811 million US dollar, of which agriculture accounted for 6 %, industry 30.7 %, and services 63.3 %. http://www.indexmundi.com/world/ ̶omy_profile.html.

 ̶ ̶estimate is based on the airlines' revenue and the world GDP of 2013, based on IATA ̶ ̶b).

Table 1.2 Air transportation industry statistics

Airlines[a]	1397 commercial airlines	49,871 routes
Airports/aircrafts[a]	3864 airports	25,332[b] aircrafts
Employment[c]	Direct 8.7 million jobs	58.1 million[d]
Handling volume[b]	Passenger: 2.97 (billion)	Cargo: 51.7 tone (millions)

[a]Base year is 2014
[b]Commercial services, 20,101 jets and 5231 turboprops
[c]Based on 2012
[d]Job supported by aviation worldwide
Source IATA (2014b) and industry statistics and IATA (2012, 2013a, b) annual report of 2012 and 2013

Airline passenger, goods, and postal services have become an intrinsic part of the modern and globalized economy. Statistics show that there is a strong interdependence between the airline industry and the world economy; for instance, the movement of cargo volume is consistent with the fluctuations in international trade.[4] The economy provides resources such as labor, education and skill, capital and energy to airlines, while airlines in turn provide services and generate jobs[5] and revenues by deploying these productive resources. More fundamentally, by transporting people and goods to locations where they are needed the most, air transportation lubricates the wheels of the world economy. As part of the two-way causal relationship, economic growth fuels the demand for airline travel, as is evident in the People's Republic of China (PRC), India, and several other emerging economies.

While the relationship between airlines' performance and the broader economy is inherently complex, it is one of mutual dependence, with each strengthening the other. Looking at the latest performance of airlines, the accumulated worldwide scheduled revenue ton kilometer (RTK) was 5.4 trillion kilometers in 2014[6] (IATA 2014b). Around 52 % of international tourists traveled by air. Approximately 35 % value of world trade was carried by air, accounting for only 0.5 % of the volume of world trade (IATA 2014b). Airlines collectively earned a total net profit of $16.4 billion in 2014 or a 2.2 % margin on revenues.

As is the case in other industries, airlines' economic performance is considerably influenced by the world's economic growth. Nevertheless, the airline industry has risen at a much faster pace than economic growth in other sectors. IATA (2011) reported that in the last 40 years, air transportation grew more than three times as fast as the world economy. Furthermore, while the airline industry suffered a slump during the global financial and economic crisis of 2008–2009, its recovery has been

---

[4]According to IATA (2014a), "Air transport is vital for world trade today, which is mostly in components rather than finished goods. IATA estimates that the value of international trade shipped by air in 2014 reached $6.4 trillion value of cargo handled by air in 2012. Tourist, people travelling by air on the other hand spent an estimated $621 billion" (IATA 2014a).

[5]In 2014, airlines created 2.39 million jobs directly and 58.1 million jobs indirectly in form of supply chain jobs (IATA 2014a).

[6]In 2013, it was 5.7 trillion.

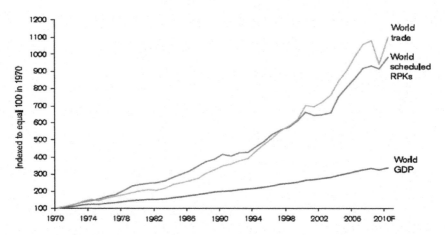

Fig. 1.1 Development of the world GDP, trade and aviation service, 1970–2010. *Source* IATA (2011)

noticeably faster and more robust than most other industries and activities. Figure 1.1 shows that world trade and world scheduled RPKs have developed much faster compared with 1970 used as the base year. Furthermore, it shows that the world scheduled RPKs recovered from the global economic crisis of 2008 much faster that world trade and GDP.

Airlines have made a huge contribution to the economy by creating jobs, business opportunities,[7] and revenues. Moreover, they have benefitted consumers by providing convenient travel, fast transportation , and fresh products delivered by air transportation.[8] Analyzing the various factors that influence the airline industry's competitiveness thus becomes a noteworthy exercise. The policy implications that emerge from our analysis will be relevant for not only the airline industry but also the broader globalized and national economies.

1.2 Background to Airlines' Competitiveness

The issues related to competitiveness of firms, industries, and even entire economies or countries have been a common subject of interest among academics, policy-makers, and the general public. In particular, in light of the rapid advent of the recent wave of globalization, which has eroded barriers between countries and catalyzed cross-border economic transactions, we find it meaningful to examine the

---

[7]Supply chains such as catering, airport services and sometimes hotel services.

[8]"Air transport plays an especially pivotal role in just-in-time global manufacturing production and in spreading fresh products from agricultural communities in developing economies to markets in the industrialized world" (IATA 2014b).

international competitiveness of the airline industry. This is because the industry is a principal actor in the globalization process as well as one of its main facilitators.

There are a number of reasons we chose the airline industry as the subject of our competitiveness analysis. First, virtually all countries operate at least one airline, which often serves as a national symbol and facilitates international business and trade development, allowing for a comparison of the competitiveness of airline industries at the international level.

Second, at first sight, the airline industry performs the simple function of transporting people and goods between different locations. However, a closer examination reveals a constellation of factors—aviation agreements, a wide range of constraints, and the economic situation of countries—that make airlines a highly complex industry. In addition, the highly competitive and technologically sophisticated nature of the airline industry means that it has many ramifications for the national competitiveness strategies.

Airline competitiveness analysis has a special resonance in Korea, which has a rapidly expanding airline industry and economy. Furthermore, Incheon airport located outside the capital city of Seoul has emerged as a major air travel hub in East Asia, and air transportation has become a key tool in Korea's dynamic export sector. Since airlines' performance is closely related with the upturn of the economic cycle, GDP and world trade growth, an analysis of airlines' competitiveness can enable an understanding of the underlying components of the services sector's competitiveness.

Lastly, while Asia, especially East Asia, now possesses a well-developed, export-oriented, and globally competitive manufacturing sector, its services sector still lags far behind the advanced economic systems as well as the optimal service sector level and organization capacity. As such, a competitiveness analysis of the airline industry, one of the most important service industries, can help Asian policymakers to better prepare for the liberalization of the services sector, which is expected to gain momentum in the near future.

Globalization, defined as the free movement of goods, people, and capital, breaks down national borders and dilutes the distinction between local and global markets. This phenomenon can be an opportunity and also a challenge for the airlines. The rapid growth of international trade and travel, facilitated by growing liberalization of trade (e.g., GATT, WTO) and travel (e.g., easing of visa requirements and agreements of terms of trade) is fueling the growth of both passenger and cargo traffics. At the same time, the growth of air transport capacity is a major impetus behind and a facilitator of the growth of international trade and travel.

Like globalization, technological progress in communication and other business sectors can create both opportunities and challenges for the airline business. In an environment of intense globalization and fierce competition among corporations for market shares and survival, the performance outcome of airlines can differ greatly depending on their business strategic choices as well as the global, regional, and national economic development and conditions. As a consequence, the airline industry is a highly competitive industry, constantly buffeted by structural changes and continuously adapting to changes in its fluctuating environment. This is self-evident and reflected in the airlines' continuous entry into and exit from local and global markets (see Appendix 1.1). In such a dynamic environment with intense competition, it is challenging for firms to achieve and sustain growth.

Mere survival is a major achievement in an industry characterized by constant bankruptcies, mergers and acquisitions of existing firms, birth of new firms, and formation of alliances. More generally, achieving a certain market size is a pre-requisite for success in a highly dynamic industry characterized by continuous and extensive structural changes. Therefore, gaining a larger market share based on cost competitiveness and product competitiveness is the primary rather ultimate goal of airlines to withstand global competition.

In addition to the airlines' overall business strategies, the market structures of the countries where the airlines are based significantly shape their national, regional, and global competitiveness. The relationship between airlines and their respective home country's market conditions is interdependent, much like the relationship between airlines and the economy as a whole. Airlines are considered a precon-dition for the economic development of many nations and their specific industries.

1.3   The Conceptual Framework

The key objective of strategic management studies has been to understand how some firms can perform better than others under fierce competition. Many researchers have tried to explain the phenomenon. Achieving a sustainable com-petitiveness in a global market has been crucial concerns for the airline industry.

In our analysis of airlines' competitiveness, the theoretical framework used will be Michael Porter's competitive advantage. Porter was the first to formulate a concept of competitive advantage as the determinant factor for firms' performance in global competition. According to him, competitive advantage results from the competitive strategies that firms choose and implement in their business practices. These choices of strategy make firms profitable and sustainable in the competition within the industry (Porter 1986). Porter argued that, "to achieve competitive success, firms must process a competitive advantage in the form of either lower costs or differentiated products that command premium prices." "To sustain advantage, firms must achieve a competitive advantage over time, through pro-viding higher quality products and services or producing more efficiently" (Porter 1990, pp. 10). "Competitive advantages statements help distinguish companies by highlighting what they offer to the customer using tangible terms and concepts" (Porter 1990).

Along with the concept of competitive advantage, we need to build a logical/systematic framework to form the backbone of this empirical study. We now provide the basic definitions and concepts that will be used in this study, especially when selecting variables for the empirical performance analysis.

Performance of the airlines is estimated in terms of efficiency of the services provided by the airlines as units of production. Several researchers who have developed the concept of efficiency have expressed their views about the framework and its importance for business operation and competitiveness. "The quest for identifying changes in efficiency is conceptually different from identifying technical change" (Diewert and Lawrence 1999). "Full efficiency in an engineering sense means that a production process has achieved the maximum amount of output that is physically achievable with current technology, and given a fixed amount of inputs used in production of goods or services" (Diewert and Lawrence 1999).

Economic efficiency is a product of technical and allocative efficiencies. Kumbhakar and Lovell (2000) Heshmati (2003) and Kumbhakar et al. (2015) provide a complete overview of the methodology and its applications to cross-section and panel data cases under different objectives, distributional assumptions, and estimation methods, as well as various generalizations of the model. "Technical efficiency gains are thus a movement towards use of "best practiced" technology, or the elimination of technical and organizational inefficiencies" (OECD 2001). However, not every form of technical efficiency makes economic sense. "This is captured by the notion of allocative efficiency, which implies profit-maximizing behavior by the firm through best allocation of resources" (OECD 2001). "One notes that when productivity measurement concerns the industry level, efficiency gains can either be due to improved efficiency in individual establishments that make up the industry or to a shift of production technology towards more efficient establishments" (OECD 2001).

According to the basic principle of economic rationality, the purpose is to achieve a given result with minimal resources or to get the maximum result with a given set of resources and technology (Vuorinen et al. 1998). However, it is not easy to measure the maximum level of performance in the production of services. Hence, it is important to examine the economic evaluation of service operations on the basis of the concept of productivity. Many studies have been undertaken in this context, and these will be examined closely in the literature review chapter.

Academics as well as international organizations such as OECD and World Bank have produced a number of studies on competitiveness. The "Global Competitiveness Report" and the "Doing Business Ranking" from the World Bank measure and compare the competitiveness of different countries. These reports are largely based on a productivity-based approach to measuring and comparing competitiveness. In order to identify and apply a precise definition of the terms and concepts that will be used in this research, the literature review chapter provides an intensive review on these issues.

1.4 The Objectives

Reflecting on the central role of the airline industry in the economy, many economists and institutions, including various government agencies, have analyzed and compared the performance and competitiveness of the international airlines. There are wide variations in the scope of analysis, both across different studies and over time.

These studies, however, have focused on highly specific issues based on origin and destination (O&D) such as route pair or city pair comparisons. According to Morrison and Winston (1987, 1990), O&D data best reflect competition among airlines, but such data is not readily available to researchers, except in the case of US international routes (see also Clougherty 2009). Considering the complexity of the airline business model and the econometric challenges linked with the analysis of issues of causality or measurement errors, this kind of approach is appropriate, especially in terms of theoretical soundness and the generation of useful information for the industry's business decision-makers.

An analysis of the global competitiveness of airlines needs to take into account not only firm-specific factors but also other situation-specific factors that airlines have to face in their competitive and highly regulated global market. Airlines' sustainable competitiveness in the global market is in fact the result of successful coordination between an overall business strategy and a well-designed market-specific strategy, which is chosen on a case-by-case basis depending on the market dynamics of each destination. Success in one particular route or city therefore does not guarantee similar results in the global market competition. Thus, instead of looking at specific routes or particular country pair comparisons, our analysis will include various strategies of main airlines such as alliances, pricing, aggregate flying frequency, and flying hours to reflect the airlines' overall strategies of their operation and sales in the global market for a period of 15 years.

Based upon the above conceptual framework and definitions, this paper will examine and provide answers to the following objectives. The first objective is to provide a comprehensive picture of developments in the airline industry and its contributions to the global economy in the recent decades. The second objective is to estimate the level of efficiency for individual airlines and changes in the efficiency of international airlines, and how this is related to their allocation factors both from production and cost function perspectives, namely, output maximization and cost minimization objectives, both of which are aimed at maximization of profits. The third objective is to investigate the components that affect the airlines' efficiency and temporal changes in relation to several characteristics such as firm's size, geographical location, specializations, and alliance memberships. The fourth objective is to investigate how airlines' efficiency affects airline's competitiveness in the global market.

In addition to providing an up-to-date presentation of the airline industry structure and conduct, this study makes at least three major contributions to the analysis of performance of the airlines with respect to competitiveness and efficiency. First, while there are many studies that analyze airline efficiency or productivity for specific routes, destinations or countries, there are only few studies which look at the overall population of major airlines from countries around the world. Second, there are few studies that link competitiveness in both production and cost, and jointly investigate the two as complementary. Looking at both sides of efficiency will improve the scope of interpretation by appropriately addressing the issue of the efficiency in airlines, while simultaneously reflecting on the ongoing process of airlines' entry and exit from the highly evolving and competitive market. Such an approach is less likely to make a biased estimation on the global competitiveness of airlines. Third, this study uses up-to-date estimation methods and long time series of individual airlines covering substantial numbers of airlines from each region of the world including the Asian region, where there have been relatively fewer studies. Each of these three contributions is valuable in its own right, and we hope collectively they will make a valuable contribution to the literature by providing a clear picture of the performance and strategic decision-making of the industry.

1.5 Data and Methodology

Among the member countries and airlines of IATA, we utilize data from 39 international airlines, with the headquarters of operations based in 33 countries, during the period 1998–2012 (see Appendix 1.2). We chose 39 airlines among the top 50 carriers in terms of the 2012 output performance of airlines that were operating during the sampled period. In principle, we selected one carrier per country, but taking into consideration demand and market size, we included 4 carriers from the United States, 3 from China, and 2 from Japan. Some airlines were excluded from the data analysis and estimation procedure due to limitations in the data availability. The airlines' performance-related data was primarily collected from the Korean Government Official Statistics site (www.airportal.go.kr) as well as each airline's homepage. Country-based indicators in air transportation and travel data were collected from the World Bank, UNWTO, UNDP, and IMF databases.

In order to specify models consistent with the objectives and conduct estimations that are efficient yet robust, both theoretically and econometrically, we will first carry out our empirical analysis of airline efficiency using economic theory-based approaches—i.e., production function and cost function approaches. In the first case, the objective of airlines is to maximize output by using available inputs and technology, while in the second case, airlines aim to minimize the cost of producing a given level of services demanded, factor prices, and available technology (Battese and Coelli 1992, 1995; Kumbhakar and Lovell 2000). A cost function approach requires access to price information, which is neither readily available nor always reliable.

With the results from this process, we will then estimate the degree of production and cost efficiency for each airline and over time and explain the temporal changes in the degree of inefficiency in terms of possible observable determinants. In addition, the production model will be estimated by the stochastic frontier methodology, which allows estimation of efficiency parametrically and identifies and estimates effects of the determinants of its level and variations. Here, one estimates a single production function but controls for different technologies and characteristics of airlines and markets to form a stochastic frontier representing the best-practiced technology. By doing this, cross-country differences in airlines' efficiency can be estimated and separated by their technology and market characteristics and differences.

The following chapter provides a review of studies on the airline industry, in particular studies on airlines' efficiency in the context of the characteristics of the airline industry and market. Chapter 3 provides an overview of airline characteristics, theoretical concepts, empirical models, and topical issues related to the industry such as "freedoms of the air" and "multilateral and bilateral agreements between the member countries." These are the areas of interest for industry participants and have implications for their business strategies. In Chaps. 4 and 5, 39 international airlines' production and cost efficiency will be estimated via stochastic frontier production and cost function models. In the conclusion, we will reveal the competitiveness position of the main and sub-variables affecting airlines' performance, survival, and growth in the industry, and discuss the factors that can increase the strength of the airlines' global competitiveness and contribute to global economic development, effectiveness, growth, and stability.

Appendix 1.1: US Carrier Exit and Entry Dates

Carrier	Carrier_name	Start_date	Thru_date
AA	American Airlines Inc.	1982-04-01	–
CL	Capitol International Inc.	1960-01-01	1984-12-31
CO	Continental Air Lines Inc.	1985-04-01	2011-12-31
DL	Delta Air Lines Inc.	1960-01-01	–
E0	EOS Airlines, Inc.	2005-10-01	2006-12-31
E0	EOS Airlines, Inc.	2007-01-01	2008-06-30
E8	US Africa Airways Inc.	1994-06-01	1995-02-28
EA	Eastern Air Lines Inc.	1985-06-01	1986-09-30
ER	Astar Air Cargo Inc.	2003-07-01	2010-12-31
ER	Astar USA, LLC	2011-01-01	2012-06-30
ER	DHL Airways	1992-04-01	2002-12-31
ER	DHL Airways	2003-01-01	2003-06-30
FF	Tower Air Inc.	1983-11-01	2000-09-30
FM	Federal Express Corporation	1986-01-01	1996-07-31
FT	Flying Tiger Line Inc.	1960-01-01	1989-07-31
FX	Federal Express Corporation	1996-08-01	–
MY	MAXjet	2007-01-01	2007-12-31

(continued)

(continued)

Carrier	Carrier_name	Start_date	Thru_date
MY	MAXjet	2005-11-01	2006-12-31
NW	Northwest Airlines Inc.	1960-01-01	2009-12-31
PA	Pan American World Airways	1960-01-01	1991-12-31
PE	People Express Airlines Inc.	1983-06-01	1986-12-31
PI	Piedmont Aviation Inc.	1987-06-01	1989-08-31
PO	Polar Air Cargo Airways	1996-05-01	–
QH	Air Florida Inc.	1979-01-01	1984-06-30
RP	Chautauqua Airlines Inc.	2012-07-01	–
TW	Trans World Airlines Inc.	1960-01-01	2001-03-31
TW	Trans World Airways LLC	2001-04-01	2001-12-31
TZ	American Trans Air Inc.	2000-01-01	2003-02-28
TZ	American Trans Air Inc.	1993-10-01	1999-12-31
TZ	ATA Airlines d/b/a ATA	2007-01-01	2008-06-30
TZ	ATA Airlines d/b/a ATA	2003-03-01	2006-12-31
UA	United Air Lines Inc.	1990-05-01	–
US	US Airways Inc.	1997-02-01	–
US	USAir	1989-08-01	1997-01-31
WO	World Airways Inc.	1980-06-01	1986-09-30
YX	Republic Airlines	2011-07-01	–

Source US DOT

Appendix 1.2: Airlines and Countries

Country	Sub total	Region	Tone rank	PAX rank	Airline	Airline code	Alliance	Starting year	AC	AC year
United States	5 countries 8 airlines	AM	1	1	American Airlines	AA	One word	1934	896	14.9
					UNITED airline	UA	Star	1931	704	13.3
					DELTA airline	DL	Sky team	1929	722	16.7
					US AIR	US	Star	1939	339	12.6
Canada		AM	12	8	Air Canada	AC	Star	1937	205	12.2
Brazil		AM	15	14	TAM Linhas Aereas	JJ	Star	1976	146	
Chile		AM	30	33	LAN Airlines	LA	One word	2004	107	5.1
Colombia		AM	31	42	AVIANCA	AV	Star	1940	71	6.9

(continued)

(continued)

Country	Sub total	Region	Tone rank	PAX rank	Airline	Airline code	Alliance	Starting year	AC	AC year
China	12 countries 15 airlines	AS	2	2	Air China	CA	Star	1988	275	6.5
					China Southern	CZ	Sky team	1988	259	6.2
					China Eastern	MU	Sky team	1989	413	6.6
Hong Kong		AS	2	2	Cathay Pacific Airways	CX	One world	1946	134	10.3
Korea		AS	6	13	Korean Air	KE	Sky team	1969	130	9.4
Japan		AS	7	7	Japan Airlines	KJL	One world	1951	180	9.5
					All Nippon Airways	NH	Star	1953	151	12.1
Singapore		AS	9	17	Singapore Airlines	SQ	Star	1972	128	6.4
Australia		AS	13	12	Qantas Airways	QF	One world	1922	141	10.8
India		AS	14	11	Air India	AI	One world	1932	88	7.3
Thailand		AS	18	19	Thai Airways	TG	Star	1960	98	10.7
Malaysia		AS	21	21	Malaysia Airlines	MH	One world	1947	108	10.3
Indonesia		AS	26	23	Garuda Airways	GA	N/A	1950	81	6.5
Philippines		AS	29	28	Philippine Airlines	PR	N/A	1941	40	9.8
New Zealand		AS	32	30	Air New Zealand	NZ	Star	1940	98	9.4
Germany	12 countries 12 airlines	EU	3	4	Lufthansa,	LH	Star	1926	427	12.3
U.K		EU	5	3	British Airways	BA	One world	1919	240	
France		EU	8	6	Air France	AF	Sky team	1933	377	9.5
Spain		EU	16	15	IBERIA	IB	One world	1927	112	9.3
Ireland		EU	17	10	Air Lingus	EI	N/A	1036	44	6.7
Turkey		EU	20	18	Turkish Airlines	TK	Star	1956	189	6.4
Italy		EU	22	22	Alitalia	AZ	Sky team	1947	160	9.4
Switzerland		EU	23	25	SWISS Air	LX	Star	1931	91	
Sweden		EU	25	24	SAS Scandinavian Airlines	SK	Star	1946	143	12.9
Portugal		EU	33	29	TAP Portugal	TP	Star	1946	71	11.5
Finland		EU	35	34	Finn air	AY	One world	1968	68	8.4
Austria		EU	36	32	Austrian	OS	Star	1958	80	14.3

(continued)

(continued)

Country	Sub total	Region	Tone rank	PAX rank	Airline	Airline code	Alliance	Starting year	AC	AC year
Russian Federation	4 countries 4 airlines	EU	11	9	Aeroflot Russian airlines	SU	Sky team	1923	123	5.5
Qatar		EU	19	20	Qatar Airways	QR	N/A	1994	111	5.1
Saudi Arabia		EU	27	27	Saudi Arabian Airlines	SV	Sky team	1947	163	10.3
Israel		EU	34	36	El Al	LY		1949	40	13.4
33 countries and 39 airlines										

Notes PAX passenger, *N/A* not applicable

References

Battese G, Coelli TJ (1992) Frontier production functions, technical efficiency and panel data: with application to paddy farmers in India. J Prod Anal 3:153–169

Battese G, Coelli TJ (1995) A model for technical in efficiency effects in a stochastic frontier production function for panel data. Empirical Econ 20:325–332

Clougherty JA (2009) Domestic rivalry and export performance: theory and evidence from international airline markets, Canadian Economics Association. Can J Econ/Revue Canadienne d'Economique 42(2):440–468

Diewert WE, LawrenceD (1999) Progress in measuring the price and quantity of capital. Discussion paper 99-17, Department of Economics, University of British Columbia, Vancouver, Canada, V6T 1Z1

Heshmati A (2003) Productivity growth, efficiency and outsourcing in manufacturing and services. J Econ Surv 17(1):79–112

International Air Transport Association (2011) Vision 2050, Singapore, 12 Feb 2011 report. www.IATA.org

International Air Transport Association (2012) Annual report 2012. www.IATA.org

International Air Transport Association (2013a) Annual report 2013. www.IATA.org

International Air Transport Association (2013b) Profitability and the air transport value chain. International Air Transport Association economics briefing, No. 10. (www.IATA.org)

International Air Transport Association (2014a) Fact sheet: industry statistics. www.IATA.org

International Air Transport Association (2014b) Aviation benefits beyond borders, pp 2–8. www.aviationbenefitsbeyondborders.org

International Monetary Fund. http://www.imf.org

Kumbhakar SC, Lovell CAK (2000) Stochastic frontier analysis. Cambridge University Press, Cambridge

Kumbhakar SC, Wan H, Horncastle A (2015) A practitioner's guide to stochastic frontier analysis using stata. Academic

Morrison SA, Winston C (1987) Empirical implications and tests of the contestability hypothesis. J Law Econ XXX:53–66

Morrison SA, Winston C (1990) The dynamics of airline pricing and competition. Am Econ Rev Pap Proc 80(2):389–393

OECD Manual (2001) Measuring productivity—measurement of aggregate and industry-level productivity. http://www.oecd.org/std

Porter ME (1986) Competition in global industries. Harvard Business Press, Boston

Porter ME (1990) The competitive advantage of nations. Harvard Business Review, Boston

Pearce B (2012) The state of air transport markets and the airline industry after the great recession. J Air Transp Manage 21:3–9

Vuorinen I, Järvinen R, Lehtinen U (1998) Content and measurement of productivity in the service sector: a conceptual analysis with an illustrative case from the insurance business. Int J Serv Ind Manag 9(4):377–396

World Bank. http://www.worldbank.org, http://www.indexmundi.com/world/economy_profile. html

Chapter 2
Survey of Studies on Airlines and Their Efficiencies

Abstract This chapter takes a closer look at previous studies on the efficiency and competitiveness of airlines. We provide a comprehensive review of the latest literature on airline efficiency, productivity and competitiveness, summarizing the main findings in chronological order. The various aspects of the airlines industry reviewed are classified into: efficiency, productivity, and factor conditions; alliances and market liberalization; market concentration, market power, and competition; and other issues. The review is used to assess the consistency of production and cost functions of airline operation with theory. The review also serves as a guide to estimations of airlines' efficiency and compares these across airlines with different characteristics. Appropriate methods are used to identify determinants of the level of efficiency and their effects.

Keywords Efficiency and productivity · Stochastic frontier functions · Competitiveness · Airline industry · Literature review

2.1 Efficiency, Productivity, and Factor Use

Economic theory mainly distinguishes between three types of efficiency: technical, allocative, and cost. Technical efficiency refers to the effectiveness with which a particular set of inputs is used to produce an output. Allocative efficiency involves selecting the mix of inputs that produce a specified set of outputs at a minimum cost (Battese et al. 2000), and cost efficiency or economic efficiency is largely the alignment of both technical and allocative efficiency (Assaf 2012). A number of sources provide a review of the literature (Schmidt 1986; Kumbhakar and Lovell 2000; Heshmati 2003; Kumbhakar et al. 2015). The methodologies of the estimation can be generally divided into parametric, semi-parametric, and nonparametric estimation methods, cost, production and profits functions, panel data and cross-sections, time-invariant and time-variant efficiency, homoscedastic and heteroscedastic variances, etc. Each category is further divided into a number of specialized cases depending on the specific examples studied and the underlying

© Springer Science+Business Media Singapore 2016   15
A. Heshmati and J. Kim, *Efficiency and Competitiveness
of International Airlines*, DOI 10.1007/978-981-10-1017-0_2

assumptions. This review focuses mainly on the models and methods that are frequently used to analyze the performance of the airline industry.

"Efficiency" can be defined in various ways depending on the perspective employed. We estimate efficiency in following chapters on the basis of the assumption that output is maximized given certain inputs and cost is minimized for a specified level of output (Battese et al. 2000; Kumbhakar and Lovell 2000). A number of studies have estimated technical efficiency using a production function approach since this approach does not require price information. Estimating allocative and cost efficiency requires estimating the cost function, in which case information on the input prices of each airline is required. The availability of such information for academic research is, however, rather limited. An alternative method is to estimate technical efficiency on the basis of input and output quantities, which are relatively easier to access. The use of technical efficiency can be consistent with the measurement of productivity, which involves a technical efficiency change component. In this setting, the distance function can be calculated using either an input-oriented assumption or an output-oriented assumption. At the same time, airlines in general have limited flexibility in setting the measure of inputs, e.g., the number of planes is relatively determined, and in most airlines, labor is also contracted in the short to medium term, with more flexibility in the long term. In such cases, input is treated as quasi-fixed. Therefore, given the assumption of output maximization, with relatively fixed inputs, airlines are trying to produce the maximum possible output. In short, the nature of the airline business is to maximize outputs and revenues from using the given inputs and allocate them optimally across spaces.

A survey of the recent literature reveals a large number of empirical studies that examine the factors affecting the efficiency of airlines. Allocative efficiency has drawn extensive debates among scholars and industry practitioners. Many studies have been conducted on the US and European-based airlines, while there have been fewer studies on other regions, particularly Asia, until the recent years. With China emerging as a major player in the airline industry, as with other industries, Asian airlines deserve due attention and research needs to be conducted to account for the substantial and growing portion of international passenger and cargo traffic in the region.

Methodologically, there is an obvious pattern in the existing studies in that they are largely confined to the nonparametric estimation of allocative efficiency. A number of studies are based on stochastic frontier cost and production functions, data envelopment analysis (DEA), and Malmquist productivity analysis. Depending on the aim of a study, the results derived from the frontier function were used in the second stage with a different methodological approach. These studies tried to seek the source of the various factors affecting key issues such as cost factors, profits, and output. For details on the models and methodology, please see Appendix 2.1, which summarizes the relevant literature for the airline industry.

2.1.1 Stochastic Frontier Production and Cost Functions

In the parametric approach, often a production, cost or profit function is specified and estimated parametrically. The objective is to maximize output, minimize cost, or maximize profit given certain conditions. Each function has different data requirements and is estimated using the Ordinary Least Squares (OLS), Corrected Ordinary Least Squares (COLS), Generalized Least Squares (GLS), or Maximum Likelihood Estimation (MLE) methods.

The Stochastic Frontier Analysis (SFA) is an analytical method that employs econometric (parametric) techniques whose models of production and cost recognize the technical inefficiency and the random shocks that may impact the output or cost (Coelli 1996; Kumbhakar and Lovell 2000). In contrast to nonparametric approaches that assume decisive frontiers, SFA permits for deviations from the frontier, whose error can be decomposed for suitable discrepancy between technical efficiency and random shocks—e.g., labor or capital performance variations. In other words, stochastic frontier models permit an analysis of technical inefficiency in the framework of production and cost functions. Production units (firms, industry, regions, countries, etc.) or cost units are assumed to produce according to a given technology, and reach the frontier when they produce the maximum (spend the minimum cost in the case of the cost model) possible output for a given set of inputs (Coelli 1996). Inefficiencies are highly correlated with structural problems or market imperfections and other factors that cause firms to yield less than the maximum possible output. SFA is therefore both a theoretical and a practical framework, whose objective is to define and estimate production and cost frontiers (Constantin et al. 2009). Koopmans (1951), Debreu (1951) used SFA, while Farrell (1957) was the first to measure production efficiency empirically. Aigner et al. (1977), Meeusen and van de Broeck (1977) introduced the SFA with a decomposed or an error component structure. Schmidt (1986), Kumbhakar and Lovell (2000), Heshmati (2003), Kumbhakar et al. (2015) provide comprehensive reviews of the literature. Battese and Coelli (1988, 1992, 1995) also provide a complete list of diverse applications of stochastic frontier models. The specification and application of production and cost models will be further reviewed in relation to estimation of models in later chapters.

Coelli et al. (1999) evaluate the efficiency of international airlines. They obtained technical efficiency scores from stochastic frontier production functions that were adjusted to account for environmental influences such as network conditions and geographical factors. The paper proposed two alternative approaches to the efficiency measurement—environmental factors influence how technology is shaped and they directly determine the level of technical inefficiency. The two sets of results provided similar rankings of airlines but derived distinctive degrees of technical inefficiency. The results also suggested that Asian/Oceanic airlines were technically more efficient than European and North American ones but that the variances are primarily due to more favorable environmental conditions. It was among Asian companies that the major improvements in managerial efficiency (technical efficiency with environmental factors netted out) took place over the sample period (1977–1990).

Oum and Yu (1998) compared unit cost competitiveness of the world's 22 major airlines over the period 1986–1993. They described the methodologies for estimating a neoclassical cost function and for decomposing the unit cost differentials between airlines into potential sources. Their study computed a unit cost index for aggregate output via a multilateral index procedure. A translog variable cost function was then estimated and the result was used to decompose the unit cost differentials into potential sources, input prices, network and output attributes, and efficiency. The results of the unit cost decomposition were again utilized to build a cost competitiveness indicator after removing the effects of network and output attributes. The key findings of the study are as follows:

- Asian carriers (except Japan Airlines and All Nippon Airways) were generally more cost competitive than the major US carriers, mostly due to their substantially lower input prices.
- Japan Airlines and All Nippon Airways were more than 50 % less cost competitive than American Airlines, largely because of their high input prices.
- Among European carriers, British Airways and Scandinavian Airlines Systems were 7 and 42 % less cost competitive, respectively, compared to American Airlines, largely due to higher input prices and lower efficiency.
- Among the US carriers, American Airlines, United Airlines, and Delta were similar in cost competitiveness, while Northwest and Continental enjoyed a 5 and a 12 % cost competitiveness gain over American Airlines.
- Exchange rate fluctuation has had considerable effects on the cost competitive position of Japan Airlines and German Lufthansa.

In another study, Oum et al. (2005) measured and compared the performance of 10 major North American airlines in terms of residual total factor productivity (TFP), cost competitiveness, and residual average yields during the period 1990–2001. Revenue Ton Kilometers (RTK) of passenger, fright, and mail service, including nonscheduled services, were used as output data. In order to incorporate incidental services into the estimation, a quantity index of incidental services output was constructed by deflating the incidental revenues with the US GDP deflator and adjusting by purchasing power parity (PPP) index. Labor, fuel, materials, flight equipment, and ground property and equipment (GPE) were employed as input variables. The number of full-time equivalent (FTE) number of employees was used for the labor input data. The following are the key findings of the study:

- North American airlines improved productive efficiency by about 12 % between 1990 and 2001 despite the substantial reduction of residual TFP between 2000 and 2001.
- Airlines need to perform well in both production efficiency and pricing to be financially successful.
- The significant productivity improvement in the 1990s enabled the airlines to cope with rising input costs and down pressure on returns.

- Airlines that aggressively expanded fleet in response to the fast-growing market during the mid-1990s suffered loss of productive efficiency.
- The 9/11 terrorist attack led to significant reductions in the airlines' yields, which in turn contributed to declining productivity and increasing unit cost.

The airlines scheduling model is estimated by Yan et al. (2008). The model includes solution algorithms based on the stochastic demand model to determine the optimization of the flight schedule of airlines. The study suggests that in order to have a well-planned flight schedule, airlines not only have to consider their fleet supply and related operations, as well as market share, but also account for stochastic variations caused by daily passenger demands in actual operations. It indicated that many earlier studies on short-term flight scheduling used the average passenger demand as an input to create the final timetable and schedule, which means that daily passenger variations in real operations were ignored. Yan et al. (2008) produced a stochastic demand-scheduling model to accommodate such stochastic disturbances and employed arc-based and path-based schemes to foster two heuristic algorithms, useful to solve the problem (Yan et al. 2008). The test results, based on a major Taiwan airline's operation, showed the desirable result in the performance of the model and the solution systems (Yan et al. 2008).

Another example of the parametric approach is that by Assaf (2009) who analyzed the technical efficiency of the US airlines using a Bayesian random stochastic frontier model with data covering the period from 2003 to 2007. A Cobb–Douglas production function was adopted to represent the frontier production technology. He used two outputs together—passenger service and cargo operation together, four inputs—total operational cost (excluding labor cost), labor cost, aircraft fuel and oil expenses, and the number of planes (proxy for capital input). Load factor (RPK/ASK) was similarly appended to the frontier model to evaluate the effects of environmental features which the airlines are able to control. The technical efficiency results showed that US airlines were running at a declining efficiency rate, with an average of 69.02 % of the airlines operating with best-practiced technology.

2.1.2 Nonparametric Approaches

The parametric approach has certain advantages over the nonparametric estimation as it can use environmental factors of the airline, industry, markets, and production rather than simple inputs and outputs in the estimation of efficiency. The disadvantage is that one must assume a functional form, which may not be correctly chosen, thus biasing the inference. However, one can test different functional forms and their generalizations.

Many of the recent Nonparametric Approaches on airline efficiency studies centered on the estimation of airline efficiency or productivity using the application of DEA. They mostly conducted the allocative efficiency test, followed by a second stage to analyze the impact of the other variables of interest on the efficiency level.

Considering the nature of airlines, which operate with multiple inputs and outputs, this approach can address the problems of spurious results and multiple equilibriums. Several studies have focused on the technical efficiency of a route or a city pair, with relatively fewer focusing on the aggregated level of analysis of the airlines' efficiency.

Barbot et al. (2008) studied the efficiency and productivity of 41 international airlines by grouping them into 4 regions.[1] The authors compared the efficiency and productivity of full-service carriers with low-cost carriers. For the empirical analysis, two different methodologies—DEA and TFP—were used. They also investigated which factors account for differences in efficiency. The result revealed that low-cost carriers were more efficient than full-service carriers. Efficiency and the dispersion of both DEA and TFP indices amongst airlines differed by geographical location. The authors argued that different legislation and deregulation processes were the main causes of the variance. As for specific competitiveness factors, labor was the only input that had a statistically significant effect on the level of productivity. Finally, larger airlines were found to be more efficient due to the economies of scale. Labor (number of core business workers), fleet (number of operating aircraft), and fuel (in gallons consumed) were used as measures of inputs, while available seat kilometers (ASK), revenue passenger seat kilometers (RPK), and revenue ton kilometers (RTK) were used as measures of outputs.

The study by Greer (2009) also used DEA and evaluated technical efficiencies of airlines by transforming inputs (labor, fuel, and fleet-wide seating capacity) into ASK (available seat-miles). The paper used data of passenger airlines in the US and employed the Tobit regression model to identify determinants of the efficiency score. This analysis defined variables in terms of physical units instead of monetary values. The result showed that the impact of unionization on airline efficiency was statistically insignificant when control variables such as the average age of an airline's fleet, the average size of its aircrafts, and the average stage length were included as determinants of inefficiency.

Lee and Johnson (2011) propose a two-dimensional efficiency decomposition (2DED) of profitability for a production system. They tried to assess the demand effect observed in the productivity data of the US airline industry from 2006 to 2008. The first process identified four components of efficiency: capacity design, demand generation, operations, and demand consumption, using Network DEA (Network DEA). The second process decomposed the efficiency measures and integrated them into a profitability efficiency framework. Each constituent of profitability transformation was evaluated on the basis of the changes in technical efficiency, scale efficiency and allocative efficiency. The result showed that the decline of productivity was mainly caused by a demand fluctuation in 2007–2008 rather than loss of technical productivity.

---

[1]They grouped airlines using the regional classification of the International Air Transport Association (IATA). The regions and their respective number of airlines are Europe and Russia (21 airlines), North America and Canada (11), China and North Asia (8), Asia Pacific (7), and Africa and Middle East (2).

Wang et al. (2013) studied the links between the operating performances of 30 US airlines and corporate governance. DEA was employed to measure the relative efficiency of airlines and to investigate the contribution of inputs and outputs that affect technical efficiency. Efficiency decomposition, combined with cluster analysis and multidimensional scaling, was utilized to explore the competitive advantage of the airlines. Furthermore, they examined whether corporate governance has an impact on the airlines' performance. They concluded that more than half of the thirty US airlines examined were less efficient than the best-performing airline in the industry. The performance of carriers was not just related to internal characteristics such as the number of committees and nonexecutive directors but also affected by external factors.

Cristina and Gramani (2012) runs a two-phase DEAto separately examine the operational and fiscal operations of airlines. The study empirically analyzed the data of 4 airlines—2 Brazilian and 2 American—observed between 1997 and 2006. To measure operational performance, the input-orientation model was embraced and the optimization of the resources in producing a gifted layer of production was investigated. On the other hand, to measure financial performance, the study used the output-oriented DEA model where output is maximized for given inputs and technology. It employed the VRS model (variable returns to scale) instead of CRS (constant returns to scale) since an increase in inputs did not generate the same increase in outputs. Aircraft fuel, wages, salaries and benefits, and cost per available seat mile (CASM) were used as input variables and revenue passenger mile (Load Factor/Available Seat Mile) as output variables in the estimation of operational performance. When investigating financial performance, the inverse of the efficiency scores obtained from the first process was used as an input, while flight revenue and flight income were used as output variables. The result revealed that for emerging markets, operational performance is better than financial performance, implying that resource optimization has been the main concern of the airlines. The study underlined that improving operational efficiency does not inevitably translate into improvement in financial efficiency in emergent airline markets.

Assaf et al. (2009) have measured the efficiency of UK airlines, which have experienced difficulties in recent times. They evaluated the technical efficiency of airlines by applying DEA and employing the bootstrap methodology. In calculating the dispersion of estimated efficiency points, they find the airline size and load factor to be positively linked with technical efficiency. In addition, factors such as higher oil prices and fierce market competition were also potential causes of technical inefficiency. This paper added to the previous studies on the measurement of efficiency and is relevant to the other chapters in this volume. For a list of various important studies on airlines' efficiency, see Table 2.1.

Merkert and Hensher (2011) evaluated the key determinants of the efficiency of 58 passenger airlines by applying a two-stage DEA with partially bootstrapped random effects to estimate standard errors for the point efficiency estimates. They deployed a Tobit regression to estimate the second stage and explain variations in the level of efficiency. This study aimed to evaluate the factors that influence the costs and efficiency of airlines in the highly competitive and challenging airline

Table 2.1 Previous studies on the measurement of airlines efficiency

Study	Inputs	Outputs	Other variables
Coelli et al. (1999)	Labor, capital	TKA	Load factor, aircraft capacity
Ahn et al. (1997)	Labor, materials fuel	Revenue	Load factor, aircraft size
Good et al. (1995)	Labor, materials planes	Revenue	Load factor, aircraft size
Baltagi et al. (1995)	Capital, labor	TKA	Load factor, aircraft size, hubs, mergers
Cornwell et al. (1990)	Labor index materials, energy, capital expenses	TKA	Stage length, service quality, seasonality
Schmidt and Sickles (1984)	Labor index materials, energy, capital expenses	TKA	Size, load factor

Source Assaf et al. (2009)

Note TKA ton kilometers available

industry environment arising from the global financial crisis, the growth of low-cost carriers, and the high and volatile fuel prices that represent a substantial cost pressure for airlines. As for input data, they use available ton kilometers (ATK) as a proxy for capital, in line with the existing literature, and FTE staff as a measure of labor. The two output measures revenue passenger kilometers (RPK) and RTK were used in all three DEA models.[2] For the second-stage explanatory variables, they use available seat kilometers (ASK) to measure the size of each airline. While the average stage length, measured in kilometers, was chosen to evaluate the impact of route/network optimization on airline efficiency, aircraft size measured in terms of average seats per aircraft across the operating fleet, was also selected to test whether the earlier discussed productivity measures of individual aircrafts would have an impact on the overall airline efficiency.

Results of the study by Merkert and Hensher (2011) showed that not only the size of airlines but also the fleet mixes of the size of aircrafts and the number of families of aircraft in the fleets have an impact on technical, allocative and, ultimately, cost efficiency. Although stage length had an impact on an aircraft's unit cost, its impact at the airline level was limited to technical efficiency. Conversely, the age of fleets had no significant impact on technical efficiency, but it delivers, on average, a small positive effect on the allocative and cost efficiency components. The analysis of individual efficiency scores yielded examples of very young fleets achieving relatively high efficiency. The authors concluded that airline managements that aim to reduce costs should focus less on stage length and fleet age and more on other variables, particularly the optimization of the fleet mix. They suggest that the effects of route optimization[3] are limited to technical efficiency. The results

---

[2]These are commonly used to reflect the output of both passenger and cargo (including mail) flight operations.

[3]They used the average stage length of the fleet as a proxy for measuring route optimization.

from this research showed that airline size and key fleet mix characteristics, such as aircraft size and the aircraft fleet series, were more pertinent to successful cost saving by airlines since they had significant impacts on all three types of airline efficiency. The results also exposed that despite the fuel-saving benefits of a younger aircraft, the age of an airline's fleet had no significant impact on its technical efficiency but did have a positive impact on its allocative and cost efficiencies.

In a recent study, Merkert and Williams (2013) applied a two-stage DEA approach and analyzed the efficiency of 18 European Public Service Obligation (PSO) airlines over two financial years (2007/08 and 2008/09). They used truncated regressions to determine the impact of specific airline characteristics and their 206 PSO contracts on efficiency. They wanted to investigate whether individual PSO operators functioned competently because most of these services are important for the social and economic development of the relevant regions. The data suggested that apart from a small number of contracts with international traffic in France, Ireland, and Finland, PSO routes were usually operated domestically by local (national) carriers and often connect different islands with the mainland. In terms of aircraft, some carriers in France, Italy, Portugal, and Spain used much bigger aircraft (e.g., A320) than carriers from other countries such as the UK. This substantial heterogeneity across countries/operators has implications for the average distance flown. In terms of data for the first-stage DEA analysis, the authors used two inputs, ASK[4] and FTE,[5] for staff employed in the relevant period. Outputs were estimated with revenue passenger kilometers (RPK) and realized departures. The results suggested that ownership has no impact on airline efficiency. By contrast, the number of remaining months before a PSO is due for renewal in these contracts has a very significant positive effect. The effect of the stage length to the efficiency of the associated airlines showed a negative impact.

In another recent study, Duygun et al. (2015) applied network DEA models and studied efficiency and productivity issues in 87 European airlines from 23 European carriers during the period 2000–2010. While estimating the impact of airline market liberalization, the influence of several events, such as the 9/11 attacks in 2001 and the global financial crisis of 2008, on the performance of European airlines had to be taken into account as they happened during the sample period. To overcome the shortcomings of the DEA estimation, which they regarded as "disentangling the black box or production process," they employed two basic stages. In the first stage, inputs consumed by airlines for delivering services (such as seats kilometers) were used. They find that the decision to use the level of service or customer satisfaction together with the level of quality offered in their previous travel experiences differ across the organization, thus they used them as a second input. In sum, they found

---

[4]Available seat kilometers to measure the offered capacity of each operator.
[5]As a proxy for employed capital and full-time employment.

that most inefficiencies are produced in the first stage of the analysis. However, when taking into account the various types of carriers, several differences emerge, with most of the budget carriers' inefficiencies are confined to the first stage. The estimation also revealed that performance of airlines is very dynamic since efficiency varied across types of airlines during 2000–2010.

Finally, Mallikarjun (2015) applies the un-oriented DEA network methodology to assess the operating efficiency and performance ratios as well as the sources of inefficiency of 14 major and 13 national US airlines. The results of the study suggest that major US airlines captured better efficiency than national US airlines in terms of spending operating expenses and gaining operating revenue, while there was no meaningful variance in their service provision and efficiencies of the demand.

2.1.3   Malmquist Productivity Analysis

Productivity measurement is different from efficiency measurement. Productivity is a measure for single factors such as labor, energy, and capital or multiple factors termed as single factor productivity (SFP) and multiple or TFP respectively. It measures the output per unit or aggregate units of inputs. Productivity studies are interested in yield per unit of input and its development over time. One can compare the productivity of two units in the same period or of the same unit over different periods. Productivity is linked to efficiency by its decomposition into scale, technical change, and efficiency changes. Productivity measure can be estimated parametrically from the production of cost function or nonparametrically using the Malmquist productivity analysis. For reviews of the literature, see Kumbhakar and Lovell (2000), Heshmati (2003).

Pires and Fernandes (2012) applied the Malmquist productivity index to estimate the financial efficiency of 42 airlines from 25 countries in 2001 (the year of 9/11) and their profitability in the following year. The Malmquist productivity index was used to investigate changes in the airlines' capital structure from 2001 to 2002. The results showed the airline capital structure management and profitability dynamics following the unexpected shock of 2001. Their main conclusion was that airlines which moved more aggressively to reduce their indebtedness showed improved profitability, for a given size, fleet, and intangible assets. In order to expand their air transportation operations, airlines require substantial financial investments, especially in aircraft, fleet maintenance, and information systems. To meet the passenger and cargo demands adequately, the authors suggested that the system must have an equilibrium that reconciles these and other factors such as operating costs and expenses, fleet suitability for each route, and company profitability.

2.1.4 Other Performance Measurement Methods

Despite the global trend toward deregulation, barriers to entry in the air transportation industry, particularly in the domestic markets, still remain high. Recently, productivity issues in the industry have been much explored by many researchers due to increased competition facing the industry, particularly in the international market. Current research on airline productivity has centered on two aspects: drivers of productivity variations and sources of productivity growth. In addition, a number of studies have examined the inadequacy of TFP as an indicator of financial improvement. These studies suggest that unit cost competitiveness and average yield indexes should be used together with TFP to get a better indicator of the performance of airlines.

Employing an alternative performance measurement method, Gorin and Belobaba (2004) investigated the effect of airline revenue management on traditional measures of airline market performance and explored the dynamics of airline markets, especially with respect to competition issues. They emphasized the role of revenue management and the new entrants' capacity in market competition. They criticized existing measures of incumbent carriers' anticompetitive actions by pointing out that "it did not constitute a reliable indication of the response of incumbent carriers and provided even less information on the strategic intent of the incumbent carriers." Their results implied that even airline-specific average fares, traffic, and revenues provide an incomplete picture of the effects of entry into a market, contrary to the findings of previous researchers.

Many of the studies cited above showed the importance of identifying factors influencing the performance of airlines. Gudmundsson (2004) studied factors associated with airline performance through an exploratory factor analysis. A two-level bottom-up hierarchical approach was used in the empirical study. The results showed that airlines with a higher relative score on productivity and brand image were less likely to be under financial distress, while airlines with a higher relative emphasis on market power were more likely to be under financial distress affecting the airlines' performance.

An empirical time series analysis of airlines' performance is rare. Okulski and Heshmati (2010) performed a time series analysis on the technology efficiency of the airline industry by using monthly data from January 2001 to April 2009 for a large panel of 130 airlines. The results showed that specialized passenger airlines could not obtain sufficient revenues to stay in the market for a long period of time. Airlines can reduce costs by adding additional products to the scope of their services. Even the worst performing joint service airlines performed better in carrying passengers than specialized best practice airlines. Therefore, in order to increase profits and improve survival chances, airlines specializing solely in passenger transportation must diversify their business and carry both passengers and cargo.

Quality and its measurement are often neglected in analysis of performance of the service industry. Parast et al. (2010) investigated both the effects of quality on profitability and the effect of productivity in the US airline industry using with

Table 2.2 Various output measures used in airline industry

Output measures	Passenger-miles and ton-miles
Proxy for productivity	Labor productivity
Measure of quality (conformance quality)	On-time performance[a]
Measure of operational cost	Gas price (average of year)
Measure of operational cost	Employee salary (average of year)
Measure of profitability	Passenger load factor[b]
Measure of operational cost	Maintenance cost per flight hours[c]

[a]The percentage of flights that were departed on-time (less than 15 min late)
[b]The number of passenger-kilometers traveled as a percentage of the total seat-kilometers available
[c]The average cost of maintaining the aircraft divided by the total number of flight hours per year
Source Parast et al. (2010)

panel data from 1989 to 2008. The results showed that labor productivity was the most significant predictor of profitability, while on-time performance had no relationship with profitability. The findings identified "labor productivity, gas price, average annual maintenance cost, and employee salary" as the most significant explanatory variables or predictors of profitability. The authors found a progressive impact of labor productivity and employee wage on profitability, while gas price and average annual maintenance cost were regressive to the level of profitability. As for methodology, they employed a correlation and multivariate regression analysis to measure the effect of airlines' operations and expenses on productivity and profitability. Stepwise regression was applied to assess the significance of each variable. Labor productivity, which is the output per unit of labor, is derived from dividing output by an extent of the labor input, typically labor hours (see Table 2.2 that provides a list summarizing the variables used for the empirical estimation of this study).

There is a plethora of studies on US airlines. Powell II (2012) evaluated the productivity performance of US passenger airlines since the airline deregulation in 1978. The paper measured and compared productivity at both the aggregate US airline industry and individual carrier groups. Productivity was measured at the aggregate airline industry level in terms of multi factor productivity (MFP) the ratio of a single output to a combination of inputs, in order to track industry productivity over from the period 1978–2009. In addition, productivity was measured at the dismantled carrier level in terms of TFP and the ratio of total inputs over total outputs in order to compare productivity growth across airlines and over time from 1995 to 2010. The key findings indicated that US passenger airlines experienced tremendous MFP improvements since deregulation despite periods of reduced productivity levels that coincide with exogenous shocks such as economic recessions, fuel price spikes, and other unforeseen events with negative impacts on airline productivity. Between 1978 and 2009, cumulative MFP in terms of airline traffic revenue passenger miles (RPMs) and network capacity available seat miles (ASM) increased by 191 and 117 % respectively. This implies that US passenger airlines have at least doubled their productivity over the past three decades. The paper argued that if RPMs are used as the measure of output, productivity increase would almost triple.

Demydyuk (2011) reviewed metric measures commonly used for analyzing the performance of the airline industry. In particular, this study examined the effectiveness of models based on two activity drivers—passenger-based revenue drivers and kilometer-based cost drivers. The study covered 27 top carriers over a 5-year period. The data was clustered according to airline type, region of origin and operation, and strong or weak financial performance. It was then analyzed in terms of specific properties, followed by a correlation analysis for three data clusters. The variables were then tested to assess the multicollinearity and fixed endogenous problems. Twelve multiple regressions were run on each data cluster with two different dependent variables, namely, operating margin percentage and returns on assets percentage. The main results indicated that operating profit per passenger or per passenger-kilometer was the most significant predictor of airline profitability compared to revenue, unit cost, and load factor, which are conventionally used by the industry. There was no significant correlation between size, business model, or region, which would explain low or high profitability of an airline. According to the regression analysis, seats were not found to be a better denominator than passenger-kilometers, since the analysis showed that operating profit per passenger-kilometer fits the industry better. A central finding is that operating profit per passenger was almost as good as operating profit per revenue passenger kilometers (RPK) in evaluating airlines' financial performance.

Service quality and sensitivity analysis are helpful in estimating performance accurately. Liou (2011) applied MCDM (multivariate statistical analysis and multiple criteria decision-making) methods to analyze airline strategies for passenger services based on passenger preferences. The study used the VC-DRSA (Variable Consistency Dominance-based Rough Set Approach) as the basic empirical framework. Flow graphs were applied to infer decision rules and variables. A large number of alternative approaches and specifications were employed to validate the robustness of the performance results obtained.

Nath (2011) proposed a way to resolve the conceptual and practical problems associated with the quantification of airlines' productivity. He claimed that conventional methodologies to quantify productivity change were inadequate. Quantifying productivity with different units of measurement, such as output per man hour, output per machine hour, and output per unit of material consumed, posed aggregation and disaggregation problems. As a solution, he proposed economic productivity measurement models for the simulations, the use of which significantly improved the estimation results.

In general, the entire airline industry is expected to suffer from immediate and lasting effects as a result of the outbreak of a recession. Pearce (2012) examined air transport markets and the airline industry after the recession of 2008–2009. This paper found that the demand for air transport has been robust in the face of repeated external shocks. International air travel and airfreight rebounded to prerecession levels within 18 months after the recession. Air travel has remained income elastic. Globalized business supply chains have continued to depend on fast air cargo services. Airlines have adjusted their fleet to overcome the demand shock. Capacity was cut, though largely by underutilizing aircraft, which accentuated financial losses. Cash flows in many regions have recuperated although returns on capital stayed below the industry's weighted average cost of capital. Pearce found that competition was restricted to parts of the supply chain that were identified as the primary source of inadequate airline profitability. The author concluded that the value created by the air transport industry has become indispensable to consumers and the wider economy.

Many studies have investigated the impact of an airline's business model, mostly by comparing full-service carriers and low-cost carriers. Different business model imply different cost structures, and this issue has been investigated in conjunction with airline efficiency. A business model reflects the degree of flexibility and independence in decision-making. Most studies have adequately addressed such structural differences using various approaches.

2.2 Alliance Formation and Market Liberalization

It is generally agreed, at least by the advocates of the free market economy, that liberalization of the air transport market leads to increased efficiency. Liberalization eases entry barriers against potential carriers and new carriers, therefore leading to high competition levels in the market. In order to attract a high volume of passengers, airlines have to cut costs and deliver a lower fare as well as a better service quality. Otherwise, passengers will turn to competitors who offer better prices and service quality. The findings from the literature reveal a direct or indirect effect on airline efficiency from opening up of the market. With regard to the effect of liberalization on airline efficiency, most studies have focused on markets in the United States and Europe probably because airline liberalization in Asia began only after 2000. So far research on open skies has centered on the challenges faced by airlines under an open skies agreement and the determinants of a successful open skies initiative. While market liberalization in general and open skies policies in particular met with a degree of success in both the US and Europe, more studies are required on the Asian market. Asia is a relatively latecomer in joining the market liberalization trend, and therefore it deserves further investigation on the progress it has made so far. An additional area that merits a closer look is the prospects of the open skies movement in Southeast Asian economies.

Kontsas and Mylonakis (2008) examined the impact of bilateral agreements on some European air routes in terms of price competition and market structure. They described a theoretical model of firm behavior in the airline industry, both in collusive oligopoly and noncooperative settings. The proposed model explained firms' behavior in the air services market and their characteristics in demand and pricing policies. The results showed that prices were determined by the mark-up on standard cost variables, and the mark-up was in turn determined by customers' goodwill.

In another related study, Fu et al. (2010) studied the traffic volume and traffic flow patterns in relation to the impact of the liberalization policies on economic growth. They investigated the mechanisms driving these changes. The main findings of this study are summarized as follows:

- Liberalization brought extensive economic and traffic growth. Such positive effects are primarily because of the extensive competition and efficiency gains in the airline industry, as well as positive externalities to the economy.
- Liberalization allows airlines to optimize their networks within and across continental markets. Consequently, traffic flow patterns will be transformed accordingly. Strategic alliance is an alternative counter measurement and will weaken when ownership and citizenship restrictions are relaxed.
- There is a two-way association between the expansion of low-cost carriers (LCCs) and liberalization. The paper found that the prevailing growth of LCCs leads to intensified competition and expanded traffic, demanding the removal of restrictions on capacity, frequency, and ticket-charging practices. In addition, it concluded that by increasing the competitiveness of the national aviation industry, emerging and future development of LCCs in the domestic market would also promote the liberalization policy. Such a perspective views the existing regulations as the cause of hindrance to LCCs' growth. More active liberalization should therefore be undertaken for the full realization of associated gains.

A common form of airline cooperation in the wake of the global trend toward liberalization in the air transport market is an increased tendency to form alliances. This is attributed to substantial regulations and the need to form a global network as a way of getting around the wide range of restrictions—legal, political, and institutional—that stand in the way of mergers and acquisitions in the aviation market. Airline alliances can have a positive impact on economic welfare, better services due to improved coordination among the airlines (e.g., flight connections) and lower unit costs. The studies find a strong evidence of efficiency gains derived from economies of scale, evident in increased passenger volume, reduced average air fare, and positive structural changes.

Consolidation and alliance formation is another aspect that plays a role in enhancing airlines' survival and competitiveness. Fana et al. (2001) examined the prospect of various aspects of airlines' consolidation and alliance developments. They conceptualized the most viable near-term airline alliance and consolidation scenario along with a possible scenario of evolution. They showed that economic factors of the industry would force airlines into a superior degree of consolidation, subject to the bound of regulatory liberalization in passenger air transport and the public's opposition to competition.

In a related study, Whalen (2005), using eleven years of the US and European region's data, estimated the various effects of airline code sharing, antitrust immunity, and open skies treaties on prices, output, and capacity. The estimation results showed that code sharing and immunized alliances were statistically significant in lowering the prices compared to traditional interline or multicarrier services, but the estimated size of the effects was significantly smaller than previous results.

Gudmundsson and Lechner (2006) investigated multilateral airline alliances through the lens of structural holes and network closure. The structural holes theory sees network ties as opportunities that link separate network segments through brokers and weak ties. The contrary view argues that network closure would generate superior social capital and thus superior economic rent since there would be more trust, reputation and cooperation within a closed group with strong internal ties. The authors argued that the two perspectives in combination can advance the ability to explain alliance processes in the airline industry.

Sjögren and Soderberg (2011) looked at how deregulation, privatization and the formation of strategic alliances have affected the productivity of international airlines. They evaluated the three factors simultaneously and disaggregated the carriers' operations into production and sales, allowing for firm-level heterogeneity through random parameters. This study used the annual data of 50 major international airlines during the period from 1990 through 2003. Estimations of stochastic frontier models revealed that at the aggregate level, deregulation increased productivity; membership in alliances had an ambiguous effect; and state ownership had no significant effect. Disaggregating the carriers' operations confirmed the productivity gains from deregulation but indicated less clear-cut positive effects for state ownership and alliances.

Finally in a more recent study, Bilotkach et al. (2012) discussed some antitrust implications of airline alliances. They categorized airline alliances in accordance with consumer benefit and the supply side, and discussed their main competitive effects. They concluded that most types of efficiencies can only be considered as partly immunity-specific and suggested an assessment of only the economic effects of antitrust immunity.

2.3　Market Concentration, Market Power and Competition

In any industry, companies can compete on the basis of lower costs, higher quality, or product innovation (see Porter 1990). In the airline industry, depending on the market situation, airlines choose the best strategies to expand their market share in the face of competition. Due to the importance of market share and market power, many studies have analyzed this issue. The analysis makes use of various tools and methodologies in evaluating the effects of market concentration, market power, and competition on airlines' performance.

In an early stage of performance evaluation, Graham et al. (1983) estimated the same type of equation used by Douglas and Miller with the data sample of 324 airline markets. In this paper, they used the Herfindahl–Hirschman Index (HHI), based on carriers' shares of departures, to measure market concentration instead of the number of carriers that Douglas and Miller relied upon. They also estimated load factor equations for the years 1976 and 1980 by applying OLS and two-stage least squares (2SLS). Due to the possible correlation between the density variable and the error term, the use of 2SLS was suggested as the better approach to deal with the endogeneity problem. The results showed that high load factors reduced service quality and thereby reduced traffic. The Herfindahl–Hirschman Index was treated as exogenously determined.

Captain and Sickles (1997) studied the market power of European airlines in an oligopoly structure with product differentiation for the period 1976–1990 and tested the monopoly hypothesis. This paper analyzed the level of competition among eight major European airlines and found little evidence of market power in the industry over that period. The main findings of this paper was that the high prices in Europe were not entirely due to the bilateral agreements, possibly leading to monopoly power, but probably a result of very high cost structures in the industry. These results were inconsistent with the previous study conducted by Good et al. (1994) who examined the same issues in European airlines by estimating a structural, two-stage game—that is, a demand function which incorporates cost and market power as explanatory variables.

In an Asian market context, Chan (2000) reviewed competition in the air transportation market, focusing on the strategy of competition. This article looked at the degree of the competition in the air travel industry located in the Asia Pacific and its impact on the economy in the 1990s. The author investigated and explained the causes of the region's explosive market growth. The air travel share in Asia exceeds 40 % of global travel, rising to 50 percent in 2010. IATA (International Air Transport Association) also projected that the growth rate of international scheduled passenger numbers in Asia will be an average of 7.1 % annually.

Clougherty (2001) empirically tested whether globalization undermines the autonomy of domestic airline competition policy. With a panel data set of twenty-one nations over the 1983–1992 period, his analysis yielded two major findings: (1) globalization undermines the autonomy of domestic airline competition policy and (2) government institutions mediate globalization's impact. The empirical tests reported in this paper utilized a random-effects specification to capture firm-specific effects, after a series of Lagrange Multiplier and Hausman tests, along with a defined period-effect to account for time-specific trends. Three additional econometric issues—nonlinearity in the explanatory variables effects, multicollinearity concerns and confounded effects—and the static nature of the domestic market structure were also addressed. The report concluded that globalization increases the importance of international competitive effects, and private and public interest related political forces are more likely to back consolidation when international competitive effects are important.

Contributing to the literature, Chang and Yeh (2001) presented an objective approach to the evaluation of airline competitiveness. The evaluation problem was formulated as a multi-attribute decision-making model, which was solved by three widely used methods—the simple additive weighting method, the weighted product method, and the technique for order preference based on proximity to an ideal solution. This approach is based on multi-attribute value theory. A new empirical validation procedure was developed to mitigate the problem of inconsistency between the outcomes produced by the three methods. It conducted an empirical study on Taiwan's three major domestic airlines and addressed the advantage of the approach in assessing the results. The estimation found that the simple additive weighting method is superior among the three alternative methodologies.

Firms' heterogeneity and the way it is captured influence unbiasedness and consistency of the estimation results. Cliberto and Tamer (2009) applied the "probability function" methodology and empirically verified if a firm's heterogeneity has a significant impact on forming the market structure in the US airline industry. They uncovered evidence that airlines in their profit functions[6] are heterogeneous across the airlines. The competitive effects of large airlines—American, Delta, and United Airlines—showed a variance with those of low-cost carriers and Southwest Airline. Also, the competitive effect of an airline increased with its airport presence, which was taken into account in measuring the observable heterogeneity in the airline industry.

Johnston and Ozment analyze concentration in the US airline industry between 1970 and 2009. Concentration is proxied by the HHI (Herfindahl-Hirschman Index) and concentration ratio, along with variation in industry costs. The results showed an industry-wide trend of declining costs per available seat mile, which is negatively correlated with the increased level of output and concentration over the last thirty years. These findings support deregulation of the airline industry in the sense that they confirm presence of the sizable economies of scale; a major rationale for deregulation was a multitude of studies showing a lack of scale economies. The concentration ratios indicated that airlines would be behaving as an oligopoly. All measures of concentration show increased concentration ratios since deregulation, and the cost per unit of output has steadily decreased as output has increased. Somewhat inconsistent with this body of evidence, the price per unit of output has decreased even faster than costs.

In a recent study, Liang (2013) analyzed the quantitative effects of airport dominance on ticket prices by routes. The Hausman-Taylor method and random effects method were employed on data from the nine largest domestic US airlines in the third quarter of 1987 for service on 5428 routes. Liang argued that an airline's share of passengers on a route was positively linked with its ability to charge prices above costs. He also reasoned that the force of market concentration in the airline industry was unclear. Higher market concentration, reflected in the market share of the dominant carrier, showed that it was often linked to increases in the average market fare level. Another finding was that high concentration at an airport might

---

[6]Airline (%)/Airport presence/Cost (%)/Market level variables/Wright amendment/Dallas airport/Market size (population)/Per capita income/Income growth rate/Market distance (miles)/Closest airport (miles)/ US centered distance (miles)/Number of markets.

Table 2.3 Testing for market concentration

Dependent variable	Average fare
Time varying exogenous variables	Fuel cost (labor cost was not included because it causes severe multi collinearity problem)
Time varying endogenous variables	Number of passengers, the largest carrier's market share on that route, the price difference between overall market fare and that charged by the largest carrier, the low fare carrier's market share, the price difference between market fare, the price charged by the low fare carrier
Time-invariant exogenous variables	Distance and hub

Source Liang (2013)

lead to more efficient operation and thus reduce the fare level. Variables used for the empirical test of this paper are listed in Table 2.3.

Clougherty (2009) investigated if the national-champion rationale fits with the airline industry's[7] performance. He produced a theoretical framework for analyzing the effect of domestic rivalry on the worldwide competitiveness of airlines by proposing three paths through which domestic rivalry can translate into enhanced international competitiveness. Data from 37 airlines across 19 nations over 1987–1992 (433 specific airline routes/total of 1889 observations) was empirically analyzed. Clougherty used an airline's international market share—i.e., share of revenue passengers in a particular international country-pair market—to measure its competitive performance. The study measured domestic market rivalry or domestic competition by the number of domestic competitors in the market where the airlines were based. Empirical analysis of the world airline industry showed that enhanced firm performance resulting from greater domestic rivalry is positively linked with improved international exports. The paper uses the following two approaches to compare the fitness and the efficiency of airlines (for details, see Table 2.4).

The results showed that domestic rivalry had a positive impact on international market shares. Both domestic network and the merger dummy variable were positively related to the international market share of airlines. International rivalry had a negative impact on market share, while an additional domestic competitor (i.e., domestic rivalry) led to an increase in an airline's market share. Clougherty (2009) confirmed that the result was consistent with Porter's (1990) idea that "International competition is not a substitute for domestic challenge".

Using a profit function approach, Okulski and Heshmati (2010) estimated profit maximization objectives of the US airlines using dynamic panel regression as suggested by Arellano and Bond (1991). He pointed out that first-order conditions can be derived from the profit functions and the competitive quantities of airline

---

[7]The author selected airlines for the test "because airline industry represents a good setting in which to consider the relationship between domestic rivalry and exports because of the ability to isolate the domestic-rivalry effects, the conformity of the airline industry to an idealized setting for the national-champion rationale, and the presence of joint economies of production".

Table 2.4 Approaches to compare estimation methods and model specifications

Methodology	Variables
Time and country specific fixed effect, LSDV	Lagged values of dependent variables, domestic-competitors, domestic-market-share, domestic-competitor-network, international rivalry, the merger dummy, home-competitors, and the airline's number of flights in the country-pair market
GMM	Two lagged dependent variables was included

Source Clougherty (2009)

seats, derived from Cournot and collusive structures, can be estimated. The conflict between these estimates and the actual seat capacities provided a measure of collusive behavior. In his second essay, conjectural variation parameters were estimated to assess the level of competition, which he then regressed on market conditions. The result demonstrated that airlines kept the quantity low to impose higher prices on some routes despite several challenges such as the issue of low-cost carriers, the 9/11 terrorist attacks, and the collusive behavior of airlines. The threat of entry, as measured by potential entrants, did not affect the probability of collusion on a route. Furthermore, he found no evidence that domestic code sharing necessarily leads to collusive behavior. The final essay explored the role of code sharing in the industry more comprehensively. It concluded that code sharing is a tool used by airlines to alleviate risk from uncertain demand and capacity constraints. Evidence from two difference-in-difference estimation studies revealed that code sharing leads to higher load factors and lower price dispersion, while the fares remained constant.

Several strategies positively influence the growth of different airline market participants. Adler and Gellman (2012) discussed strategies that would aid the airlines, airports, airframe, and engine manufacturers, and their first-tier suppliers as well as bodies governing the industry. They proposed that airlines need to employ strategies that can protect them from the risk of fuel price instability, the introduction of carbon cap, and trade regulations. They proposed a number of proactive strategies to ensure further industry growth in an economically, politically, and environmentally sustainable manner.

Price formation and level strongly influence the survival and profitability of airlines. Obermeyer et al. (2012) examined the effects of competition on price dispersion in the European airline markets. By conducting a cross-sectional analysis of 1200 flights between 130 European airport pairs, they confirmed that the characteristic of the European airline industry could be summarized as a non-monotonic link between competition intensity and price distribution. They connected the results of the paper with other studies on efficiency and productivity of airlines. Ticket price information on routes between the airports of European capitals and other international airports with more than one million departing passengers traveling within Europe in 2008 was collected for the analysis. Price dispersion for each flight was calculated on the basis of commonly used indices such as the Gini coefficient of inequality. The following variables listed in Table 2.5 were used for the empirical estimation of this study.

Table 2.5 Variables used in computation of Gini Coefficient

Variables	Definition
Flights	Variable that measures the number of flights on route during a fixed time interval. It is the capacity offered by all airlines operating on this route
LCC	Dummy variable indicating if a low-cost carrier is operating on route. It aims to capture the potential influence of low-cost carriers on competition
Tourist	Dummy variable indicating whether at least one of the cities on the route is a potential tourist destination. It intends to eliminate the potential influence of tourist traffic on price dispersion
Distance	A continuous variable that measures the distance between origin and destination airport, serving as a proxy for operating costs
Population	Average number of inhabitants in the metropolitan areas of the two end points on route. It was calculated as the arithmetic mean of passengers departed at the origin and destination airport on route
Airline fare	Control variable for systematic differences in price dispersion behavior between airlines

Source Obermeyer et al. (2012)

The results of this study confirmed the hypothesis that efficient airlines are better positioned to differentiate fares than their less efficient counterparts, providing empirical evidence of a non-monotonic relationship for the European airline market. The study also confirmed an inverse U-shaped association between the extent of competition and the scale of price dispersion for economy-class flights. Depending on the actual level of market concentration, an increase in competition can either increase or decrease the price dispersion.

Recently Cosmas et al. (2013) attempted to segment the US origin and destination (OD) markets into peer groups by performing statistical cluster analysis on OD city-pair data. The data was categorized by the market concentration, passenger volume, and yield. The study thoroughly reviewed the OD market structure, in much more detail compared to previous studies such as one by Belobaba and Van Acker (1994), which merely employed market concentration measured by the Herfindahl–Hirschman Index   (HHI) or by the competitors' numbers to classify the market structures. The OD market clusters were defined using a two-step clustering process—first assigning cases to pre-clusters and subsequently grouping pre-clusters using a hierarchical clustering algorithm. The results showed that high-yield markets have, on average, consistently made the industry underperform in both passenger and revenue growth, whereas low-yield markets have led the industry in both areas.

2.4   Other Issues

The literature has focused on several other issues apart from the ones discussed above. Shan and Hamilton (1991) examined the hypothesis that land-specific advantage embedded in firms of a particular nationality is a motivation for

Table 2.6 Determinants of air travel demand

Oil gross domestic product	Exchange rate (Saudi Riyals/special drawing rights—SDR)
Private non-oil gross domestic product	Exchange rate (Saudi Riyals/US$)
Government non-oil gross domestic product	Population size
Total non-oil gross domestic product	Total expenditures
Total gross domestic product	Private consumption expenditures
Consumer price index	Total consumption expenditures
Per capita income	Yield
Import of goods and services	

Source Ba-Fail et al. (2000)

international inter-firm cooperation. A sample of domestic and international cooperative relationships formed by Japanese firms in the commercialization of biotechnology is applied to identify elements that differentiate domestic from foreign partners. The findings supported their hypothesis that country-specific advantage is a significant variable in explaining differences between cooperative relationships with partners of different countries.

In order to shed light on the issue of land-specific advantage, Ba-Fail et al. (2000) identified the components that influence the domestic air travel demand in Saudi Arabia. They built models for domestic air travel demand in the country with different combinations of explanatory variables, utilizing a stepwise regression technique. The model, which included total expenditures and population size as explanatory parameters, was proposed as the most suitable approach to embody the demand for domestic air travel in Saudi Arabia. The remaining models introduced in the paper were reported as suffering from a multicollinearity problem. The paper suggested implementing this model to specify and measure the relationship between domestic air travel demand and economic and demographic forces in the country. The following explanatory variables listed in Table 2.6 were selected to examine the relationship with air travel demand.

In focusing on the price and income responsiveness of consumers, Ferguson et al. (2007) looked into the specific issues of: (i) how does the role of price elasticity and cross-price elasticity improve previous models and (ii) how income elasticity improves market demand functions. They discussed the conditions for optimality using estimated market demand functions. Econometric modelling was applied to construct market demand functions. The role of multiple linear regressions improved the results on elasticity, cost degradation, and passenger diversion. The authors then built a model to optimize revenue generations for domestic flights.

Berry and Jia (2008) introduced a structural model of the airline industry and approximated the impact on profitability of demand and supply shocks caused by turbulence in the airline industry in the early 2000s. They revealed that the four major bankruptcies and two mergers, all involving legacy airlines, resulted in a large profit reduction. The study reported that the expansion of low-cost carriers

Table 2.7 Determinants of air and sea travel demands

Air travel demand	Number of airline passengers
Relative price	Fare ratio of air fare to sea fare levels
Relative frequency	Frequency ratio of the total number of flights to the total number of sea and ferry itineraries
Relative capacity	Seat ratio of the total number of aircraft seats to the total number of vessel seats
Relative time	Time ratio of the air travel times to the sea ferry travel times
Income GDP	Sum of the gross domestic product (GDP) of the origin zones and each destination island (in constant 1995 prices in million drachmas)
Tourism bed	Total number of visitor beds in hotels and other legal accommodation
Population POP	Product of the population size of the origin zones and of each destination island (in billions)

Source Tsekeris (2009)

(LCCs) significantly dented the legacy carriers' variable profits, and air-travel demand became more price-sensitive in 2006 compared to the late 1990s. Passengers showed a stronger preference for direct flights and the change in marginal cost favored direct flights. These factors, along with the expansion of LCCs, led to a more than 80 % reduction in the legacy carriers' profits. Along with escalating fuel costs and competition from LCCs, changes in demand patterns were also an important reason behind the legacy carriers' lower profits.

In another study on sensitivity and shifts in demand to fare changes, Tsekeris (2009) described a dynamic demand model, referred to as a dynamic abstract mode model, for estimating both short- and long-term responses of air passengers to relative changes in air and sea travel fares in competitive markets. The implementation of the model in the competitive market of Aegean islands in Greece showed that the volumes of air passengers and the relative travel costs explained current air travel demand to a significant degree (see Table 2.7).

Tourism has expanded dramatically in recent years. Assaker et al. (2011) applied structural equation modeling (SEM) methodologies to a cross-sectional data of 162 countries, evaluating the measurement and use of structural models on the relationship between the economy, society, environment, and tourism. Using SEM estimation, they examined the interconnection between the prime constituents of the tourism destination paradigm[8] and the demand for tourism at that destination. They found that although the economy construct had no direct influence on tourism, it did have a mediating positive impact on tourism through the society and environment constructs, with the society construct paralleling the condition of the infrastructure. Furthermore, society and environment were found to have a straight, positive influence on producing tourism undertakings and revenues. For a list of different categories of variables used in the specification of the models, see Table 2.8.

---

[8]The economy, society, and the natural and infrastructural environments.

Table 2.8 List of variable categories

Economic variables	Infra structure related variables	Society construction variables
Consumer price index (CPI); Purchasing power parity (PPP) Trade volume (TRADE) Foreign direct investment (FDI) Industry value added (IVA)	Road index (ROAD) Sanitation access (SAN) Electricity index (ELEC) Number of vehicles (AUTOS) Internet access (INT) Telephone mainlines (TEL) Mobile phones (CEL)	Education (EDU) Life expectancy (LEXP) Income (INC) Television index (TV) PC index (PC) Newspaper index (NEWS)

Source Assaker et al. (2011)

In 2012, IATA published a report on air travel demand entitled "Measuring the responsiveness of air travel demand to changes in prices and incomes." The report suggested various ways of measuring income and price elasticity on the basis of short-haul versus long-haul flights and by the regions. The report also presented various estimation methodologies.

The two-way or higher form of causality effects in airline studies reviewed above is not common. Koo et al. (2013) introduced a cause and effect structure into the relationship between tourism demand and air transport capacity. They then applied a vector error-correction model to assess whether capacity or passenger demand could be a significant cause for the return to long-run equilibrium following short-run deviations. Using data on international aviation between Australia, China, and Japan, they found that demand in the Japan–Australia market modifies for short-run nonconformities from the long-run equilibrium faster than the China–Australia market. The possible reasons for such variation in the adjustment speeds were discussed. The results were robust to the phenomenon of airlines preempting demand when setting capacity. In the short run, airline seats were generally static due to schedule commitments. Passenger demand, however, was responsive to economic conditions. The result suggested that the speed at which the equilibrium between supply and demand is reached is different for Japan and China.

Low-cost carriers (LCC) are seen as a source of changes in the airlines market. Pearson and Merkert (2014) examined whether LCCs are a critical danger to the sustainability of network airlines. The fast expansion of LCCs, particularly within the Asia-Pacific region, has impaired the growth of network airlines. The latter have responded to this phenomenon by forming lower-cost subsidiaries, identified as airlines-within-airlines (AWAs). The study attempted to delineate the criteria for successful AWAs and revise the analysis of past, present, and proposed and announced AWAs. With a thorough review of the previous studies, it found that AWAs have limited accomplishments, as 27 out of 67 AWAs failed, including three in the Asia-Pacific region. Of those presently operating, 58.1 % are from Asia Pacific, accounting for almost 40.0 % of the proposed and announced carriers. The study concludes that these AWAs are operating under ill-defined strategies, with rather late entrance into the market, excess management control from the parent airline which makes the AWAs very similar to the parent, higher costs and less efficiency vis-à-vis low-cost competitors. It concludes that operating AWAs with excess capacity and comparatively low fares in intensively competitive markets are the vital causes for failure. In contrast, the most successful AWAs have considerable independence from their parent, and have market dominance and decisive leadership. In this sense, they are not much different from the pure LCC model unless an ample revenue premium is realized.

In a recent study, Lowa et al. (2014) examines the performances of 114 major international airlines and 6 LCCs for the period between 1987 and 2010, using the resource-based theory. Results show that among the human, physical, and intangible resources at the aggregate industry level, intangible resources are the most critical factor behind performance success. Furthermore, the study noted that to become effective, airlines should provide satisfactory services at comparatively cheaper costs. Country-specific components such as the extent of liberalization—calculated by a bilateral open skies agreement between states—and the regions where airlines are located are important factors responsible for the higher profits made by some airlines and not others. The increasing consumer acceptance of new airlines indicates that established airlines cannot be complacent. Following the emergence of budget airlines that offer point-to-point service for short-distance destinations, full legacy carriers can distinguish themselves by providing direct services on long-distance flights.

2.5   The Conclusion

This chapter provides a review of studies, focusing mainly on the competitiveness of airlines. In our view, we have provided useful and up-to-date information on the modeling of airline efficiency, productivity, and competitiveness, and the results obtained. The review is classified into a wide variety of themes: efficiency, productivity, factor conditions; alliances and market liberalization; market concentration, market power, competition; and other issues such as price and income sensitivity of demand, tourism and the entry of low-cost airlines into the market. The review provides a comprehensive understanding of the literature. The information provided will be useful in influencing the specification of production and cost functions of airlines' operation in a manner that is consistent with both theory and practice. The review also serves as a guide to the best approaches in estimating airlines' efficiency through a comparative analysis of airlines with different characteristics. Finally, suitable policy recommendations have been provided on the basis of the results and the determinants of performance.

Appendix 2.1: Summary of Productivity and Efficiency Studies

Author(s)	Type of data	Sample and period	Estimation structure	Dependant variable(s)	Independent variable(s)	Estimation method(s)	Findings/issues
Oum and Yu (1998)	Panel data	22 international airlines (1986–1993)	A translog variable cost function	Unit cost difference	Share of variable cost, Size, Output mix (RTK), Input prices—(labor, fuel, flight, equipment, ground property, equipment (GPE), and materials), Operating characteristics, Time effects	Maximum likelihood estimation	Capital input (negative) Stage length (negative) Efficiency (negative) Incidental (negative)
Oum et al. (2005)	Panel data	10 full-service carriers in Canada and US (1990–2001)	A multilateral index using the s translog function	Total factor productivity cost competitiveness, residual average yields	Output: RTKs Inputs: labor, fuel, materials, flight equipment, and ground property and equipment GPE, Output scale (size); Average stage length of flights; Composition of outputs (scheduled passenger services, scheduled freight services, non-scheduled services incidental services). Average load factor; Rate of fleet capacity, year dummy	Log-linear TFP regressions	Output size (positive) Average stage length (positive) Passenger load (positive) Fleet adjustment (negative) The year dummy (significant) Residual TFP and productive efficiency (the industry's average residual TFP decreased). Unit cost competitiveness (overall, the industry's average level of cost competitiveness was improved steadily from 1990 to 1997)

(continued)

(continued)

Author(s)	Type of data	Sample and period	Estimation structure	Dependant variable(s)	Independent variable(s)	Estimation method(s)	Findings/issues
Barbot et al. (2008)	Cross-sectional data	49 intl. full-service airlines plus 10 LCC (2005)	Output/Input	Efficiency and TFP	Inputs: Labor, fleet fuel Outputs: ASKs, RPKs, RTKs	Data envelopment analysis and OLS	LCCs perform better than full-service airlines (DEA and TFP consistent) The majority of European and American carriers have higher effectiveness than Asia Pacific and China/North Asia airlines
Assaf et al. (2009)	Panel data	15 major UK airlines (2002–2007)		Efficiency	Output: TKA (ton kilometers available), total operational revenues, Inputs: labor expenses, aircraft fuel and oil expenses, load factor and airline size	DEA bootstrap methodology	The efficiency of UK airlines has continuously declined since 2004. Airline size and load factor were found to be significantly and positively related to technical efficiency variations. Factors such as increase in oil price and fierce market competition were also potential inefficiency determinants
Assaf (2009)	Panel data	of major 12 US airlines (2004–2007)	Cobb–Douglas production function	Input/output	Output: total operating revenues Inputs: Total operational cost (excluding labor cost), aircraft fuel and oil expenses, number of planes (proxy for capital input). Load factor (RPK/ASK)	Random effects (the Bayesian stochastic random frontier model)	Bayesian random stochastic frontier model fits data well with all coefficients correctly signed. Satisfy the theoretical requirements. The efficiency estimates: performance of US airlines has declined over time to reach a value of 69.02 % in 2007. Return to scale support the efficiency results. Confirmed that US airlines are not operating at an optimum level of scale

(continued)

(continued)

Author(s)	Type of data	Sample and period	Estimation structure	Dependant variable(s)	Independent variable(s)	Estimation method(s)	Findings/issues
Greer (2009)	Panel data	16 US airlines (1999–2008)		Efficiency	Inputs: labor, fuel and fleet-wide seating capacity. Output: ASK (available seat-miles). Union density. Average aircraft size, Average stage length, Degree of hubbing, Legacy carrier, Percent passengers-flying internationally	Data envelopment analysis and Tobit regression model	Due to the left- and right-censored variable problem of DEA, union density/aircraft size, (negative). Hubbing (influence a lot) unionized (exhibit lower levels of efficiency) Aircrafts age (not statistically significant). Result found that the more heavily unionized carriers are generally less efficient than the lesser unionized ones
Parast et al. (2010)	Panel data	US domestic airlines (network and low-cost carriers) (1989–2008)		Profitability	Quality and productivity; Passenger and ton-miles; Labor productivity; On-time performance; Gas price; Employee salary; Maintenance cost per flight hours; Passenger load factor	Correlation and multivariate regression analysis. Stepwise regression analysis	Labor productivity is the most significant predictor of profitability. On-time performance has no relationship with profitability. Labor productivity, gas price, average annual maintenance cost and employee salary are significant predictors of Profitability. The relationship between labor productivity and employee salary with profitability is positive. Gas price and average annual maintenance cost have a negative relationship with Profitability

(continued)

(continued)

Author(s)	Type of data	Sample and period	Estimation structure	Dependant variable(s)	Independent variable(s)	Estimation method(s)	Findings/issues
Lee and Johnson (2011)	Panel data	5 US airline (2006–2008)	Profitability production function	Profitability efficiency and efficiency	Firm's fleet, Fuel expenses; Number of employees, scheduled revenue passenger miles (RPM); available seat miles (ASM); Production system: Capacity, design, demand generation, operations, demand consumption. Efficiency change: Efficiency was decomposed via a rational Network DEA model and decomposed into: Technical efficiency change, Scale efficiency change, allocative efficiency change	Two-dimensional efficiency decomposition (2DED) and OLS	Productivity was mainly caused by demand fluctuation than technical change in Production probabilities. The profitability efficiency in cargo service was 21 % more efficient than civil service. Capacity design significantly affect efficiency
Wang et al. (2013)	Cross-sectional data	30 airlines including 22 US carriers and 8 non-US (2006)		Output/input Technical efficiency	Input variables: Employees, Fuel expense, Aircraft. Output variables: ASMs, RPMs, Non-PAX Rev. Performance: Board size, Committees. Meetings, Non-executive director, CEO duality, CEO and chairman	Data envelopment analysis (DEA) and Multivariate analysis	More than half of US airlines less efficient than the best in the industry. performance of carriers is not just related to their characteristics such as the number of committees and non-executive directors But affected by the external factors
Merkert and Hensher (2011)	Panel data	58 of the largest passenger airlines		Output/Input Efficiency	Input: available tome kilometers (ATK) (proxy for capital), FTE (measure of labor).	Two-stage data envelopment analysis (DEA) with partially	Overall efficiency of the airlines has decreased over the two years. The relatively poor cost efficiency was a result of

(continued)

(continued)

Author(s)	Type of data	Sample and period	Estimation structure	Dependant variable(s)	Independent variable(s)	Estimation method(s)	Findings/issues
		(2007/2008, 2008/2009)			Output: revenue passenger kilometers (RPK) and revenue ton kilomtres (RTK), Airline Size (ASK), Stage Length (km), Aircraft Size (seats), Fleet Age (years), Aircraft Families Aircraft Manufacturers	bootstrapped random effects regression	allocative inefficiency rather than of the technical inefficiency of the airlines
Cristina and Gramani (2012)	Panel data	4 airlines (2 Brazilian and 2 American) (1997–2006)		Operational performance and Financial performance	Inputs: Aircraft fuel, wages, salaries and Benefits, Cost per Available Seat Mile (CASM). Output: Revenue Passenger Mile 1/4 load factor, available seat mil, Input: 1/score, Efficiency, Outputs: flight revenue, Flight income	A two-step data envelopment analysis (DEA)	Emergent market, operational performance is always much better than the financial one. Resources optimization has been the main concern for these companies. Improving the operational efficiency does not necessarily generate an improvement in financial efficiency
Pires and Fernandes (2012)	Cross-sectional data	42 airlines from 25 countries (2001)	Catch-up effect (input-orientation) frontier-shift effect	Malmquist productivity index	Input: Financial leverage. Output: firm size, tangibility of assets, and intangible assets	Malmquist productivity analysis	Airlines which moved more aggressively to reduce their indebtedness showed improved profitability, for a given size, fleet and intangible assets. To expand their air transportation operations, airlines require substantial financial investments, especially in aircraft, fleet maintenance and information systems

(continued)

(continued)

Author(s)	Type of data	Sample and period	Estimation structure	Dependant variable(s)	Independent variable(s)	Estimation method(s)	Findings/issues
Powell II (2012)		US airline industry level data and the disaggregated carrier level data (1978–2009)		Productivity	Outputs: RPM (scheduled revenue passenger-miles), RTK (Scheduled, revenue ton-miles of freight), RMK (Scheduled revenue ton-miles of mail), Incidental revenue. Inputs: Labor, Fuel, Capital; Intermediate expense	MFP and TFP estimation	Despite of reduced productivity levels that coincide with exogenous shocks such as economic recessions, fuel price spikes, and other unforeseen events with negative impact, US passenger airlines experienced tremendous MFP improvements since deregulation
Merkert and Williams (2013)	Panel data	18 European Public service obligation (PSO) airlines (2007/08, 2008/09)	A semi-parametric approach	Technical efficiency	Inputs: available seat kilometers (ASK) and full-time equivalent (FTE). Outputs: revenue passenger kilometers (RPK) and realized departures. 2nd stage: Stage Length (km), PSO contracts, Duration (months), PSO_Share (in %), Ownership, year	Two-stage approach including DEA and truncated regressions	DEA models (VRS and CRS) the average bias-corrected technical efficiency scores are smaller than the average uncorrected scores. Technical efficiency suggest that stage length has a negative impact on the operators' efficiency. Operators that are in an early stage of their contracts are more efficient than those that are close to the renewal/re-tendering of their contracts. That this impact is significant regardless of CRS or VRS assumption. Operators with a large number of PSO contracts to be more efficient than those with only a few contracts

(continued)

(continued)

Author(s)	Type of data	Sample and period	Estimation structure	Dependant variable(s)	Independent variable(s)	Estimation method(s)	Findings/issues
Mallikarjun (2015)	27 US domestic airlines			Airline operating efficiency, cost efficiency, service effectiveness, Revenue Generation	Input: Operating expenses the first stage: ASM(available seat miles) is an output the 2nd stage: ASM is input revenue passenger miles (RPM) is output and Fleet size (FS) and destinations (DS) are the two site characteristics the 3rd stage: operating Revenue	The unoriented DEA network methodology	Major US airlines are more efficient than national US airlines in spending operating expenses and achieving operating revenue while not much significant difference in their service supply and demand efficiencies
Duygun et al. (2015)	Panel data	87 European airlines from 23 European countries (2000–2010)	A network Data Envelopment Analysis (network DEA) approach which comprises two sub-technologies	Efficiency	Inputs: Capital (flight capital) —number of aircrafts; Labor —Quantity of pilots, cabin crew, mechanics, passenger and aircraft handlers, and other labor (Divisia index); Materials Quantity of supplies, outside services, and non-flight equipment (Divisia index). Intermediate output: Revenue Ton Kilometers (RTK)/ (LOAD FACTOR) Output: Revenue Ton Kilometers (RTK)	A network data envelopment analysis	In over all, most of the inefficiencies are produced in the first stage of the analysis. Most of the budget carriers' inefficiencies are restrained to the first stage. Performance of airlines are very dynamic and efficiency varied across types of airlines

References

Adler N, Gellman A (2012) Strategies for managing risk in a changing aviation environment. J Air Transp Manage 21:24–35

Ahn SC, Good D, Sickles RC (1997) A dynamic frontier approach to assessing the relative efficiency of Asian and North American airline firms. Paper presented at the Taipei international conference on efficiency and productivity growth, Taipei

Aigner DJ, Lovell CAK, Schmidt P (1977) Formulation and estimation of stochastic frontier production function models. J Econometrics 6:21–37

Arellano M, Bond S (1991) Some tests of specification for panel data: Monte Carlo evidence and an application to employment equations. Rev Econ Stud 58(2):277–297

Assaf A (2009) Are US airlines really in crisis? Tour Manag 30:916–921

Assaf A, George JA (2009) The operational performance of UK airlines: 2002–2007. J Econ Stud 38(1):5–16

Assaf A, George JA (2012) European versus US airlines: performance comparison in a dynamic market. Tour Manag 33(2):317–326

Assaker G, Vinzi VE, O'Connor P (2011) Modeling a causality network for tourism development: an empirical analysis. J Model Manag 6(3):258–278

Ba-Fail AO, Abed SY, Jasimuddin SM (2000) The determinants of domestic air travel demand in the Kingdom of Saudi Arabia. J Air Transp Worldwide 5(2):72–86

Baltagi BH, Griffin JM, Rich DP (1995) Airline deregulation: the cost pieces of the puzzle. Int Econ Rev 36:245–259

Barbot G, Costa A, Sochirca E (2008) Airlines performance in the new market context: a comparative productivity and efficiency analysis. J Air Transp Manage 14:270–274

Battese GE, Coelli TJ (1988) Prediction of firm-level technical efficiencies with a generalized frontier production function and panel data. J Econometrics 38:387–399

Battese G, Coelli T (1992) Frontier production functions, technical efficiency and panel data: with application to paddy farmers in India. J Prod Anal 3:153–169

Battese G, Coelli TJ (1995) A model for technical in efficiency effects in a stochastic frontier production function for panel data. Empirical Economics 20:325–332

Battese GE, Heshmati A, Hjalmarsson L (2000) Efficiency of labor use in the Swedish banking industry: a stochastic frontier approach. Empirical Economics 25:623–640

Belobaba P, Van Acker J (1994) Airline market concentration: an analysis of US origin-destination markets. J Air Transp Manage 1:5–14

Berry S, Jia P (2008) Tracing the woes: an empirical analysis of the airline industry. NBER working paper series, working paper 14503

Bilotkach V, Hüschelrath K (2012) Airline alliances and antitrust policy: the role of efficiencies. J Air Transp Manage 21:76–84

Captain PF, Sickles RC (1997) Competition and market power in the European airline industry: 1976–1990. Manag Decis Econ 18(3):209–225

Chan D (2000) Air wars in Asia: competitive and collaborative strategies and tactics in action. J Manage Dev 19(6):473–488

Chang YH, Yeh CH (2001) Evaluating airline competitiveness using multiattribute decision making. Omega 29:405–415

Ciliberto F, Tamer E (2009) Market structure and multiple equilibria in airline markets. Econometrica 77(6):1791–1828

Clougherty JA (2001) Globalization and the autonomy of domestic competition policy: an empirical test on the world airline industry. J Int Bus Stud 32(3):459–478

Clougherty JA (2009) Domestic rivalry and export performance: theory and evidence from international airline markets, Canadian Economics Association. Can J Econ/Revue Canadienne d'Economique 42(2):440–468

Coelli T (1996) FRONTIER version 4.1: a computer program for stochastic frontier production and cost function estimation. Working paper 96/7, CEPA, Department of Econometrics, University of New England, Armidale, Australia

Coelli T, Perelman S, Romano E (1999) Accounting for environmental influences in stochastic frontier models: with application to international airlines. J Prod Anal 11:251–273

Constantin PD, Martin DL, Rivera EB, de Rivera Bastiaan (2009) Cobb-Douglas, translog stochastic production function and data envelopment analysis in total factor productivity in Brazilian agribusiness. J Oper Supply Chain Manage 2(2):20–33

Cornwell C, Schmidt P, Sickles RC (1990) Production frontiers with cross-sectional and time-series variation in efficiency levels. J Econometrics 46:185–200

Cosmas A, Love R, Rajiwade S, Linz M (2013) Market clustering and performance of US OD markets. J Air Transp Manage 28:20–25

Cristina M, Gramani N (2012) Efficiency decomposition approach: a cross-country airline analysis. Expert Syst Appl 39:5815–5819

Debru G (1951) The coefficient of resource utilization. Econometrica 19:273–292

Demydyuk G (2011) Optimal financial key performance indicators: evidence from the airline industry. Acc Taxation 4(1):39–51

Duygun M, Prior D, Shaban M, Emili TA (2015) Disentangling the European airlines efficiency puzzle: a network data envelopment analysis approach. Working paper Castellon, 2014/04

Fana T, Vigeant L, Geissler C, Bosler B, Wilmking J (2001) Evolution of global airline strategic alliance and consolidation in the twenty-first century. J Air Transp Manage 7:349–360

Farrell MJ (1957) The measurement of productive efficiency. J Roy Stat Soc, Series A 120:253–290

Ferguson BR, Hong D (2007) Airline revenue optimization problem: a multiple linear regression model. J Concr Appl Math 5(2):153–167

Fu X, Oum TH, Zhang A (2010) Air transport liberalization and its impacts on airline competition and air passenger traffic. Transp J 49(4):24–41

Good DH, Röller LH, Sickles RC (1994) US airline deregulation: implications for european transport. Econ J 103–419:1028–1041

Good D, Roller LH, Sickles RC (1995) Airline efficiency differences between Europe and the US: implications for the pace of EC integration and domestic regulation. Eur J Oper Res 80:508–518

Gorin T, Belobaba P (2004) Impacts of entry in airline markets: effects of revenue management on traditional measures of airline performance. J Air Transp Manage 10:259–270

Graham DR, Kaplan DP, Sibley DS (1983) Efficiency and competition in the airline industry. Bell J Econ 14(1):118–138

Greer M (2009) Is it the labor unions' fault? Dissecting the causes of the impaired technical efficiencies of the legacy carriers in the United States. Transp Res Part A 43:779–789

Gudmundsson SV (2004) Management emphasis and performance in the airline industry: an exploratory multilevel analysis. Transp Res Part E 40:443–463

Gudmundsson SV, Lechner C (2006) Multilateral, airline alliances: balancing strategic constraints and opportunities. J Air Transp Manage 12:153–158

Heshmati A (2003) Productivity growth, efficiency and outsourcing in manufacturing and services. J Econ Surv 17(1):79–112

Kontsas S, Mylonakis J (2008) Pricing competition policy in the European airlines industry: a firm behavior model proposal. Innov Mark 4(4):23–27

Koo TR, Tan DT, Duval DT (2013) Direct air transport and demand interaction: a vector error-correction model approach. J Air Transp Manage 28:14–19

Koopmans TC (1951) An analysis of production as an efficient combination of activities. In: Koopmans TC (ed) Activity Analysis of production and allocation, proceeding of a conference. John Wiley and Sons Inc., New York, pp 33–97

Kumbhakar SC, Lovell CAK (2000) Stochastic frontier analysis. Cambridge University Press, Cambridge

Kumbhakar SC, Wan H, Horncastle A (2015) A practitioner's guide to stochastic frontier analysis using stata. Academic, Cambridge

Lee CY, Johnson AL (2011) Two-dimensional efficiency decomposition to measure he demand effect in productivity, analysis. Eur J Oper Res 216:584–593

Liang J (2013) An econometric analysis on pricing and market structure in the US airline industry. Adv Econometrics 3(2):1–28

Liou JH (2011) Variable consistency dominance-based rough set approach to formulate airline service strategies. Appl Soft Comput 11:4011–4020

Lowa JMW, Lee BK (2014) Effects of internal resources on airline competitiveness. J Air Transp Manage 36:23–32

Mallikarjun S (2015) Efficiency of US airlines: a strategic operating model. J Air Transp Manage 43:46–56

Meeusen W, van den Broek J (1977) Efficiency estimation from Cobb-Douglas production function with composed errors. Int Econ Rev 18(2):435–444

Merkert R, Hensher DA (2011) The impact of strategic management and fleet planning on airline efficiency—a random effects Tobit model based on DEA efficiency scores. Transp Res Part A 45:686–695

Merkert R, Williams G (2013) Determinants of European PSO airline efficiency: evidence from a semi-parametric approach. J Air Transp Manage 29:11–16

Nath DH (2011) Economic productivity quantification and simulation models for the air transport industry. In: 2011 international conference on modeling, simulation and control IPCSIT, vol 10. IACSIT Press, Singapore

Obermeyer A, Evangelinos C, Püsche R (2012) Price dispersion and competition in European airline markets. J Air Transp Manage 26:31–34

Okulski RR, Heshmati A (2010) Time series analysis of global airline passengers. Transportation industry. Technology management, economics and policy program, TEMEP discussion paper no. 2010:65

Oum TH, Yu C (1998) Cost competitiveness of major airlines: an international comparison. Elsevier Sci 32(6):407–422

Oum TH, Fu X, Yu C (2005) New evidences on airline efficiency and yields: a comparative analysis of major North American air carriers and its implications. Transp Policy 12(2):153–164

Parast MM, Fini EH (2010) The effect of productivity and quality on profitability in US airline industry: an empirical investigation. Managing Serv Qual 20(5):458–474

Pearce B (2012) The state of air transport markets and the airline industry after the great recession. J Air Transp Manage 21:3–9

Pearson J, Merkert R (2014) Airlines-within-airlines: a business model moving East. J Air Transp Manage 38:21–26

Pires HM, Fernand E (2012) Malmquist financial efficiency analysis for airlines. Transp Res Part E 48:1049–1055

Porter ME (1990) The competitive advantage of nations. Harvard Bus Rev. March/April 1990

Powell II RA (2012) Productivity performance of US passenger airlines since deregulation. Master thesis, Massachusetts Institute of Technology, Department of Civil and Environmental Engineering

Schmidt P (1986) Frontier production functions. Econometric Rev 4:289–328

Schmidt P, Sickles RC (1984) Production frontiers and panel data. J Bus Econ Stat 2(4):367–374

Shan W, Hamilton W (1991) Country-specific advantage and international cooperation. Strateg Manag J 12(6):419–432

Sjögren S, Soderberg M (2011) Productivity of airline carriers and its relation to deregulation, privatization and membership in strategic alliances. Transp Res Part E: Logistics Transp Rev 47:228–237

Tsekeris T (2009) Dynamic analysis of air travel demand in competitive island markets. J Air Transp Manage 15:267–273

Wang Z, Hofer CH, Dresner ME (2013) Financial condition, safety investment and accident propensity in the US airline industry: a structural analysis. Transp Res Part E 49:24–32

Whalen WT (2005) A panel data analysis of code sharing, antitrust immunity and open skies treaties in international aviation markets. Antitrust Division, US Department of Justice, Economic Analysis Group

Yan S, Tang CH, Fu TC (2008) An airline scheduling model and solution algorithms under stochastic demands. Eur J Oper Res 39(1):22–39

Chapter 3
A Review of the Airline Industry

Abstract This chapter provides an overview of the key issues in the passenger airline industry, in particular its current status and the challenges it faces in going forward. The air transportation industry is faced with the many global issues such as the cost burden from the fuel price fluctuations, epidemics, global economic downturn, environmental issues, and tightened regulations. We have briefly introduced these issues here to provide a context for the remaining parts of the manuscript.

Keywords Stochastic frontier functions · Performance · Productivity · Airline industry

3.1 Terms Related to Air Transportation[1]

The areas covered in the remaining chapters are mainly related to the passenger services of the airline industry. To enable a better understanding, we first introduce here the terms and scope defined by the "Statistics of International Trade in Services 2010" published by the UN.

"*Air transport* covers all international freight and passenger transport services provided by aircraft" (UN 2010).

Most of the technical terms and definition covered in this chapter are summarized without any major alteration from the publications of IATA, ICAO, UK Department for Transport, United States Department of Transportation, and WTO. In addition to these official reports, some parts of this chapter, in particular the key drivers of the airline economy, have been summarized from both IATA and "The Global Airline Industry" (Belobaba et al. 2009), which has been widely used as the formal guideline for the airline industry's study. In the case of issues related to airline liberalization and freedom of the skies, from the WTO and IATA manual has been quoted without any alteration.

---

[1]For the details on the terms used in the airline industry and in the chapters in this volume, see Appendix 3.3.

"*Passenger services* include fares and other expenditure related to the carriage of passengers, including any taxes levied on passenger services, such as sales or value-added taxes. Fares that are a part of package tours, charges for excess baggage, vehicles, or other personal accompanying effects, and food, drink or other items purchased on board carriers are also included. The valuation of passenger transport should include fees payable by the carriers to travel agencies and other providers of reservation services. Also included are rentals provided by residents to non-residents, and vice versa, of vessels, aircraft, coaches or other commercial vehicles with crews, for limited periods (such as a single voyage), for the carriage of passengers" (UN 2010).

"*Freight services* cover the transport of objects. Freight services may be divided into three types. The first two are associated with the fact that, in line with the recommendations of the BPM6, goods are valued f.o.b. at the customs frontier of the exporting economy. The third type encompasses the freight of goods which do not change ownership. These three types of freight services are further described below. The service charge may be charged directly or be included in the price" (UN 2010).

In most cases, both IATA (International Air Transport Association) and ICAO (International Civil Aviation Organization) provide data related to air transportation to international organizations such as UN (the United Nations), UNWTO (World Tour Organization), World Bank, IMF (International Monetary Fund), and WTO (World Trade Organization). The above definitions can therefore be considered as the standard for empirical studies.

3.2   Industry Status

Market outcomes of the airline industry have expanded faster over the last few decades, with increasing customers, routes, and additional frequency in flights. In the 1970s, markets in the US started getting liberalized, followed by those in Europe in the 1980s, and then to some degree in other regions as well. Costs have decreased to a sizeable degree, driven by improved technology and sophisticated operational management. Such cost reduction created much value, especially for consumers and the broader economy, but became the main cause behind restructuring airline employees and procurements. It also initiated a growing global phenomenon of a new business model in the airline industry, namely, the emergence of low-cost carriers. The economy induces a travel demand for air transportation services, and the provision of air transportation services offers an economic enabling effect that provides access to people, markets, ideas, and capital. Air transportation therefore enables the economic system to function at a regional and national level. The interactions between supply, demand, and the economy illustrate the rudimentary macro functionality of the air transportation system (Tam and Hansman 2003).

Most airlines, however, have failed to recover the cost of their investment and capital, even over airline business cycles of 8–10 years (IATA 2012). Many studies, including those by IATA, have argued that such poor profitability in the airline industry is not due to lack of efforts on the part of airlines, but rather due to the market structure and policy changes that involve a heavy toll on airlines' profitability. In fact, airlines have made several efforts at streamlining their operations and cutting down their operational costs. Good examples of such attempts include outsourcing of activities like electronic ticketing, maintenance, and ground handling; cutting down unnecessary services; and introducing a more sophisticated yield management. In addition, airlines have tried to improve their productivity by increasing aircraft utilization rates, providing additional revenue streams, introducing a wide range of customer loyalty programs, and establishing alliances or code-sharing. All these efforts have contributed to reducing the operating costs, but the margin above cost still lags far behind that of other industries.

3.3   Growth of the Airline Industry

The global airline industry has expanded by almost 5 % per year over the past 30 years (IATA 2011). The reports from IATA indicate that there are substantial yearly variations due to both changing global economic conditions and differences in the economic growth of each region. Operating to and from virtually every country in the world, airlines have played an intermediary role in building and supporting the global economy. Table 3.1 shows the airline industry's growth during the 2004–2015 period. The industry's revenue comes from passengers and cargos, which declined in 2009 due to the 2008 global economic crisis. As a result of the crisis, the world economy declined from a 4.0 % growth rate in 2007 to 1.5 % in 2008 and −2.0 % in 2009—a decline of 6.0 % from the peak in 2007.

Figure 3.1 shows the development of growth in the airline industry and the world economy. The growth rate in the airline industry is in general higher than the growth rate in the world economy, with the two indicators being highly correlated. Cargo services follow a similar development pattern, but it is subject to larger fluctuations, e.g., it had a larger decline in relation to the 2008 crisis but also a much faster recovery after 2009.

The airline industry itself performs several economic activities in terms of both its own operations and its impact on related industries. "Few other industries generate the amount and intensity of attention given to airlines, not only by those directly engaged in its operations, but also by government policy makers, the news media, as well as its billions of people who travelled from one country to countries" (Belobaba et al. 2009).

According to a recent IATA publication, the global airline industry consists of over 1397 airlines operating more than 23,844 commercial aircrafts providing services to over 3846 airports. In 2014, the world's airlines carried over 2.97 billion

Table 3.1 Airline industry's growth trend, 2004–2015

Category	2004	2005	2006	2007	2008	2009	2010	2011	2012	2013	2014	2015F[a]
Revenues, $ billion	379	413	465	510	570	476	564	642	706	717	733	727
% change	17.7	9.1	12.5	9.6	11.7	−16.5	18.4	14	9.8	1.7	2.2	−0.7
Passenger ($ billion)	294	323	365	399	444	374	445	500	541	555	563	556
Cargo ($ billion)	47	48	53	59	63	48	66	67	64	61	63	62
Traffic volumes												
Passenger growth, RPK (%)	14.9	8.9	6.9	8	2.4	−1.2	8	6.3	5.3	5.7	6	6.7
SKD passenger numbers (million)	2078	2225	2350	2556	2594	2479	2681	2858	2989	3143	3327	3542
Cargo growth, FTK (%)	11.6	2.5	6.4	4.7	−0.7	−8.8	19.4	0.4	−0.9	0.6	5.8	5.5
Freight tones (millions)	36.2	37.1	39.4	41.9	40.5	40.2	47.9	48.9	48.2	49.3	51.5	54.2
World economic growth (%)	4	3.5	4	4	1.5	−2	4.1	2.9	2.4	2.5	2.6	2.9
Passenger yield (%)	2.8	1.7	6.6	1.7	8.2	−13.7	9.6	5	2.9	−3	−4.2	−7.5
Cargo yield (%)	3.9	0.3	4.4	5.6	7	−15.2	14.3	0.8	−4.2	−4.9	−2	−7

[a]The 2015 data is forecasted
Source IATA (2014a)

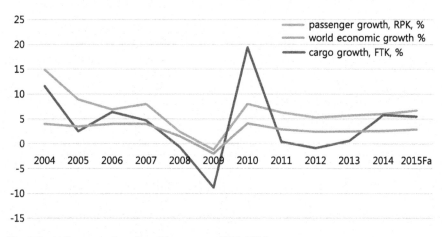

Fig. 3.1 Airlines growth and world economy, 2004–2015

passengers, created 8.38 million jobs, and generated revenue of 708 billion dollars (IATA 2014b). Table 3.2 reports the airlines' key milestones and carried passengers over the period 1914–2011.

3.4 Cost Reduction

As briefly stated in the introduction, airlines grew substantially over the study period while reducing their operating costs by up to 60 % (IATA 2011). Improved technology and operational efficiencies were the main driving forces behind this success. The advantages created from these cost efficiencies were, however, mostly passed on to consumers in the form of lower real air transport prices, while the benefit did contribute to improving airlines' yield (Pearce 2012).

The trend in airline cost reductions is shown in Table 3.3. The table shows that expenses have developed positively but with large year-to-year variations. Variations in the fuel share of expenses are large. The variation is a result of fluctuations in fuel and jet kerosene prices. While fuel use efficiency has improved, the overall CO_2 emissions have increased over time. The weight load factor and passenger load factor also show a positive trend.

3.5 Airline Industry's Central Role in Globalization

Being rooted in the world economy and its rapid development, the airline industry has grown along with the advent of the recent wave of globalization. By taking advantage of technological developments, the airlines facilitate international trade,

Table 3.2 Airlines' key milestone and carried passengers

1914	1919	1921	1922	1930
1205 passengers	6549 passengers	13,559 passengers	19,285 passengers	290,000 passengers
First commercial passenger flight, commercial airline	KLM starts operations: oldest airline still in service	First air traffic controllers employed at Croyden Aerodrome, London	First use of aircraft for government business by Colombian president	First flight attendant with Boeing Air Transport (today's United)
1934	1935	1936	1939	1944
652,000 passengers	976,000 passengers	1,300,000 passengers	2,000,000 passengers	5,500,000 passengers
First transatlantic airmail services operated by Deutsche Luft Hansa (Lufthansa)	First transpacific airmail services operated by Pan American's China clipper	Douglas DC-3 enters service with American Airlines	First scheduled passenger transatlantic flights operated by Pan American	Chicago convention signed—the foundation of global aviation today
1945	1952	1971	1970	1976
2,000,000 passengers	39,500,000 passengers	39,500,000 passengers	383,000,000 passengers	576,000,000 passengers
The International Air Transport Association (IATA) founded in Havana	First commercial jet passenger service by BOAC	First low-cost carrier, Southwest Airlines, enters service	The Boeing 747 enters service with Pan American	Concorde enters service as first supersonic passenger aircraft
1978	1981	1998	2007	2011
679,000,000 passengers	752,000,000 passengers	1,471,000,000 passengers	2,422,000,000 passengers	2,824,000,000 passengers
United States deregulates the airline industry	First frequent flyer program launched by American Airlines	First transpolar passenger flight by Cathay Pacific	The Airbus A380 enters passenger service with Singapore Airlines	First passenger biofuel flights by KLM and Lufthansa

Source IATA (2014b)

international business, and international tourism, thus contributing significantly to economic growth in most countries of the world. Without fast and efficient airlines services, one can hardly imagine the current level of cross-border economic activities and transactions.

Figure 3.2 shows the indexed development of trade since 1993 for advanced and emerging economies. The development was identical during the period 1993–2000 for the two groups of countries, but from 2000 onward, the country groups deviate in their development. Following the 2008 economic crisis, both groups faced

Table 3.3 Airline cost trend, 2004–2015

Category	2004	2005	2006	2007	2008	2009	2010	2011	2012	2013	2014	2015[a]
Expenses ($ billion)	376	409	450	490	571	474	536	623	687	692	699	677
% change	16.2	8.9	10.1	8.8	16.5	−16.9	13.1	16.2	10.4	0.7	1	−3.1
Fuel ($ billion)	65	91	127	146	205	135	152	192	227	228	226	191
% of expenses	17	22	28	30	36	28	28	31	33	33	32	28
Crude oil price, Brent ($/b)	38.3	54.5	65.1	73	99	62	79.4	111.2	111.8	108.8	101.4	65
Jet kerosene price ($/b)	49.7	71	81.9	90	126.7	71.1	91.4	127.5	129.6	124.5	116.6	78
Fuel consumption (billion gallons)	66	68	69	71	70	67	70	72	73	74	77	80
CO_2 emissions (million tons)	620	644	651	667	664	629	658	678	683	694	724	757
Non-fuel ($ billion)	311	318	323	344	366	339	384	431	460	464	473	487
Cents per ATK[b] (non-fuel unit cost)	39.1	37.9	36.7	36.6	38	36.7	40.1	42.4	44	42.8	41.4	40.2
% change	1	−3	−3	−0.3	3.6	−3.3	9.3	5.8	3.7	−2.7	−3.1	−3.1
Capacity growth, ATK (%)	10.1	5.7	4.8	6.6	2.7	−4.2	3.7	6	3	3.6	5.4	6.2
Flights (million)	23.8	24.9	25.5	26.7	26.5	25.9	27.8	30.1	31.2	32	33.6	35.4
Break-even weight load factor (%)	60.9	61.2	60.7	60.3	62.2	61.8	63.5	64.1	64.7	64.5	64.1	62.7
Weight load factor achieved (%)	61.5	61.8	62.7	62.7	62.1	62	66.8	66.1	66.4	66.9	67.2	67.3
Passenger load factor achieved (%)	73.5	74.9	76	77	76	76.1	78.6	78.4	79.3	79.7	79.8	80.2

[a]The 2015 data is forecasted
[b]Available ton kilometers
Source IATA (2014b), IATA economic industry performance (IATA economics)

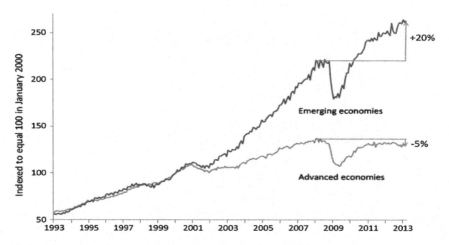

Fig. 3.2 International trade in goods by emerging and advanced economies, 1993–2013. *Source* IATA (2013a)

significant declines in economic development. The emerging economies recovered and grew by 20 % by 2013 compared with the level prior to the 2008 crisis. However, the advanced countries are still 5 % below the 2008 level.

Air transport is more closely linked to trade developments than GDP since a substantial portion of airline output comprises the cargo handling volume. Thus, when trade volumes increase, the airline outputs increase. In fact, the boom in international trade between countries in recent years is reflected in the air transport developments.

3.6 Airlines' Impact on Related Industries

The tourism industry is possibly the most closely related to the airline industry because its expansion was greatly facilitated by the growth of the airline industry. Tourists from all over the world travel long distances in less time to reach attractive destinations, often in developing countries. Tourist expenses are often a major source of foreign exchange and income for the destination countries. As we have witnessed, countries like Greece, Italy, and Spain in the EURO zone are heavily dependent on tourism, with the economic growth of these countries heavily fluctuating with changes in the tourism demand. Tourism revenue contributes to the development of poor countries, enabling their citizens to seek participation in the labor market of other countries, which further fuels the growth of the air transportation industry and the overall economy.

Therefore, airlines and tourism are interdependent, helping each grow and expanding. "The evidence suggests that once real GDP per capita reached $15,000–$20,000, the average number of flights per capita levels out" (IATA 2011). The US and Europe markets, typical samples of large markets, are approaching a saturation point. However, BRICS[2] and other fast-growing economies are still underdeveloped and require a substantial timespan before they can fully realize their capacity and accommodate their potential demand. They are thus the major source of future growth for the airline industry. There is also a well-established historical relationship between airline profits and global GDP. In the past, whenever global economic growth slowed down, the airline industry profits would slip into loss.

3.7   Issues of the Airline Industry

Air transport continues to create high value for users, passengers, shippers, and others in the value chain. The industry has been successful to some extent in getting decent returns for capital investors compared to other sectors of the economy (IATA 2014a). Overall, as an industry, airlines have experienced low profitability. Most airlines are publicly owned and as such have a different objective compared with private corporations. When fuel costs climb, when a new tax or surcharge is imposed, or when some airports charge very high fees, the airlines usually cannot raise their fares in proportion to their rising input costs, and as a consequence, the profitability of the airline industry suffers. For instance, airlines in the United States have been continuously struggling with challenges arising from a highly competitive industry structure. The poor profitability of the industry has long been a major concern among market participants. "Airline returns are highly cyclical in response to the economic cycle and various demands and cost shocks" (IATA 2011). When demand falls, airlines cut prices as in any other competitive market, but the charges levied by external parties such as the government and suppliers (e.g., aircraft suppliers, airports) do not decline accordingly, thereby putting the industry's profitability under pressure.

At the same time, the airline industry can be classified as one of the most capital-intensive industries due to the high amount of initial investment for the procurement of aircrafts and the very high standard of facilities and equipment needed for operation and maintenance. Investment in the industry is very long term in nature and subject to much risk where the recovery of the investment in reasonable time is concerned. The risk remains high in spite of massive public investment in airports, security and transportation.

High fixed costs are required to enter this market, and this could be one of the plausible explanations for the chronic low profitability of the airline industry. Without achieving of economies of scale, high fixed cost cannot be recovered in the short run, especially when there is downturn in the national or global economy. Such constraints are also experienced by other industries such as the automobile industry to some extent, but the effect on airlines is much bigger because air travel

---

[2]Brazil, Russia, India, China, and South Africa.

in most countries is still a luxurious good, the consumption of which tends to be cut when there is a downturn in the economy. This explains why there have been many incidences of bankruptcies, mergers and acquisitions in the airline industry. See also Appendix 1.1. This challenging business environment forces airlines to seek mergers and acquisitions as a way of reducing their unit costs by achieving greater economies of scale.

3.8   Airlines' Performance

3.8.1   The Factors Influencing Airlines' Performance

The airline industry is particularly vulnerable to external economic factors because the industry heavily depends on a wide range of other industries and support. A large portion of the industry involves operating across borders, which means that economic conditions of the world other than that of the domestic market also affect its performance.

The major costs for airlines are fuel, labor, and operating costs (IATA 2012). Fuel constitutes around 25–35 % of the total operating costs of an airline (IATA 2014a). Any political, social, or economic instability in the oil-producing nations causes the prices to rise, which adversely and significantly affects the profitability of airlines. For instance, jet fuel prices that were about USD 83 per barrel in August 2010 but escalated to USD 129 per barrel in March 2011 implied a surge of 55.4 % in only 8 months (see Fig. 3.3). In a similar way, the drops in the fuel price can be as drastic. Taxes and environmental concerns also subject the industry to large fuel price fluctuations.

Labor is another major cost for the airline industry and data suggests that flight and cabin crew capture a substantial portion of the value created in the industry.

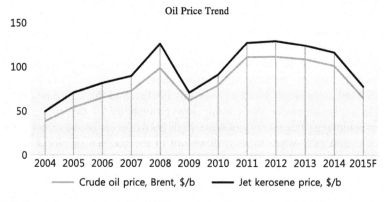

Fig. 3.3 Development of price of jet and Brent crude oil products, 2004–2015. *Source* www.iata. org/economy (IATA 2014b)

Table 3.4 Example of airline staffs' net monthly incomes (USD 2005 constant, and PPP)

Category	Germany	UK	US	Philippines	China	Brazil
Airline pilot	8448	5323	4206	5639	3249	4851
Engineer	3146	3832	4710	1827	1876	3687
Flight attendant	2605	1628	2949	914	627	2319

Source IATA (2013b)

"The airline industry has wage inequality issues, for instance pilots in one airline/country can earn much higher salaries than the pilots of another airline" (IATA 2011). See also Table 3.1. The high degree of wage inequality across countries is reported in Table 3.4. Other than unequal wage levels across airlines, the labor cost has increased due to many welfare reforms carried out by the employers. The within-airline wage inequality is another dimension that is very high but not shown in Table 3.4.

This trend becomes evident when one analyzes some of the union data available within the countries. Various reports have indicated that due to wage inequality, the aviation industry has been subject to very high levels of employee turnover. However, it should be noted that most countries deregulated airline wage costs. Consequently, under many circumstances, in order to protect the national airlines, wage payments have been left in the hands of airlines' management.

Due to the shortage of skilled pilots resulting from the high demands in fast-growing countries like China, there is not much that the airlines can do to address this issue. States manage pilot education, and the training program and certification process is lengthy and not easily adaptable to market demand. A recent report from IATA found that pay per block hour has fallen from its peak in the early 2000s but a sizable pay gap between the large airline average and the cost leaders in the industry still remains. Despite repeated recessions, fuel price shocks and many other external factors such as epidemics (e.g., SARS) and new environmental regulations and charges, airlines have successfully managed to reduce their costs. The main driver of the cost-reduction trend is the industry's continuous efforts to increase labor productivity and minimize costs through various strategies. A significant reduction of costs was possible by increasing the efficiency of new aircraft, improved usage of airplanes, and better operational performance of airlines.

The fuel cost efficiency gains of the new aircraft models achieved over the past 40 years contributed to the pattern of real travel cost and real unit operating cost decline. Aircrafts have 20–30 years of an economic life cycle; thus it takes time for newly launched efficient models to have an evident effect on fleet efficiency (IATA 2013b). However, the extent of fuel efficiency improvement in the past 40 years closely mirrors the improvement of unit costs and the fall in the actual cost of cargo shipping. These cost improvements supported by upgraded technology expand the consumers' surplus by charging lower fares and freight rates (IATA 2013b).

3.8.2 Improving Performance Despite Difficult Conditions

Airlines' financial performance continues to improve slowly, despite difficult business conditions. IATA (2014a) has forecasted net post-tax industry profits of $29.3 billion for 2015. Although the direction of change is positive, the implicit margin of only 4.0 % on revenues of over $727 billion is still markedly lower than most other sectors of the economy (Table 3.5).

The development of the airline's EBIT margin as a percentage of revenues and net profit for aggregate global and the three main regions—America, Europe, and Asia Pacific—are reported in Figs. 3.4 and 3.5, respectively, for the period 2009–2015. The figures show evidence of an initial recovery from the 2008 global economic crisis but significant heterogeneous development among the regions with respect to both indicators of performance post the crisis. Despite the enormous expansion of the market, price competitiveness , and high service quality, airlines in

Table 3.5 EBIT margin and net profits of global and regional airline, 2009–2015

Airlines	EBIT margin % revenue							Net profit $ billion						
Year	09	10	11	12	13	14	15F	09	10	11	12	13	14	15F
GLOBAL	0.4	4.9	3.1	2.6	3.5	4.6	6.9	−4.6	17.3	8.3	6.1	10.6	16.4	29.3
North America	1.2	5.7	3.0	3.4	6.8	9.7	12.1	−2.7	4.20	1.70	2.30	7.4	11.2	15.7
Europe	−2.2	2.4	0.8	0.7	2.0	3.0	5.0	−4.3	1.9	0.3	0.4	1.0	3.3	5.8
Asia Pacific	2.8	8.0	6.6	4.7	2.9	2.6	5.3	2.7	9.2	5.0	2.7	1.9	1.2	5.1

Source IATA (2014a)
Note The 2015 data is forecasted

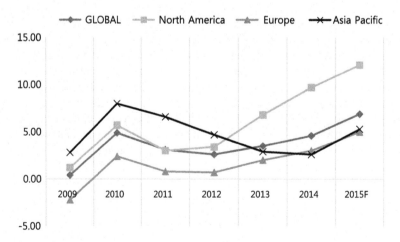

Fig. 3.4 Airlines' EBIT margin % revenue, 2009–2015

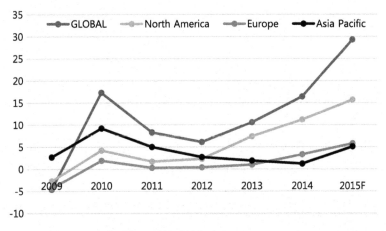

Fig. 3.5 Airlines' net profit $ billion, 2009–2015

the Asia-Pacific region do not seem to perform better than their American and European counterparts.

3.8.3 Productivity Enhancement

"The industry has managed to halve unit costs in real terms over the past 40 years" (IATA 2012). The efficiency gains were mostly distributed in the form of consumer welfare through lower prices. These productivity gains have been driven by restructuring and improved business models adopted by the airlines. The emergence of low-cost carriers and technological progress in the reservation, check-in, and baggage handlings are the good examples of such changes within the industry. The market price of air transport services reflects airlines' actual operating costs. Consumers have experienced a large increase in economic benefits due to the halving of the real price of air transport. Figure 3.6 shows the value proposition for air passengers for the 1990–2013 period. As expected, there is a positive trend in fuel efficiency and negative trend in fares and fatal accidents.

3.8.4 Liberalization

Airline liberalization in the 1980s and 1990s created opportunities for new entry of airlines into the market and stimulated considerable innovation, in particular in short-haul markets to meet the demand of price-sensitive consumers. This facilitated the entry of no-frills, low-fare airlines. Incumbent airlines responded with further efficiency improvements but, except for the EU, deregulation did not reach to the

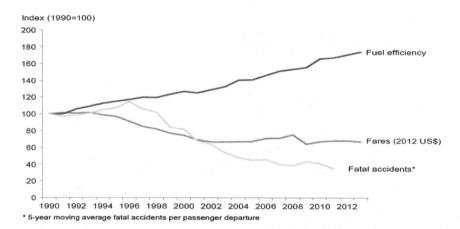

Fig. 3.6 Value proposition for air passengers, 1990–2013. *Source* www.IATA.org/Economics, IATA (2013a)

extent of ownership and control. This has prevented cross-border restructuring, which has been realized in the manufacturing industry, despite its necessity in these economic conditions. "Even where industry consolidation has taken place, economies of scale in operations have proved elusive beyond a certain fleet size" (IATA 2012). Economies of scale is clearly important for marketing—with economies of scale from aggregating passenger movement and capturing the economic benefits created from route density, operating a larger aircraft to be deployed on city-pairs eventually lower the unit costs. This important issue will be thoroughly reviewed again in the section on market structure and liberalization (IATA 2011).

3.9   Other Issues

The airline industry generates a number of positive externalities. This includes promoting tourism, rising employment, greater investment, and an overall increase in the GDP. On the other hand, the industry also entails negative externalities. These include noise emission and pollution resulting from the excessive emission of harmful gas into the atmosphere (IATA 2011). A major external cost is thus the environmental cost of noise, local air pollution, and greenhouse gases. Some studies found that these will not have a significant impact on airline profitability, but there will be indirect effects through government regulations. Together with airlines, the suppliers of airframes and engine manufacturers have made considerable reductions in the economic costs of aircrafts (IATA 2012).

The airline industry is also disproportionately affected by changes in government policy. The costs of complying with policy changes often affect the aviation industry negatively and thus contribute to higher production costs. An example of this is the high standard of environmental rules and regulations. Another example of policy-induced costs is labor costs, which affect all sectors in the same way. In addition, infrastructure investment within the aviation sector affects the performance of the industry. For instance, if the government makes large investments in infrastructure facilities that support airlines such as building more airports or improving existing ones, it is likely that the performance of the industry will improve. It should be noted that such investments are determined by the government and directly affect the allocation of resources. Infrastructure development is therefore closely intertwined with government policy. Moreover, there is a need for the government to facilitate maximizing the impact of supporting infrastructure such as airports, for instance, by building good access roads and railroads to airports.

3.10   Market Structure, Liberalization and Access

Airlines are typically highly regulated due to political, economic, and safety concerns. In such regulated markets, it is difficult to enter and establish a new airline. Over time, the industry has, however, been moving toward more deregulation, with the US leading the way in 1978 and Europe following. Deregulation promotes competition and it enables the more competitive participants to enter the market. Airlines have a history of being severely regulated throughout the world, creating the circumstances in which technological development and government policy took precedence over profitability and competition (IATA 2012). When deregulations prevail, cost efficiency, operating profitability and competitive behavior become the dominant priorities for airline management (IATA 2012). Airline deregulation has now expanded beyond the US to most countries, impacting domestic air travel within each country as well as promoting the continuous evolution of a highly competitive and changing international airline industry (IATA 2012).

3.10.1   Current Restrictions and Barriers

International aviation is governed by a compound series of bilateral air service agreements (ASAs) that were first developed according to the principles of the 1944 Chicago Convention[3] (IATA 2012). IATA estimates that there are over 3000 ASAs in existence, though just 200 of them account for around 75 % of the total traffic covered by the agreements. There has been a degree of airline liberalization in some regions and on some routes (e.g., the intra-EU market, Australia, and New Zealand, the March 2007, US-EU "open-skies" bilateral agreement). But only 17 % of international air traffic is currently conducted in a liberalized operational environment. Even in many of

---

[3]See Appendix 3.1.

these cases, such as intra-EU flights, there are still some restrictions on airline ownership and control over investors based outside the region.

While liberalization might result in a price decrease in general, it may also lead to a substantive degree of price volatility, at least in the short term, because firms will respond quickly to accommodate the changes in market conditions. Imposing a fuel surcharge to the tickets based on real price fluctuations of the fuel is illustrative of such a response. But changes in prices can also act as an effective signal for new investment or capacity restructuring. In addition, removing capital restrictions creates opportunities for industry consolidation, with the risk of a firm maintaining a dominant market position. Liberalization encourages privately owned airlines compete with firms' own capability and service quality rather than their superior market power supported by a monopoly position.

3.11 Summary of the Airline Industry and Its Evolution

This chapter has reviewed various characteristics of the airline industry, as well as the opportunities and challenges facing consumers, service providers, and regulators in the rapidly expanding market. One distinctive aspect of the airline industry that although there has been an increasing pressure of competition in the global market due to the ongoing liberalization of air services such as the open skies policy and ASA, it has achieved a high degree of productivity and cost reduction through the various forms of strategic management.

This chapter has laid down the context of the airlines industry and discussed the various efficiency improvements it has achieved. Based on this, the following chapters will examine the specific causes and effects of the airlines' efficiency improvements in production increase and cost reduction. They also suggest possible policy measures that can enhance the airlines' efficiency to overcome the lower yield and poor profitability of this industry compared with other industries as well as investment alternatives, an issue most of the major airlines are struggling with.

Appendix 3.1: The Chicago Convention[4]

In 1944, before the end of World War II, the representatives of 54 states[5] attended the International Convention on Civil Aviation, a conference on the future of international air transport held in Chicago. This conference and the international treaty that was signed as a result became known as the "Chicago Convention."

---

[4]The content in this is quoted from IATA and WTO without any alteration to correctly convey the terms and definitions.

[5]The term "state" is used in this chapter interchangeably with the less formal "country" or "nation."

The treaty marks a critical milestone in the history of aviation, as it laid the foundation for the present global air transportation system. The Convention made several fundamental contributions to the conduct of domestic and, especially, international civil aviation, and thus underpinned the industry's enormous growth over time. At a broader level, the Convention crystallized the growing realization that civilian air transportation is an activity of potentially enormous global importance, deserving to be nurtured and promoted through a set of internationally accepted rules for the rights of access to markets.

In trying to define what these rules would be, the Convention, for the first time in the history of aviation, had to seriously confront the choice between a liberal and a protectionist regulatory environment for international services. This fundamental choice has been at the center of much controversy ever since. At that time, the US advocated a liberal framework based on a regime that would place few restrictions on access to the world's air transportation markets and permit open competition among airlines, including the right to set market-driven flight frequencies and airfares. However, most other states, led by the UK, advocated a much more restrictive system, guided by the rationale of national security and airspace sovereignty, as well as protecting the then-nascent domestic airline industry. An apparent underlying concern of this group was that a liberal competitive environment might lead to dominance by US airlines, which were believed to be much stronger, financially and in many other respects, compared to the airlines of other nations at the time. Using the threat of refusing landing rights as their bargaining tool, the protectionist group largely prevailed.

Rather than establishing a universal set of rules, the Convention thus decided to simply create a *framework* within which such rules could be established for regulating air transport services on a *bilateral* basis, i.e., between *pairs of countries*. As a result, bilateral *air service agreements* (ASAs) between states emerged as the instrument for initiating or modifying international transportation services and for regulating these services. The principal initial "model" for such agreements was developed only two years later, through the 1946 "Bermuda I" Agreement, which established the ground rules for US–UK air services. Bilateral ASAs continue to be prevalent today, but multilateral ASAs have also become increasingly common and important in recent years. As noted earlier, the Chicago Convention established a framework for regulating international air transportation services on the basis of ASAs. All bilateral and multilateral ASAs make a reference to the following four critical aspects of the services to be provided:

(a) Market access: the *potential* city pairs to be served between the states involved in the ASA, as well as any Freedoms beyond the Third and Fourth critical aspects, which may be granted under the ASA.

(b) Airline designation: the number of airlines[6] from each of the states that have the right to provide service in each city pair included in the agreement.

---

[6]Note that, by specifying the number of airlines, but not necessarily their identity, the ASA allows a state to change designated airlines over time, if needed.

(c) Capacity: the frequency of flights and the number of seats that can be offered in each city pair.
(d) Airfares (tariffs): the manner in which passenger fares and/or cargo rates to be charged are determined and any steps necessary for government approval of these fares.

Appendix 3.2: Freedoms of the Air[7]

The Chicago Convention created the concept of the so-called "Freedoms of the Air." The Convention specified only the first five of the nine freedoms described below. The remaining four were subsequently defined informally over time, in response to the development of additional types of international aviation services. The freedoms refer to the rights that an airline of any state may enjoy with respect to another state or states. The nine freedoms are as follows:

First Freedom of the Air—the right or privilege, in respect of scheduled international air services, granted by one State to another State or States to fly across its territory without landing (also known as a *First Freedom Right*).

Second Freedom of the Air—the right or privilege, in respect of scheduled international air services, granted by one State to another State or States to land in its territory for non-traffic purposes (also known as a *Second Freedom Right*).

Third Freedom of The Air—the right or privilege, in respect of scheduled international air services, granted by one State to another State to put down, in the territory of the first State, traffic coming from the home State of the carrier (also known as a *Third Freedom Right*).

Fourth Freedom of The Air—the right or privilege, in respect of scheduled international air services, granted by one State to another State to take on, in the territory of the first State, traffic destined for the home State of the carrier (also known as a *Fourth Freedom Right*).

Fifth Freedom of The Air—the right or privilege, in respect of scheduled international air services, granted by one State to another State to put down and to take on, in the territory of the first State, traffic coming from or destined to a third State (also known as a *Fifth Freedom Right*). ICAO characterizes all "freedoms" beyond the Fifth as "so-called" because only the first five "freedoms" have been officially recognized as such by international treaty.

Sixth Freedom of The Air—the right or privilege, in respect of scheduled international air services, of transporting, via the home State of the carrier, traffic moving between two other States (also known as a *Sixth Freedom Right*). The so-called Sixth Freedom of the Air, unlike the first five freedoms, is not incorporated as such into any widely recognized air service agreements such as the "Five Freedoms Agreement".

---

[7]Quoted from the "Manual on the Regulation of International Air Transport (Doc 9626, Part 4)" without any alteration.

Seventh Freedom of The Air—the right or privilege, in respect of scheduled international air services, granted by one State to another State, of transporting traffic between the territory of the granting State and any third State with no requirement to include on such operation any point in the territory of the recipient State, i.e., the service need not connect to or be an extension of any service to/from the home State of the carrier.

Eighth Freedom of The Air—the right or privilege, in respect of scheduled international air services, of transporting cabotage traffic between two points in the territory of the granting State on a service which originates or terminates in the home country of the foreign carrier or (in connection with the so-called Seventh Freedom of the Air) outside the territory of the granting State (also known as an *Eighth Freedom Right* or "consecutive cabotage").

Ninth Freedom of The Air—the right or privilege of transporting cabotage traffic of the granting State on a service performed entirely within the territory of the granting State (also known as a *Ninth Freedom Right* or "*stand alone" cabotage*).

Appendix 3.3: Abbreviations and Their Definitions

Abbreviation	Description
ACPRD[a]	Measure of aircraft productivity: calculated by dividing aircraft block hours by the number of aircraft days assigned to service on air carrier routes. ACPRD is typically presented in block hours per day
AFTK	Available freight ton kilometers: the measure of a flight's freight carrying capacity. AFTK is calculated by multiplying the number of tons of freight on an aircraft by the distance traveled in kilometers. It is used to measure an airline's capacity to transport freight
ASK	Available seat kilometers: the measure of a flight's passenger carrying capacity. ASK is calculated by multiplying the number of seats on an aircraft by the distance traveled in kilometers. It is used to measure an airline's capacity to transport passengers
ASM	Available seat mile: the measure of a flight's passenger carrying capacity. ASM is calculated by multiplying the number of seats on an aircraft by the distance traveled in miles. It is used to measure an airline's capacity to transport passengers
CASK	Cost per available seat kilometer: measure of unit cost in the airline industry. CASK is calculated by taking an airline's total operating expenses and dividing it by the total number of available seat kilometers produced. It is used to compare costs between airlines. The lower the CASK, the lower the cost of transporting a passenger
CASM	Cost per available seat mile: measure of unit cost in the airline industry. CASM is calculated by taking an airline's total operating expenses and dividing it by the total number of available seat miles produced. It is used to compare costs between airlines. The lower the CASM, the lower the cost of transporting a passenger

(continued)

(continued)

Abbreviation	Description
FLF	Freight load factor: the percentage (%) of AFTK is used to measure FLF
FTK	Freight ton kilometers: the equivalent of RPK for freight. One FTK is one metric ton of revenue load, carried one kilometer. The sum of FTKs for every segment flown by every aircraft over a specific period is the FTK of an airline over that period
LF[a]	Load factor: the percentage of seats sold on an aircraft irrespective of fare. The number of revenue passenger miles (RPMs) expressed as a percentage of ASMs, either on a particular flight or for the entire system. Load factor represents the proportion of airline output that is actually consumed. To calculate this figure, divide RPMs by ASMs. Load factor for a single flight can also be calculated by dividing the number of passengers by the number of seats
NFARE[a]	Net fare: fares available for sale specifically by a distributor/s that is negotiated between the individual distributor and the airline
OP_COST[a]	Operating cost: costs spent for total airline operations including scheduled and non-scheduled services. Sources of revenue include passenger, cargo, excess baggage, and certain other transport-related costs
OP_REV[a]	Operating revenue: revenues received from total airline operations including scheduled and non-scheduled services. Sources of revenue include passenger, cargo, excess baggage, and certain other transport-related revenue. For passenger airlines, the large majority of revenue generally comes from passenger revenue
PFARE	Published fare: a fare "published" by an airline and available for sale to everyone (as distinct from "net" fares provided either directly by the airline or a third party distributor, e.g., travel agent)
PLF	Passenger load factor: see load factor definition provided above
PRASK[a]	Passenger revenue per available seat kilometer: often referred to as a measure of passenger "unit revenue". It is calculated by dividing passenger revenue by available seat kilometer. Typically the PRASK measure is presented in terms of cents per kilometer. This measure is equivalent to the product of load factor and yield
PRASM[a]	Passenger revenue per available seat mile: often referred to as a measure of passenger "unit revenue". It is calculated by dividing passenger revenue by available seat miles. Typically the PRASM measure is presented in terms of cents per mile. This measure is equivalent to the product of load factor and yield
PREV[a]	Passenger revenue: received by the airline from the carriage of passengers in scheduled operations
PRRPK[a]	Stage length adjusted passenger yield (passenger revenue per revenue passenger kilometer): a common practice utilized to normalize comparisons of passenger yield between carriers. The distance flown significantly impacts operating costs and revenues, and this analytical approach is designed to compare results as if all carriers fly the same missions
PRRPM[a]	Stage length adjusted passenger yield (passenger revenue per revenue passenger mile): a common practice utilized to normalize comparisons of passenger yield between carriers. The distance flown significantly impacts operating costs and revenues, and this analytical approach is designed to compare results as if all carriers fly the same missions

(continued)

(continued)

Abbreviation	Description
PYLD[a]	Passenger yield: measure of average fare paid per mile per passenger, calculated by dividing passenger revenue by revenue passenger miles. Typically, the measure is presented in cents per mile and is a useful measure in assessing changes in fares over time. Yield is not useful for comparisons across markets and/or airlines, as it varies dramatically by stage length and does not incorporate load factor (unlike the PRASM measure)
RASK	Revenue per available seat kilometer: used to compare revenue between airlines. Determined by dividing operating revenue by available seat miles (ASM/ASK)
RASM	Revenue per available seat mile: used to compare revenue between airlines. Determined by dividing operating revenue by available seat miles (ASM/ASK)
REV_EMP[a]	Revenue per employee: one measure to determine an airline's labor productivity. It is calculated by dividing an airline's total revenue by the number of airline employee full-time equivalents as reported to the United States Department of Transportation
RPK	Revenue passenger kilometers: RPK is created when a paying passenger flies one kilometer. This is the basic measure of airline passenger traffic. It reflects how many of an airline's available seats were actually sold. For example, if 200 passengers fly 500 km on a flight, this generates 100,000 RPKs
RPM	Revenue passenger miles: RPM is created when a paying passenger flies one mile. This is the basic measure of airline passenger traffic. It reflects how many of an airline's available seats were actually sold. For example, if 200 passengers fly 500 miles on a flight, this generates 100,000 RPMs. On a typical day in 2007, American Airlines produced 380 million RPMs
RTK	Revenue tone kilometer
SDEN[a]	Seat density: average seating configuration of an airline's operating fleet. The measure is derived by dividing total available seat miles flown by the number of aircraft miles flown. It is important to understand the average aircraft size as it is an important determinant of the number of employees needed to service the operation of a particular airline. Further, economies of scale generally mean that all other things being equal, an airline's CASM declines with increasing seat density (for instance, two small jet engines on a small commercial jet aircraft generally cost not much less to maintain than two large jet engines on a large commercial jet aircraft)
SLA	Stage-length adjustment: all other things being equal, the same airline will have lower CASM, RASM, and yield as stage length increases, since fixed costs are spread over increasingly larger average flight lengths. Therefore, to properly compare these quantities across airlines (or even across the same airline for two different periods if the airline's average stage length has changed significantly) requires settling on a standard assumed stage length and then adjusting CASM, RASM, and yield appropriately. This requires some judgment and different observers may use different stage-length adjustment techniques. A common method, for instance, would be looking at a detailed cost breakdown of a particular airline and deciding whether each cost category varies with stage length, and how

(continued)

(continued)

Abbreviation	Description
SLA_PRESM	Stage length adjusted passenger revenue per equivalent seat mile: a common practice utilized to normalize comparisons of PRASM between carriers. The distance flown significantly impacts operating costs and revenues, and this analytical approach is designed to compare results as if all carriers fly the same missions
SLA_TRASM	Stage length adjusted total revenue per equivalent seat mile: a common practice utilized to normalize comparisons of TRASM between carriers. The distance flown significantly impacts operating costs and revenues, and this analytical approach is designed to compare results as if all carriers fly the same missions
SR[a]	Stage-length (the average distance flown): measure in statute miles per aircraft departure. The measure is calculated by dividing total aircraft miles flown by the number of total aircraft departures performed
TCOST[a]	Transport-related costs: costs that result from service operated by a regional affiliate of a network carrier. Such costs are often excluded from RASM or CASM calculations to allow network carriers to be compared directly with carriers that do not offer service using regional affiliates
TREV[a]	Transport-related revenues: revenues that result from service operated by a regional affiliate of a network carrier. Such revenues (or costs) are often excluded from RASM or CASM calculations to allow network carriers to be compared directly with carriers that do not offer service using regional affiliates
YLD[a]	Yield airline term for revenue per unit, e.g., revenue per mile per passenger

[a]Author's own description
Source http://centreforaviation.com/about-capa/glossary/

References

Belobaba P, Odoni A, Barnhart C (2009) The global airline industry. Wiley. ISBN: 978-0-470-74077-4

International Air Transport Association (2011) Vision 2050. Singapore, 12 Feb 2011 report. www.IATA.org

International Air Transport Association (2012) Annual report 2012. www.IATA.org

International Air Transport Association (2013a) Annual report 2013. www.IATA.org

International Air Transport Association (2013b) Profitability and the air transport value chain. In: Economics briefing, vol 10. International Air Transport Association. www.IATA.org

International Air Transport Association (2014a) Fact sheet: industry statistics. http://www.iata.org/pressroom/facts_figures/fact_sheets/Documents/fact-sheet-industry-facts.pdf

International Air Transport Association (2014b) Aviation benefits beyond borders, pp 2–8. www.aviationbenefitsbeyondborders.org

Pearce B (2012) The state of air transport markets and the airline industry after the great recession. J Air Transp Manage 21:3–9

Tam R, Hansman RJ (2003) An analysis of the dynamics of the US commercial air transportation system. Technical Report ICAT-2003-2, MIT International Center for Air Transportation

United Nations (2010) Tourism satellite account: recommended methodological framework. United Nations Publication, Sales No. E.01.XVII.9

United Nations Statistics Division: http://unstats.un.org/unsd/

Chapter 4
Stochastic Frontier Production Function Model Specification and Estimation Results

Abstract This chapter compares production efficiency of the world's major 39 airlines over the 1998–2012 period. Using the stochastic frontier function methodology, we estimated airlines' production efficiency and analyzed factors accounting for differences in their level. Our findings confirmed that airlines have successfully achieved production efficiency over the sample period. Airlines with a higher market share achieved relatively better production efficiency. Airlines' operation performance measured in terms of stage, flying hours, and frequency showed a positive correlation with the production efficiency and their statistical significance were very robust. The effect of airline alliances was, however, not progressive. Our main findings show that carriers based in the Asia region are in generally more efficient than carriers based in Europe and North America regions. Out of the seven hypotheses that we tested, five were consistent and robust with our assumption, while two were found to be inconsistent.

Keywords Stochastic frontier functions · Production efficiency · Panel data · Airlines

4.1 Introduction

In this chapter, we empirically analyze the efficiency of international airlines using a stochastic frontier production function approach. We estimate the production frontier function in terms of two competing error components and technical efficiency effects models. The first approach estimates a production function and the firm-specific level of efficiency, while the second, in addition to estimating firm-specific efficiency, explains factors determining the variations in the level of efficiency as well.

The chapter is structured as follows. The next section provides a general introduction to stochastic frontier production function models. The model specifications are given in Sect. 4.3, including two particular models—the Battese and Coelli (1992) error components model and the Battese and Coelli (1995) technical

© Springer Science+Business Media Singapore 2016
A. Heshmati and J. Kim, *Efficiency and Competitiveness of International Airlines*, DOI 10.1007/978-981-10-1017-0_4

efficiency effects model, which are then applied in the empirical analysis provided in Sect. 4.5. The data and variables used in the empirical analyses are discussed in detail in Sect. 4.4. The empirical results are presented and discussed in Sect. 4.5, and a brief summary is given in Sect. 4.6. Finally, the chapter includes four appendices that provide additional empirical results reported as part of the sensitivity analysis of the results.

4.2   Stochastic Frontier Production Function

In general, the most popular methods used in airline efficiency research are Data Envelopment Analysis (DEA) and Stochastic Frontier Analysis (SFA). As discussed in the review of the literature in Chap. 2, one of the major limitations of DEA is that it is a deterministic technique and thus does not account for measurement errors in deriving the efficiency measures (Assaf et al. 2009). In addition, the DEA method cannot include characteristics of the airlines and the market in the estimation of production efficiency. The method utilizes only the input–output relationship. Here, we use SFA as a tool for estimating the individual airlines' efficiency scores and the relationship between explanatory variables of production and efficiency with the dependent variables or the output. Therefore, the input–output relationship allows for the accounting of production environmental variables and airline characteristics.

Meeusen and van den Broeck (1977) and Aigner etal. (1977) were among the scholars who first introduced the SFA where the error component of the production function is decomposed into a random error term and an inefficiency component. Kumbhakar and Lovell (2000), Heshmati (2003) and Kumbhakar et al. (2015) give a comprehensive overview of the SFA methodology and the various ways in which it can be applied. The underlying idea behind SFA is to introduce an additive error term, which has two components—a noise and an inefficiency term. Distributional assumptions have to be made for both the error term and the inefficiency term. The most common assumption is the half normal distribution, but some studies assume a number of alternative distributions for the inefficiency error component. These include the exponential, truncated normal, and gamma distributions (Coelli 1996). The random error term is assumed to be normally distributed.

It is well known that the technological relationship between the level of inputs and the resulting level of outputs is defined by the production function. "A given level of inputs, it indicates that the average level of outputs that firms can produce, if estimated from observed data on inputs and outputs using econometric techniques" (Schmidt 1986). A wide range of studies have used either individual firm-level or aggregate industry-level data to investigate the relative contributions of different factors of production—i.e., capital and labor. The studies include Hanesson (1983) (Cobb-Douglas production function), Campbell and Lindner (1990) (CES production function), Pascoe and Robinson (1998) (Translog production function) and various studies by Kumbhakar (1991, 1996, 1997). Heshmati (2013) provides a comprehensive review of the literature on efficiency and productivity in manufacturing and services and provides guidelines on the use of data and definitions of variables.

In addition to estimating an input–output relationship, the stochastic frontier production function also postulates that firms involved in the production process suffer from technical inefficiencies that reduce their potential output. For a given combination of input levels, the upper bound for the realized production of a firm is assumed to be set by the sum of a parametric function of known inputs, unknown parameters, and a random error associated with the measurement error of the production level or other factors such as the business cycles, labor disputes, and bad weather.

The larger the gap between the realized production and the stochastic frontier production function, the higher is the size of technical inefficiency. Production functions implicitly assume that all firms are subject to technical inefficiencies in their production and, as a result, the representative or average firm defines the frontier. Based on the production frontier approach, the boundary of the production function is defined by the best practiced firms in the sample through the estimation of the production frontier.

The frontier thus refers to the maximum potential output produced with the use of a given set of inputs along a ray from the origin. The nature of stochastic frontier production estimation procedures accommodates some white noise. However, an additional one-sided error captures any other deviation of the firms from (within) the boundary. "Since observations inside the frontier are viewed as inefficient, it is possible to measure, from the estimated production frontier, the relative efficiency or inefficiency of certain groups or sets of practices from the relationship between some ideal production on one hand and actual observed production on the other" (Greene 1993).

4.3 Model Specification[1]

Aigner et al. (1977) and Meeusen and van den Broeck (1977) developed the stochastic frontier production function almost simultaneously but independently. The original production function was specified for cross-sectional data that contained an error term, which consisted of two components. One component accounted for random effects and the other for technical inefficiency in production. This model has the following form:

$$Y_i = X_i \beta + (V_i - U_i), \quad i = 1, \ldots, N \qquad (4.1)$$

---

[1]The model specification is summarized and quoted from Coelli (1996).

where Y_i is the production or output (or the logarithm of the production) of the ith firm; X_i is a $k \times 1$ vector of (logarithmic transformations of the) input quantities of the ith firm; β is a vector of unknown parameters or input elasticities measuring responsiveness of output to changes in inputs; V_i are random variables that are assumed to be i.i.d. $N(0, \sigma_v^2)$ and independent of U_i, which are nonnegative random variables that are assumed to account for technical inefficiency in production and are often assumed to be i.i.d. $\left|N\left(0, \sigma_u^2\right)\right|$. This original specification provided the basic framework for a large number of empirical studies during the past two decades. "Furthermore, as might be expected, the specification has been modified and extended in several different directions" (Kumbhakar and Lovell 2000).

"Such extensions encompass the specification of more general distributional assumptions for the technical inefficiency term, including the truncated normal or two-parameter gamma distributions; the incorporation of panel data and time-varying technical efficiencies; the application of the methodology to cost functions; its application to the estimation of systems of equations; and so forth" (Coelli 1996). Schmidt (1986), Bauer (1990), Greene (1993), and Heshmati (2003), among others, provide comprehensive reviews of this vast and growing empirical literature.

4.3.1 The Error Components Specification

Battese and Coelli (1992) expanded the basic efficiency model significantly. More specifically, they developed a stochastic frontier production function for unbalanced panel data with firm-specific effects. These effects are expected to have the distribution of a truncated normal random variable and vary systematically with time. The Battese and Coelli (1992) model can be written as

$$Y_{it} = X_{it}\beta + (V_{it} - U_{it}), \quad i = 1, \ldots, N, \quad t = 1, \ldots, T, \tag{4.2}$$

where as before, Y_{it} is (the logarithm of) the production of the ith firm in the tth time period; X_{it} is a $k \times 1$ vector of (logarithmic transformations of the) input quantities of the ith firm in the tth time period; β is as defined earlier; V_{it} are random variables that are assumed to be i.i.d. $N(0, \sigma_v^2)$ and independent of $U_{it} = (U_i \exp(-\eta(t - T)))$. The error terms U_i are nonnegative random variables that are assumed to account for technical inefficiency in production and as such are assumed to be i.i.d. as truncations at zero of the $N(\mu, \sigma_u^2)$ distribution. The unknown parameter η is to be estimated, and the panel of data does not need to be complete. The use of unbalanced panel data allows the inclusion of the entry and exit of firms to maintain the sample representativeness of the population. For more details, see Coelli (1996).

We adopt the application of Battese and Corra (1977) who replace σ_v^2 and σ_u^2 with $\sigma^2 = \sigma_v^2 + \sigma_u^2$ and $\gamma = \sigma_u^2/(\sigma_v^2 + \sigma_u^2)$. The parameter γ must lie between 0 and 1, and this constrained range can thus generate an ideal starting value for use in an iterative maximization process such as the Davidon–Fletcher–Powell (DFP) algorithm (Coelli 1996) . The application of this particular model appeared in the literature that reports the consequence of imposing one or more restrictions on this model formulation. For example, setting γ to be zero generates the time-invariant model set out in Battese et al. (1989). To give another example, the production function assumed in Battese and Coelli (1988) is the result of restricting the formulation to a full balanced panel of data. These issues are discussed in further detail in relation to the review of the literature in Chap. 2.

4.3.2 The Technical Efficiency Effects Specification

A wide range of empirical studies have estimated stochastic frontiers and used the estimated functions to predict firm-level production efficiencies. These studies then regressed the predicted efficiencies on a number of firm-specific variables—e.g., ownership characteristics, firm size and managerial experience—in order to identify the causes that affect the differences in predicted efficiencies between firms in an industry. One of the good examples of this two-stage procedure is Pitt and Lee (1981). The two-stage estimation procedure has continued to be regarded as a highly useful exercise.

At the same time, many have argued that the procedure is inconsistent in its assumptions about the independence of the inefficiency effects in the two separate stages of the estimation. The two-stage procedure is unlikely to generate estimates that are as efficient as those that could be obtained from a single-stage procedure. Kumbhakar (1991) and Reifschneider and Stevenson (1991) have addressed this issue. More specifically, they set forth stochastic frontier models that explicitly express the inefficiency effects (Ui) as a function of a vector of firm-specific variables and a random error. Battese and Coelli (1995) proposed a model that is analytically identical to the Kumbhakar (1991) specification, with a few exceptions. More precisely, Battese and Coelli (1995) impose allocative efficiency, remove the first-order profit maximizing conditions, and allow for use of panel data in the analysis. Therefore, it is possible to express the Battese and Coelli (1995) model specification as the following model. The model is a simple generalization of the earlier models with panel data

$$Y_{it} = X_{it}\beta + (V_{it} - U_{it}), \quad i = 1, \ldots, N, \quad t = 1, \ldots, T, \tag{4.3}$$

where Y_{it}, X_{it}, and β are as defined earlier; $V_{it}^{\,2}$ are random variables that are assumed to be i.i.d. $N(0, \sigma_v^2)$ and independent of U_{it}, which are non-negative

---

[2]"In the stochastic frontier literature, the V_{it} are nothing but "statistical noise" that is, the V_{it} are unexplainable error components which should not be systematically related with firms' input or output decisions. Thus, a firm's input decisions X_{it} should be strictly exogenous to the V_{it}; all leads

random variables that help explain technical inefficiency in the production process and are assumed to be independently distributed as truncations at zero of the $N(m_{it}, \sigma_u^2)$ distribution, where

$$m_{it} = Z_{it}\delta, \tag{4.4}$$

Z_{it} is a $p \times 1$ vector of variables that may influence the efficiency of a firm; δ is $1 \times p$ vector of unknown parameters to be estimated. As before, we follow the parameterization of Battese and Corra (1977), replacing σ_v^2 and σ_u^2 with $\sigma^2 = \sigma_v^2 + \sigma_u^2$ and $\gamma = \sigma_u^2/(\sigma_v^2 + \sigma_u^2)$.

4.4 Data and Variables

The data used in the empirical analysis covers 39 airlines from 33 countries over the period 1998–2012. Data related to airline perfomance has been collected primarily from two sources—the Korean government's official statistics site (www.airportal. go.kr) and each airline's home page. The countries we analyzed are evenly distributed across different parts of the world. The 33 countries (see Table 4.1) in the data set can be grouped into the three main regions of America; Europe, Middle East, and Russia; and Asia Pacific (see Table 4.2).

The data contains a number of variables including input, output, and airlines' characteristics, which are used in estimating the production models. There are many ways to choose input and output variables and their definitions. In general, inputs are asset and cost related, while outputs are revenue related. There is an external demand for the services or goods provided or produced by the decision-making units, i.e., individual airlines. We select the input and output variables to reflect the operational characteristics of the industry. Inputs generally refer to operations-related factors such as aircraft utilization, fuel and labor costs, flight schedule, pricing of service, and so forth. As such, they are the variables over which airlines exercise discretion for the most part and are thus largely independent from the service demand environment. Outputs are the results or achievements of service operations. The variables are defined below.

A. Output

The output (Y) for production function is the sum of the revenue ton kilometers (RTK) of passenger and cargo (FTK) for both international (INTL) and domestic (DOM) flights. While it is known that the outputs of different airlines can exhibit differences in their production, it is not possible to treat disaggregated output data

---

(Footnote 2 continued)

and lags of X_{it} are uncorrelated with V_{it}. That is, $X_{i,t-1}$ and X_{it} should be uncorrelated with it, since it simply equals V_{it}." (Coelli 1996).

Table 4.1 Characteristics of the airlines

Country	Sub TTL	Region[a]	Rank[b]	Rank[c]	Airline	Alliance[d]	Start year	AC[e]	AC years
United States	5 countries 8 airlines	AM	1	1	American Airlines	OW	1934	896	14.9
					UNITED Airline	ST	1926	704	13.3
					DELTA airline	SK	1924	722	16.7
					US AIR	ST	1939	339	12.6
Canada		AM	12	8	Air Canada	ST	1937	205	12.2
Brazil		AM	15	14	TAM Linhas Aereas[f]	OW	1976	146	–
Chile		AM	30	33	LAN Airlines	OW	2004	107	5.1
Colombia		AM	31	42	AVIANCA	ST	1940	71	6.9
China	12 countries 15 airlines	AP	2	2	Air China	ST	1988	275	6.5
					CHINA Eastern	SK	1988	259	6.2
					CHINA Southern	SK	1989	413	6.6
Hong Kong		AP	2	2	Cathay Pacific Airways	OW	1946	134	10.3
Korea		AP	6	13	Korean air	SK	1969	130	9.4
Japan		AP	7	7	Japan Airlines	OW	1951	180	9.5
					All Nippon Airways	ST	1953	151	12.1
Singapore		AP	9	17	Singapore Airlines	ST	1972	128	6.4
Australia		AP	13	12	Qantas airways	OW	1922	141	10.8
India		AP	14	11	Air India[f]	ST	1932	88	7.3
Thailand		AP	18	19	Thai Airways	ST	1960	98	10.7
Malaysia		AP	21	21	Malaysia Airlines	OW	1947	108	10.3
Indonesia		AP	26	23	GARUDA	NA	1950	81	6.5
Philippines		AP	29	28	Philippine Airlines	NA	1941	40	9.8
New Zealand		AP	32	30	Air New Zealand	ST	1940	98	9.4

(continued)

Table 4.1 (continued)

Country	Sub TTL	Region[a]	Rank[b]	Rank[c]	Airline	Alliance[d]	Start year	AC[e]	AC years
Germany	12 countries 12 airlines	EU	3	4	Lufthansa,	ST	1926	427	12.3
UK		EU	5	3	British Airways	OW	1919	240	–
France		EU	8	6	Air France	SK	1933	377	9.5
Spain		EU	16	15	IBERIA	OW	1927	112	9.3
Ireland		EU	17	10	Air Lingus	NA	1036	44	6.7
Turkey		EU	20	18	Turkish Airlines	ST	1956	189	6.4
Italy		EU	22	22	Alitalia	SK	1947	160	9.4
Switzerland		EU	23	25	SWISS air	ST	1931	91	–
Sweden		EU	25	24	SAS Scandinavian Airlines	ST	1946	143	12.9
Portugal		EU	33	29	TAP Portugal	ST	1946	71	11.5
Finland		EU	35	34	Finn air	OW	1968	68	8.4
Austria		EU	36	32	Austrian	ST	1958	80	14.3
Russian Federation	4 countries 4 airlines	EU	11	9	Aeroflot Russian Airlines	SK	1923	123	5.5
Qatar		EU	19	20	Qatar Airways	NA	1994	111	5.1
Saudi Arabia		EU	27	27	Saudi Arabian Airlines	SK	1947	163	10.3
Israel		EU	34	36	El Al	NA	1949	40	13.4

33 countries 39 airlines

[a]*AM* America, *EU* Europe and Middle East, *AP* Asia Pacific

[b]2011 Rank for revenue passenger tone kilometer (*Source* IATA, 2011)

[c]2011 Rank for revenue passenger kilometer (*Source* IATA, 2011)

[d]*ST* Star Alliance, *OW* One World, *SK* Sky Team

[e]Number of aircrafts

[f]Air India and TAM airlines changed their membership in 2013 and 2014 so when we estimated the efficiency, their alliance were counted as the One World and Star Alliance, respectively

Table 4.2 Regional distribution of airlines

Region 1	Europe and Middle East, Russia	16 countries 16 airlines	33 countries 39 airlines
Region 2	Asia Pacific	12 countries 15 airlines	
Region 3	America	5 countries 8 airlines	

for cross-country productivity comparisons and analyses. The output aggregates used here refer exclusively to the final output (RTK_INTL, RTK_DOM, FTK_INTL, FTK_DOM), which is one of the efficient ways to measure the two commodity groups—i.e., passenger and cargo—in different countries. As for production efficiency, a majority of previous studies used the revenue passenger kilometers (RPK) or revenue tonne kilometers (RTK) such as Wang et al. (2011), Greer (2009), Barbot et al. (2008) Oum et al. (1998, 2005), Merkert, and William (2013). See also Appendix 3.3 for more details.

Airlines' revenue can be used as an output of the production function, and in such a case, input variables should include the cost information (Coelli 1996). Since we want to estimate the separate analyses for production and cost efficiency, we used RTK as the output indicator. At the same time, while the main performance of airlines is in terms of passenger and cargo handling, airline revenue also includes various aspects of non-airline performance such as catering, duty-free services, ground transportation services, and sometimes the hotel business.[3] Thus, in order to focus on airlines' core activities in terms of performance, we decided to use RTK as the output measurement instead of revenue for the analyses of airlines' production efficiency.

The choice between quantities and revenues as measures of outputs in aggregate or disaggregate forms each has its benefits and limitations. A quantity measure is simple and consistent with the theory but difficult to aggregate if different output quantities are measured differently. Revenues, on the other hand, are based on prices in their calculation, which accounts for quality differences, but then it is difficult to obtain prices accurately. Availability of information is often the key determinant of the approach (quantity or value) chosen in empirical studies. For a detailed discussion on the data and definitions of variables used in the empirical analysis of performance in manufacturing and services, see Heshmati (2003).

B. **Inputs**

Since the application of stochastic frontier production analysis requires that the number of input variables to be kept at reasonable levels, we consider seven important input variables in this research. As for the inefficiency measurement, we include five variables, along with three regional dummy variables and four airline alliance dummies. Detailed descriptions of these variables are given below.

---

[3]For example, Korean Air has hotel services within the airline.

Employment (EMP): This variable encompasses cockpit crew, cabin crew, maintenance staff, marketing personnel, airport staff, and other service staff of each airline (for the period 1998–2012). Considering that the airlines typically report only the aggregate number of employees each year, it is not possible to get separate figures for the number of staff engaged in passenger and cargo services. Therefore, in the absence of disaggregation of labor, we use total employment in line with many previous studies of airline productivity and efficiency—e.g., Oum and Yu (1998), Oum et al. (2005), Barbot et al. (2008), Greer (2009) and Wang et al. (2011) —which use the same measure. Alternatively, one can use aggregate wages that account for differences in human capital.

Aircraft number (AC): The number of aircrafts is used to measure the capital assets of airlines. Since financial information on airlines such as their current capital assets is not readily available, the number of aircrafts has been applied as a proxy of the capital assets of airlines. Existing studies such as Assaf (2009), Lee and Johnson (2011), Merket and Hensher (2011) used the same variable as a proxy for capital input in estimating the production efficiency of airlines. This is motivated by non-aircraft capital, which is proportional to the number of aircrafts, and aircrafts are assumed to be of a similar size and quality, which is a strong assumption. If available, the value of aircrafts would be a better measure of capital.

Energy (ENERGY): Energy is the most important factor among airlines' operating costs. The product of international jet fuel price index multiplied by distance flown and quantity of energy per distance has been calculated, and is used as the proxy of energy consumption. A number of previous studies, including Oum and Yu (1998), Oum et al. (2005), Barbot et al. (2008), Assaf (2009), Greer (2009), Lee and Johnson (2011), Wang et al. (2011), and Cristina et al. (2012), included this variable when they estimated the production efficiency of airlines. The energy variable might also be subject to measurement errors due to differences in energy use intensity by aircrafts despite the use of passenger kilometers.

Load factor (LF_INT & LF_DOM): The load factors of both international and domestic passenger flights are included to measure productivity. "Airlines operating with a high load factor coefficient would expect to have a stronger demand, and thus consequently a higher production/efficiency" (Assaf et al. 2009). At the same time, airlines' productivity is heavily dependent on the revenue realized per supplied capacity. Therefore, this factor will analyze the significant aspect in measuring productivity and efficiency. Studies such as Graham et al. (1983), Assaf et al. (2009), Parast et al. (2010) and Johnson and Ozment (2011) included the load factor in the empirical analysis of airline productivity and efficiency.

Time Trend and its square: In order to capture the effects of technological changes in production and the time-varying effect on production efficiency, both in the short and long term, we include time trend and its square as technology variables. Technological changes are represented by a shift in the production function over time. The square term captures the nonlinear shift in the production function.

C. **Airline characteristics**

Stage length (STAGE): Oum et al. (1998, 2005), Greer (2009) and Merkert and Hensher (2011) included stage length in the estimation of airline efficiency. The average distance flown is measured in statute miles per aircraft departure. The measure is calculated by dividing total aircraft miles flown by the number of total aircraft departures per year. This can be regarded as the output of airlines depending on the estimation approach, but here we use this measure as an input factor to evaluate the optimization of resources to enhance airlines' efficiency.

Flying hour (FHRS): Flying hours measures the airlines' capacity in operation, including the capability of airlines in their aircraft resource utilization. Inclusion of flying hours will thus help to specify the airlines' efficient use of their capital resources in a systematic manner.

Frequency (Flight frequency): Parast et al. (2010) and Tsekeris (2009) used flight frequency as an input variable to measure the airlines' efficiency and productivity. This characteristic variable also measures the demand intensity for airline services.

Age of aircraft (AGE): Greer (2009) and Merkert and Hensher (2011) used aircraft age to investigate the impact of the average years of operation on airlines' productivity. Airlines equipped with new fleets and reduced average years of aircraft operation need huge investment on procurement, which affects the relative investment allocations to other airline services. Hence, both positive and negative effects are expected from the use of aircraft age, and we will test the direction of the effect.

Market share (MS): Market share is a central dimension in the estimation of global competitiveness. This variable is included to see if the market share affects the productivity and efficiency of the firms. By doing so, we can also investigate whether an airline's global competitiveness can explain the level and variations in its productivity and efficiency. Assaf (2009), Clougherty (2009) and Cosmas et al. (2013) used market share in the estimation of airlines' efficiency.

Price index (Price): Airline ticket price varies with routes, time of departure, and season as well as among the airlines and types of services supplied. As a result, price information at the country level is not readily available. Most models of aviation demand use a measure of yield[4] or carrier revenue divided by RTKs. In order to estimate a country's relative price index, we use an airline's revenue per aggregate output. Table 4.3 gives a detailed list of the variables that are selected on the basis of other studies of airline productivity and efficiency, following the standard measurement of airline performance as well as data availability. Table 4.4 provides a snapshot of the statistics of key variables used in this study.

Alliance: Most airlines in our sample belong to the major alliances such as One World, Star Alliance, and Sky Team. In order to investigate the airlines'

---

[4]Yield means revenue per unit—e.g., revenue per mile or revenue per passenger. See Appendix 3.3 for details.

Table 4.3 Description of variables used in the stochastic frontier production function estimation

Category		Code	Description
Dependent variable	Output	RTK_INTL	Revenue passenger tone kilometers, international
		RTK_DOM	Revenue passenger tone kilometers, domestic
		FTK_INTL	Flight tone kilometers, international, includes mail delivered
		FTK_DOM	Flight tone kilometers, domestic, includes mail delivered
Independent variables X	Determinants of production	EMP	Number of employment
		AC	Number of aircraft
		ENERGY	Fuel consumption expenses
		LF_INT	Load factor international
		LF_DO	Load factor domestic
		YEAR	(Year 1998 = 1. 1992 = 2… 2012 = 15)
		YEAR_SQ	Square of trend 1
Independent variables Z	Determinants of inefficiency	STAGE	Stage length
		FHRS	Flying hours
		FREQ	Flight frequency
		AGE	Average years of aircraft
		MS	Market share in international market
		PRICE	Price index
		A1	Alliance 1 (One World)
		A2	Alliance 2 (Star Alliance)
		A3	Alliance 3 (Sky team)
		A4	Alliance 4 (No Alliance)
		EU	Region 1 (Europe)
		ASIA	Region 2 (Asia)
		America	Region 3 (America)
		YEAR	(Year 1998 = 1. 1992 = 2 … 2012 = 15)

See also Appendix 3.3 for airlines' terms and descriptions

membership effects on efficiency and productivity by expanding a network and cooperation, alliance dummies are included.

Region: Airlines are grouped into three major regions by the headquarter countries of airlines to evaluate the geographical effect on the productivity and efficiency of airlines (for details, see also Tables 4.1 and 4.2).

D. **Expected effects from the use of variables**

Each variable's effects in the estimation of the specified production model are assumed to be as follows:

Table 4.4 Summary statistics of the variables

Variable	Unit	Mean	Std. dev.	Minimum	Maximum
OUTPUT	RTK (1000)	7,151,922	6,178,596	139,690	33,900,000
EMP	Number of employee	22728.56	21345.06	1034	119084
AC	Number of aircraft	179.7282	133.2754	40	827
ENERGY	USD	1,150,000,000	1,420,000,000	9,446,048	10,100,000,000
LF_INTL	Percentage	0.729	0.060	0.502	0.847
LF_DOM	Percentage	0.609	0.227	0.000	0.860
STAGE	Kilometer (1000)	408,181	308,896	0	1,667,315
FHRS	Flying hours	572,289	534,403	18,914	2,848,633
FREQ	Number	226,583	204,409	7447	994,559
AGE	Years of AC	9.55	2.73	5.10	14.90
MS	Share	0.016	0.014	0.000	0.062
PRICE[a]	USD[a]	0.895	1.379	0.019	25.932

- In the production function model, three major input variables, EMP, AC, and ENERGY, are expected to be positively correlated with the level of output. Oum and Yu (1998), Oum et al. (2005), Lee and Johnson (2011), Barbot et al. (2008), Assaf et al. (2009), Greer (2009) and many others who estimated airlines' production function models used these variables as fundamental inputs with expectation of positive association with output. (For details, see Appendix 2.1).
- Load factors of both international flights and domestic flights measure the yield of airlines' operation. A higher load factor requires higher input; thus it is assumed to be positively correlated with output. Cristina et al. (2012), Assaf et al. (2009), Parast et al. (2010) and Demydyuk (2012) used the load factor as an input variable in efficiency estimation and the correlation with output was found to be positive. In the case of domestic load factor, according to Clougherty (2009), it is related with the home rivalry effect because only a limited number of countries allow foreign carriers to operate within the nation; therefore, domestic and international airline markets are usually segmented. Clougherty's empirical study showed that an airline that has a relatively larger domestic operation performs better in international markets as well (Clougherty 2006). Thus, a higher load factor in the domestic market results in a better performance of the airline in the international market too. We thus assume that both domestic and international load factors will positively increase the output of airlines.
- The trend in the level of output is assumed to increase over time due to the continued technological progress that the airline industry has achieved through the 'learning by doing' effect of labor that accumulates skills, experience, and

knowledge. Considering airlines' output have been adjusted to the demand shocks related to the financial recession and other experienced obstacles such as epidemics and terror attacks, we expect the overall output to increase over the study period.

The characteristics and input variables listed above and treated as determinants of the technical inefficiency in the inefficiency part of the model are as follows:

- STAGE (stage length), FREQ (flight frequency) and FHRS (flight hours) will improve output because longer flying hours will improve airlines' efficiency by minimizing the time spent on the ground and consequently maximize the utilization of resources such as aircraft and manpower. A higher flight frequency implies that the airlines extend their flight schedules and routes, and thus improve their production efficiency. All other things being equal, the same airline will have a lower cost per supplied kilo capacity or yield as stage length, frequency, and flying hours increase, since fixed costs are spread over increasingly larger average flight lengths and frequency; thus these will improve the level of their production efficiency.

- AGE of the aircrafts is assumed to negatively affect their production efficiency. Intuitively, the higher the average age of an aircraft, the less efficient is the aircraft. Longer years of aircraft fleet in operation will burden airlines with higher maintenance costs and huge fuel bills. Merkert and Hensher (2011) and Greer (2009) included the aircraft age in the input variables and, surprisingly, both of them showed that the age of airlines' fleet had no impact on the technical efficiency of airlines. Merkert and Hensher (2011) showed, however, that it did have a positive impact on its allocative and cost efficiency.

- MS (market share) and PRICE (average output price) are important factors in the evaluation of airlines' efficiency. In particular, market share can measure an airline's global competitiveness. The sign of MS is therefore assumed to be negative, or positively associated with the level of efficiency. The sign of PRICE is assumed to be negatively associated with production efficiency. The airline market is very sensitive to price changes due to the intense price competition that prevails in both international and domestic markets. Therefore, higher fares charged by airlines will reduce demand and sales. Oum et al. (1998), Demydyuk (2012), Obermeyer et al. (2012), Feurguson (2007), Gorin and Belobaba (2004) and Tsekeris (2009) included the price index in their efficiency estimation. These analyses showed mixed results, but the major conclusion drawn was that price has a negative effect on the travel demand, thus creating less output, which in turn reduces production efficiency.

- The airline alliance formation effect is expected to be positively associated with production efficiency due to expanded networks and a greater variety in the scope of services provided. Alliance members also offer a wider selection of flight schedules and membership benefits to passengers; thus it will have a positive impact on the demand for the airline members. At the same time, the airline members under the same alliance can share information and jointly promote their service demand. All these activities will increase the ticket sales of the members. Variation of efficiency among the different alliances is assumed not to be so significant because most alliances provide a similar scope of services to their customers and the extent of cooperation among member airlines tend to be aligned.

• The regional effect will be examined to investigate whether there are differences in airline efficiency across different regions of the world. Since regions differ in the extent of market access and market competition, the location effect may influence the output efficiency of airlines. Because of rising tour demand in countries in the Asian region, especially the drastic increase in the demand for Chinese tourism,[5] we assume that airlines based in the Asian region will have a higher production efficiency than airlines in other regions.

On the basis of the above description and assumptions, the hypotheses to be tested can be summed up as follows:

H1	Longer stage and flying hours and larger airline flying frequency will have a positive effect on the production efficiency of airlines
H2	Increasing age of aircraft will negatively affect the production efficiency of airlines
H3	Airlines' higher market share in global competition will have a positive effect on production efficiency
H4	Higher ticket price will trim the sales, thus leading to higher output and subsequently less production inefficiency
H5	Airline alliance has a positive effect on the improvement of the production efficiency of airlines
H6	Asian carriers have a higher production efficiency than carriers based in other regions of the world
H7	Airlines achieve production efficiency improvement over the observed study period as a result of technological progress

4.5 Estimation and Analysis of Results

A core underlying assumption of the stochastic frontier production function is the existence of technical inefficiency in production compared with the best-practiced technology. In this chapter, we use two different model specifications of the stochastic production frontier—i.e., the efficiency effects (EE) and the error components (EC) models. The EC model estimates a production role and efficiency point for each observation. The EE model additionally explains the level of inefficiency attributed to its determinants. The factors considered as determinants of inefficiency in the EE model are in the EC model and they are considered as

---

[5]This situation affects not only the Chinese domestic market but also the markets of neighbouring countries.

characteristics of production, and their effects are estimated together with the production input parameters (Heshmati 2003). The functional shape of the stochastic production frontier to be specified and estimated is

$$\log(\text{Output}_{it}) = \beta_0 + \beta_1 \log(\text{EMP}_{it}) + \beta_2 \log(\text{AC}_i) + \beta_3 \log(\text{ENERGY}_{it})$$
$$+ \beta_4(\text{LF\_INT}_{it}) + \beta_5(\text{LF\_DOM}_{it}) + \beta_6 \text{TREND}$$
$$+ \beta_7 \text{TREND}^2 + V_{it} - U_{it} \quad (i = 39 \text{ airlines}, t = 1998-2012)$$

$$(4.5)$$

where V_{it} is a random error term and U_{it} is the inefficiency component. In the case of the EE model, U_{it} is modelled in the following way:

$$U_{it} = \delta_0 + \delta_1 \log(\text{STAGE}_{it}) + \delta_2 \log(\text{FREQ}_{it}) + \delta_3 \log(\text{FHRS}_{it}) + \delta_4 \log(\text{AGE}_i) + \delta_5(\text{MS}_{it})$$
$$+ \delta_6 \text{PRICE}_{it} + \delta_7 \text{A1} + \delta_8 \text{A2} + \delta_9 \text{A3} + \delta_{10} \text{EU} + \delta_{11} \text{ASIA} + \delta_{12} \text{TREND} + W_{it}$$

$$(4.6)$$

The stochastic production model specified above is estimated. The result from the Maximum Likelihood Estimation (MLE) method for both the EC and the EE model is reported in Table 4.5.

4.5.1 Analysis of the Estimation Results

A. Specifications tests

We tested a number of null hypotheses that the parameter estimates are statistically and insignificantly different from zero both in individual and joint levels, and they are rejected. The followings are the results of the specification tests conducted (see Table 4.6).

The first and second null hypothesis in Table 4.6 show the results of the test for whether all parameters in the production model (both EC and EE) are simultaneously equal or jointly equal to zero; thus these variables are not relevant to output increase or changes. The null hypotheses that all coefficients are zero are rejected as the χ^2 test results exceed the critical value (CV); thus all estimated parameters are considered statistically significant and different from zero.

The log likelihood values and likelihood ratio (LR) statistics at the bottom of Table 4.6 allow us to test for the presence of technical inefficiency. The LR statistics in the table gives the test statistics for the null hypothesis of no technical inefficiencies presented in production. LR $= -2[\log \text{L}_R - \log \text{L}_u] \sim \chi^2(J)$, where $\log \text{L}_R$ and $\log \text{L}_u$ are log likelihood of the restricted model and unrestricted models, respectively, and J is the number of restrictions imposed on the restricted model. The test statistics follow the χ^2 distribution. If the null hypothesis is rejected, it means that when estimating the production efficiency of airlines, a model that

Table 4.5 Maximum likelihood estimation result

Variables	Parameters	EC			EE		
		Coefficient	STD-error	Z	Coefficient	STD-error	Z
	Production frontier function						
CONSTANT	β_0	0.527*	0.279	1.89	4.060***	0.135	30.13
EMP	β_1	0.275***	0.034	8.06	0.080***	0.018	4.49
AC	β_2	0.055	0.077	0.71	0.107***	0.024	4.52
ENERGY	β_3	0.588***	0.031	18.76	0.268***	0.02	13.6
LF_INT	β_4	0.726***	0.158	4.6	0.302***	0.07	4.3
LF_DOM	β_5	−0.125*	0.072	−1.740	−0.109***	0.015	−7.420
TREND	β_6	−0.054***	0.007	−7.970	−0.018***	0.003	−5.420
TREND^2	β_7	0.001***	0	4.06	0.001***	0	3.22
	Determinants of inefficiency (U_{it})						
CONSTANT	δ_0				2.474***	0.128	19.37
STAGE	δ_1				−0.075***	0.01	−7.270
FHRS	δ_2				−0.092***	0.03	−3.010
FREQ	δ_3				−0.144***	0.023	−6.140
AGE	δ_4				−0.220***	0.032	−6.780
MS	δ_5				−21.969***	1.006	−21.850
PRICE	δ_6				0.040***	0.003	15.88
A1	δ_7				0.068***	0.016	4.27
A2	δ_8				0.107***	0.016	6.7
A3	δ_9				0.036**	0.018	1.98
EU	δ_{10}				0.013	0.011	1.21
ASIA	δ_{11}				−0.083***	0.011	−7.380

(continued)

Table 4.5 (continued)

Variables	Parameters	EC			Parameters	EE		
		Coefficient	STD-error	Z		Coefficient	STD-error	Z
TREND	δ_{12}					−0.007***	0.001	−5.130
Log likelihood		422.364				774.681		
σ^2		0.037***	0.007	5.488	U_σ	−5.692***	0.159	−35.850
$\gamma = \sigma_u^2/(\sigma_v^2 + \sigma_u^2)$		0.708***	0.039	18.04	V_σ	−6.243***	0.162	−38.560
μ		0.324***	0.052	6.262	σ_u	0.058***	0.005	12.6
η		0.005	0.007	0.713	σ_v	0.044***	0.004	12.35
					λ	1.317***	0.008	172.71

1. *EC* Error Component model and *EE* Technical Efficiency Effect model

2. Number of cross-sections is 39, number of time periods is 15, and total number of observation is 585

*$p < 0.05$; **$p < 0.01$; ***$p < 0.001$

Table 4.6 Generalized likelihood ratio tests (LRT)

Model	Null hypothesis, H_0	Test statistic	Prob $\chi^2 >$ CV
EC model	H_0: $\beta_i = 0$, i $\leq$ 1,2 …,7	$\chi^2(7) = 838.46$	0.000
	H_0: $\beta_i = \beta_j$ j = 2…,7	$\chi^2(5) = 824.66$	0.000
EE model	H_0: $\beta_i = 0$ i = 1,2…,7	$\chi^2(7) = 764.29$	0.000
	H_0: $\beta_i = \beta_j$ j = 2…,7	$\chi^2(6) = 681.93$	0.000
	H_0: $\gamma = \delta_1 = \cdots = \delta_{12} = 0$	$\chi^2(11) = 964.92$	0.000

This result comes from the LR test with assumption: model without inefficient variables can be nested in the EE

The test statistics has been conducted by STATA 'sfpanel' command using model BC92 and BC95 because the test statistics obtained from Frontier 4.1 and STATA statistical packages were similar results. The STATA program has the advantages that one can conduct much easier test and analyses

includes the technical inefficiency variables is more appropriate than a model without these inefficiency determinant variables. "One can also test whether any form of stochastic frontier production function is required at all by testing the significance of the γ parameter" (Coelli 1996). "If the null hypothesis, that γ equals zero, is accepted, this would indicate that is σ_u^2 is zero and hence that the U_{it} term should be removed from the model, leaving a specification with parameters that can be consistently estimated using ordinary least squares" (Coelli 1996). In this case, the production function is reduced to an average production function with no inefficiency presented, where all deviations from the average are attributed to positive and negative random events beyond the control of the producers.

Table 4.7 reports the results of the model tests, and it describes that the production model without the inefficiency variables are less complex and fit better because usually the simpler model fits well and is less complex. Because our intention with choosing the inefficiency model is to capture the individual airlines' efficiency score together with estimation results that we could not attain otherwise, there was a trade-off between the model fitness and the relevance when selecting the model and variables.

The test that we have used with the stochastic frontier panel command provides options for the estimation models in which all time-invariant unobserved heterogeneity is considered as inefficiency. We have dealt with the time-invariant unobserved heterogeneity and the result was found to be robust.

Table 4.7 Model specification test results

Model	LL (model)	DF	AIC[a]	BIC[b]
Error components model (EC)	422.364	12	−820.729	−768.269
Production frontier model (EE)	292.218	11	−562.436	−514.348
Production frontier inefficiency model (EE)	774.681	23	−1503.361	−1403.814

1. Observations 585, *DF* degrees of freedom
[a,b] Akaike's information criterion and Bayesian information criterion

Finally, multicollinearity concerns exist. Appendix 4.4 presents the correlation coefficients (and summary statistics) for variables used in the production frontier function. Among the variables, AC, EMP Energy, and LF_INT show a correlation coefficient above 0.5 that serves as the upper-level benchmark indicating serious multicollinearity. While multicollinearity concerns appear small, recall that collinearity does not lead to unbiased estimates, but it does make it more difficult to obtain significant coefficient estimates. No explanatory variables were dropped for this reason.

B. **Input elasticity results**

The estimation results indicate that the independent variables of both the EC and the EE models are statistically significantly different from zero. The sign of β coefficients are as expected and same for the two model specifications but the size of the coefficients is different from model to another. The maximum likelihood estimates, are reported in equation form below together with their standard errors in parentheses. The superscripts a, b, and c indicates significant probabilities of $p < 0.001$, $p < 0.01$, and $p < 0.05$, respectively.

EC Model result

$$
\log Y = \underset{(0.279)}{0.527} + \underset{(0.034)}{0.275^{a}} \log \text{EMP} + \underset{(0.077)}{0.055^{a}} \log \text{AC} + \underset{(0.031)}{0.588^{a}} \log \text{ENERGY}
$$
$$
+ \underset{(0.158)}{0.726^{a}} \text{LF\_INT} - \underset{(0.072)}{0125} \text{LF\_DOM} - \underset{(0.007)}{0.054^{a}} \text{YEAR} + \underset{(0.000)}{0.001^{a}} \text{YEAR}^{2}
$$

$$(4.7)$$

EE Model result

$$
\log Y = \underset{(0.135)}{4.060^{a}} + \underset{(0.018)}{0.080^{a}} \log \text{EMP} + \underset{(0.024)}{0.107^{a}} \log \text{AC} + \underset{(0.020)}{0.268^{a}} \log \text{ENERGY}
$$
$$
+ \underset{(0.070)}{0.302^{a}} \text{LF\_INT} - \underset{(0.015)}{0.109^{a}} \text{LF\_DOM} - \underset{(0.003)}{0.018^{a}} \text{YEAR} + \underset{(0.000)}{0.001^{a}} \text{YEAR}^{2}
$$

$$(4.8)$$

Since the output and input variables are in logarithmic form, the coefficients are elasticities and directly interpreted as a percentage change in output in response to percentage changes in an input, everything else given. The sum of the input elasticities is a measure of returns to scale or the effects of a proportional increase in all inputs and their effects on the output level. The elasticity with respect to time measures the rate of technical change or annual shift in the production function over time. The estimated coefficients that represent the elasticity of the inputs with respect to output are larger than their standard errors such that the t-values are large enough and consistent with the rejection of the first null hypothesis provided in Table 4.6, which suggests that all the parameters of the production function are equal to zero.

- The estimation results of both the EC and the EE models indicate that the coefficient signs of EMP and ENERGY are positive and both statistically significant at the 1 % level. In the case of the EE model, AC is positively affecting output and is statistically significant at the 1 % level, while it is statistically insignificant in case of the EC model. These results are overall consistent with our expectations. These parameters are the major determinants of airlines' output that have been represented by RTK in our analyses.
- According to the EE model, the coefficient of EMP is 0.080 and statistically significant at the 1 % level. This can be interpreted as a 1 % increase in the number of employees raising output by 0.080 %. Variables such as AC and ENERGY also have sizable impacts on output, which increases by 0.107 and 0.268 %, respectively, and they are all statistically significant at the 1 % level of significance. The result of EC model yields the same coefficient signs, but the magnitude of the coefficients is larger than those in the EE model due to different model specifications. Studies on these variables such as Oum et al. (2005) and Lee and Johnson (2011) revealed more or less similar results. The results of Parast et al. (2010), in particular, showed that energy price and employment were identified as the most significant factors affecting airlines' output.
- The sign of the LF_INT[6] coefficient is positive and statistically significant at the 1 % level in both the EE and the EC models. This result suggests that the higher the load factors of international flight, the larger the output of airlines. Because international routes are mostly longer than domestic flights, the output of revenue ton kilometers will increase more when the international passenger load factor increases. Somewhat inconsistent with our assumption is the result of LF_DOM, the load factor for domestic flight, which shows a negative correlation with airline output. One of the alternative explanations for this result is that a higher domestic load factor means airlines use more resources for domestic flights, which might lead to a reduction in international flights. The same result has been presented by Oum et al. (2005) and Assaf (2009) but contrary to Clougherty (2009) who observed a positive effect of domestic load factor on output. In recent years, many countries' domestic markets have been dominated by low-cost carriers (LCCs), which are growing rapidly, particularly in the Asia-Pacific region. To counteract the threats from LCCs, many network airlines introduced the AWAs (airlines-within-airlines) such as Jin Air of Korean Air or German wings of Lufthansa[7] (Pearson and Merkert 2014). By substituting their domestic and short international routes with AWAs, airlines can concentrate their efforts on the international routes. Taking this fact into account, airlines that still have a higher load factor in domestic routes probably have a greater focus on domestic market operation—they would thus have less

---

[6]The load factor is defined as similar to the occupancy rate. When 100 seats are provided in one segment and only 50 seats are sold, then the load factor of that flight is 50 %.

[7]Please refer to the appendix for the currently operating AWAs.

output efficiency in international flights due to the limited resource allocation for these.

- The coefficient sign of the time trend is negative, while the sign of square of trend is positive, which indicates that productivity decreases over time but in a decreasing manner. As described in previous chapters, the airlines industry has improved its productivity over the past decades through the utilization and development of IT as well as the introduction of new technology in airline networks management. According to the Powell II (2010), US passenger airlines experienced tremendous productivity improvements since deregulation in 1978. According to the study, between 1978 and 2009, cumulative productivity in terms of airline traffic (revenue passenger miles, RPMs) and network capacity (available seat miles, ASMs) increased by 191 and 117 %, respectively, which is consistent with our estimation result. Time $TREND^2$ in both the EC and the EE model is statistically significant at the 1 % level.

Generally, partial production input elasticity (E_i) is calculated by using the formula $E_i = (dX_i/dY_i) * (X_i/Y_i)$. The total production input elasticity equals the sum of all the partial production elasticities: RTS $= \sum E_i (i = 1, 2, \ldots, K)$ (Coelli 1996). In our EC model, the sum of coefficients is larger than 1, and it exhibits an increasing returns to scale of airlines' production. This result is consistent with the findings of Assaf (2009)—the sum of the coefficients of input parameters in his model was larger than "1", which suggests that the production technology of the different airlines exhibits an increasing returns to scale.

In the context of the parameters in the technical efficiency model, the signs of parameters δ reported below are as per our expectation and consistent with the findings from existing studies on airline production efficiency.

$$
\begin{aligned}
\hat{U} = \; & \underset{(0.128)}{2.474^a} - \underset{(0.010)}{0.075^a} \log \text{STAGE} - \underset{(0.030)}{0.092^c} \log \text{FHRS} - \underset{(0.022)}{0.144^a} \log \text{FREQ} - \underset{(0.032)}{0.220^a} \log \text{AGE} \\
& - \underset{(1.006)}{21.969^a} \text{MS} + \underset{(0.003)}{0.040^a} \text{PRICE} + \underset{(0.016)}{0.068^a} \text{A1} + \underset{(0.016)}{0.107^a} \text{A2} + \underset{(0.018)}{0.036^a} \text{A3} + \underset{(0.011)}{0.013} \text{EU} \\
& - \underset{(0.011)}{0.083^a} \text{ASIA} - \underset{(0.001)}{0.007^a} \text{YEAR}
\end{aligned}
$$

$$(4.9)$$

The estimated efficiency effect coefficients are larger than their corresponding standard errors, which reconfirms the rejection of the third null hypothesis reported in Table 4.6 that all the inefficiency effect coefficients are jointly equal to zero. In other words, using the technical inefficiency effect model helps specify the effects of airline output better than the reduced forms of the model. A positive sign of a determinant means that an increase in the determinant will result in an increase in the inefficiency of the airline, while a negative sign indicates a reduction in inefficiency. The results are explained below.[8]

---

[8]The superscripts a, b, and c indicate significant probabilities $p < 0.001$, $p < 0.01$, $p < 0.05$, respectively, and estimated standard errors are in parentheses.

- The signs of STAGE length, FHRS (flying hours) and flight FREQ (frequency) are consistent with our prior assumptions. A longer length of flights would naturally lead an airline to use its aircraft and manpower more efficiently, and this will generally increase the airline's capacity to sell more seats to passengers. Merkert and Hensher (2011) evaluated the key determinants of the efficiency of 58 airlines by applying a two-stage data envelopment analysis (DEA) and found that although stage length and flying hours had impacts on an aircraft's unit cost, their impact on the airline technical efficiency was very limited. Efficient utilization of resources is significant for the output maximization objective, and it is reconfirmed by minus signs of Stage Length, Flying Hours and Flight Frequency, which are statistically significant at 1 % level of significance. This means that a 1 % increase in Stage Length, FHRS (flying hours) and FREQ (flight frequency) reduces production inefficiency by 0.075, 0.092 and 0.144 %, respectively, or, equivalently, enhances production efficiency by 0.075, 0.092 and 0.144 %, respectively. We expected that these three parameters would improve airlines' efficiency by minimizing the time spent on the ground, which, in turn, would maximize the utilization of resources. Statistical significance and the signs of the coefficients confirmed that our assumptions are valid. Among the three, the magnitude of the impact of frequency on the efficiency of airlines' output is the highest.
- In contrast to our expectations, the coefficient sign of AGE of aircrafts is negative, which means that aircraft age has a positive effect on airline efficiency. Our hypothesis of a negative effect of AC age on output efficiency is drawn from the fact that a higher average aircraft age will decrease the efficiency of airlines due to higher maintenance costs and less efficient fuel consumption. Greer (2009) and Merkert and Hensher (2011) showed that AGE has no statistically significant correlation with an airline's productivity, while Oum et al. (2005) argued that AGE has a negative effect on productivity. One possible interpretation could be that huge investment on aircraft procurement leaves less capacity to allocate more capital for activities such as staff training or marketing due to the capital burden with financing of aircraft procurement or leasing. This is one possible interpretation, and existing studies have provided different results on this issue. Another explanation might be the time required for airlines to adapt to the new technologies and operate them effectively. In any case, further analysis is required to shed light on this unexpected result.
- Both market share (MS) and airfare (PRICE) have a statistically significant effect on airline efficiency, and the sign of the estimated coefficients of market share is consistent with our expectation of a statistically significant effect at the 1 % level. The result indicates that a 1 % increase of the market share leads to more than 21.97 % increase of efficiency. While this is a somewhat overestimated figure, we

can at least capture clear evidence of the correlation between the market share and an airline's efficiency level. In addition, this result also confirms the Porter's hypothesis that "firms' global competitiveness, measured at the market share, ultimately comes from the firms' productivity" (Porter 1990). A higher international market share will enable airlines to use the inputs more economically, and this will result in an increase in both passenger and cargo sales.

- We expected PRICE to have a negative effect on efficiency, and our result is in accordance with our expectation. Demand elasticity for air travel is highly sensitive to price changes. Therefore, higher airfare will reduce the sales of airlines by shifting demand to other means of transportation or competitor airlines or sometimes cancellation of the travel. This conjecture has been confirmed by the coefficient of 0.040, which means that a 1 % increase in airfare reduces output efficiency by 0.040 % via reduction in sales. This is consistent with the findings of Berry and Jia (2008) who suggest that air-travel demand in 2000 became more price-sensitive than in the 1990s. On the other hand, according to the study by Liang (2013),[9] an airline's share of passengers on a route is positively associated with its ability to charge prices above marginal costs. In other words, when an airline can charge a higher price, it has a market power over its competitors in the domestic market. Less competition in the domestic market will eventually lead to less competitiveness for airlines in the international market; thus a positive sign of price eventually results in a lower level of total output. Oum et al. (2009) also confirmed that "Liberalization, as a consequence of airlines' optimization of the operation, reduces price, and stimulates traffic growth thus leading to a productive efficiency and pricing strategy forces airlines to improve productivity, and eliminates inefficient carriers out of the market" (Oum et al. 2009). Thus, our result that price has a negative effect on efficiency can be interpreted as airlines that charge a higher fare have a certain degree of market power and such market power can negatively affect the airlines' production efficiency.

- The coefficient signs of airline alliance membership dummies reveal that alliance members are less efficient in service production than airlines that did not join any alliance, and they are statistically significant at the 1 % level of significance. This result does not support our hypothesis that airlines that join an alliance experience an output increase due to the positive membership effect, but none of the alliances showed higher production efficiency. The estimation with stochastic frontier models by Sjogre and Soderberg (2011) revealed that at the aggregate level, membership in alliances had an ambiguous effect on productivity, which is consistent with our result. Bilotkach et al. (2012) studied

---

[9]The study used data of 5428 routes of the nine largest domestic airlines in the third quarter of 1987.

antitrust implications of airline alliances and concluded that most types of efficiencies can only be considered as partly immunity-specific and suggested an assessment of only the economic effects of antitrust immunity. On the other hand, Whalen (2005) showed that alliances are associated with large increases in passenger volumes. Oum et al. (2009), Fana et al. (2001) and Gudmundsson (2006)[10] have arrived at the same result.

- The regional effect is statistically significant at the 1 % level and has a positive effect on airlines' efficiency compared with the reference region of America. In particular, the coefficients of the Europe dummy (EU) and Asia dummy (ASIA) are 0.013 and −0.083, respectively. This result indicates that the production efficiency of airlines in the ASIA region is higher than that of carriers in America, while it is the opposite in the case for the carriers in the Europe region. The coefficient of ASIA is statistically significant at the 1 % level, but the dummy variable EU is statistically insignificant. One of the plausible explanations for this result is that the demand for air travel in the Asia region is expanding substantially, especially in countries like China and India. Another possible reason for the Asian carriers' advantage could be the regulation of market access as explained in Chap. 3. Cheaper labor cost as well as the higher education level of the labor force and service quality in the Asia region could be other reasons for the output efficiency in the region. Our result is especially interesting when compared with findings of previous studies such as Oum and Yu (1998), who found that Asian carriers (except Japan Airlines and All Nippon Airways) were generally more competitive than the major US carriers, mostly due to their substantially lower input prices and high service quality. According to these studies, among the European carriers, British Airways and Scandinavian Airlines Systems were 7 and 42 % less competitive, respectively, than American Airlines because of higher input prices and lower efficiency. All these results are similar with the results of our analysis. Other studies such as Barbot et al. (2008) have argued that airlines from regions that have more homogeneous regulatory structures, like North America, are more uniform in their productivity.
- The time trend coefficient is −0.007 and is statistically significant at the 1 % level. This result indicates that efficiency is time-variant and that the airline industry is improving its efficiency over the period. A close review of the trend will be further discussed in the airline efficiency section.

In sum, including the coefficient signs of the variables, our hypotheses test each of the determinant variable's impact on the production efficiency, which is consistent with our prior assumption. For a summary of the results, see Table 4.8.

---

[10]Details of airline alliances and regional comparison across airlines will be explored in Sect. 4.5.2.

Table 4.8 Summary of the result (based on the EE model)

Variables		Assumption	Result	Effect to production	Statistically significant	Result
EMP		+	+	$\uparrow \rightarrow \uparrow$	o	Consistent
AC		+	+	$\uparrow \rightarrow \uparrow$	o	Consistent
ENERGY		+	+	$\uparrow \rightarrow \uparrow$	o	Consistent
LF_INT		+	+	$\uparrow \rightarrow \uparrow$	o	Consistent
LF_DOM		+	−	$\uparrow \rightarrow \uparrow$	o	Inconsistent
TREND		−	−	$\uparrow \rightarrow \downarrow$	o	Consistent
TREND^2		+	+	$\uparrow \rightarrow \uparrow$	o	Consistent
Variables	Hypothesis	Assumption	Result	Effect to efficiency	Statistically significant	Result
STAGE	H1	−	+	$\uparrow \rightarrow \uparrow$	o	Consistent
FREQ	H1	−	+	$\uparrow \rightarrow \uparrow$	o	Consistent
FHRS	H1	−	−	$\uparrow \rightarrow \uparrow$	o	Consistent
AGE	H2	+	−	$\uparrow \rightarrow \downarrow$	o	Inconsistent
MS	H3	−	−	$\uparrow \rightarrow \uparrow$	o	Consistent
PRICE	H4	+	+	$\uparrow \rightarrow \downarrow$	o	Consistent
A1	H5	−	+	Yes	o	Inconsistent
A2	H5	−	+	Yes	o	Inconsistent
A3	H5	−	+	Yes	o	Inconsistent
ASIA	H6	−	−	Yes	o	Consistent
TREND	H7	−	−	$\uparrow \rightarrow \uparrow$	0	Consistent

4.5.2 Airline Efficiency

A. Frequency distribution of efficiency

The mean efficiency in the EC and EE models is 0.709 and 0.879, respectively, implying that the airlines in our sample produce only 70.9 and 87.9 % of their potential output using the best performing airline as a reference. This implies that the airlines could on the average produce 29.1 and 22.1 % more services by using the same amount of inputs but by employing the best-practiced service production technology in the sample. Alternatively, they could produce the same amount of services but by using fewer inputs and at a lower cost.

The frequency distribution of efficiency, which is summarized in Table 4.9 and Fig. 4.1, shows that a large proportion of the efficiency level is concentrated between 0.55 and 0.80 efficiency intervals in the EC model, while the EE model's frequency is evenly distributed between the intervals 0.80 and 1.00. This suggests that a large number of airlines are operating at efficiency levels close to the frontier airline with the best-practiced technology in the case of the EC model and very close to the frontier in the case of the EE model. For the mean efficiency of each airline and its evolution over time, see Appendices 4.1 and 4.2. The two models produce very different levels and distributions of efficiency, which is unexpected. It

Table 4.9 Frequency distribution of technical efficiency based on the EC and EE models

EC range	Frequency	Percentage	EE range	Frequency	Percentage
0.00–0.55	12	2.051	0.00–0.55	4	0.684
0.55–0.60	48	8.205	0.55–0.60	1	0.171
0.60–0.65	110	18.803	0.60–0.65	8	1.368
0.65–0.70	127	21.709	0.65–0.70	19	3.248
0.70–0.75	129	22.051	0.70–0.75	48	8.205
0.75–0.80	80	13.675	0.75–0.80	66	11.282
0.80–0.85	19	3.248	0.80–0.85	72	12.308
0.85–0.90	0	0.000	0.85–0.90	69	11.795
0.90–0.95	30	5.128	0.90–0.95	74	12.650
0.95–100	30	5.128	0.95–1.00	224	38.291
Observation	585	100.000	Observation	585	100.000

Fig. 4.1 Frequency distributions of technical efficiency based on EC and EE models

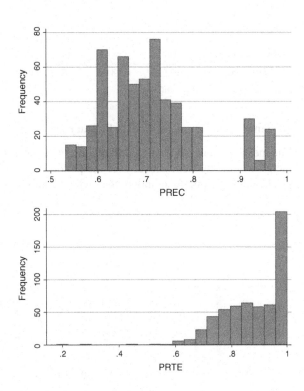

should be noted that since our sample contains almost all international airlines, the best-practiced technology in the sample is the same as the best technology in the population since the sample and population of large airlines are very likely to be the same.

Table 4.10 Development of average technical efficiency in production over time

Year	EC model				EE model			
	Mean	Std. dev.	Min	Max	Mean	Std. dev.	Min	Max
1998	0.701	0.106	0.532	0.973	0.841	0.134	0.465	0.994
1999	0.702	0.105	0.533	0.974	0.846	0.128	0.541	0.994
2000	0.703	0.105	0.535	0.974	0.846	0.125	0.565	0.994
2001	0.705	0.105	0.537	0.974	0.866	0.115	0.620	0.995
2002	0.706	0.104	0.538	0.974	0.870	0.108	0.644	0.994
2003	0.707	0.104	0.540	0.974	0.875	0.104	0.667	0.995
2004	0.708	0.103	0.542	0.974	0.878	0.105	0.670	1.000
2005	0.709	0.103	0.543	0.974	0.878	0.101	0.678	1.000
2006	0.710	0.103	0.545	0.974	0.882	0.099	0.684	0.995
2007	0.712	0.102	0.547	0.975	0.889	0.094	0.693	1.000
2008	0.713	0.102	0.548	0.975	0.889	0.094	0.697	0.994
2009	0.714	0.102	0.550	0.975	0.910	0.080	0.721	1.000
2010	0.715	0.101	0.551	0.975	0.898	0.129	0.268	1.000
2011	0.716	0.101	0.553	0.975	0.896	0.140	0.180	0.995
2012	0.717	0.100	0.555	0.975	0.915	0.086	0.603	0.994
Average	0.709	0.102	0.531	0.975	0.879	0.112	0.179	1.000

Note Each year, 39 observations

B. Time variation of technical efficiency

The mean efficiency estimated through the EC and the EE models shows a gradual increase in the efficiency level over the period (see Table 4.10 and Fig. 4.2). This result confirms our assumption that with technology development and various efforts of airlines, the overall production efficiency improves through 'learning by

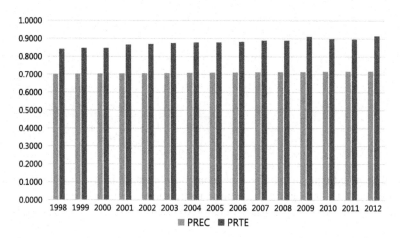

Fig. 4.2 Trend in average technical efficiency

doing' and alliance cooperation and the consequent spillover of technology within alliances and between airlines. While maximum efficiency remains within a similar range, the minimum efficiency has improved over the period, which means that the efficiency gap between the airlines is reduced probably due to technology development and high competition among the airlines and alliances. It must be noted that the mean numbers are averages of all airlines' efficiency in a given year. Hence, the within-year variations in the form of standard deviation and difference between minimum and maximum are reported.

C. **Airlines' efficiency rank**

The average technical efficiency for individual airlines and their efficiency ranks estimated by the two different EC and EE models are reported in Table 4.11. In the case of the EC model, 8 Asian carriers and 2 European carriers—BA (British

Table 4.11 Mean production efficiency of airline and their ranks (1998–2012)

EC rank	Airline	Mean	Output rank	EE rank	Airline	Mean	Output rank
1	KE	0.974	9	1	KE	0.996	9
2	SQ	0.953	7	2	LH	0.993	4
3	JL	0.924	10	3	CX	0.992	8
4	CX	0.920	8	4	SQ	0.990	7
5	TG	0.803	14	5	BA	0.990	6
6	NH	0.801	15	6	QF	0.988	11
7	QF	0.791	11	7	JL	0.986	10
8	BA	0.773	6	8	AF	0.985	5
9	MH	0.757	19	9	TG	0.983	14
10	LH	0.757	4	10	MH	0.980	19
11	LY	0.753	32	11	AA	0.979	1
12	CA	0.743	12	12	UA	0.978	2
13	LX	0.732	22	13	DL	0.968	3
14	SV	0.724	24	14	CA	0.948	12
15	GA	0.719	33	15	MU	0.944	16
16	LA	0.717	23	16	NZ	0.935	27
17	AF	0.714	5	17	NH	0.926	15
18	UA	0.712	2	18	AI	0.905	31
19	PR	0.706	36	19	AC	0.904	13
20	MU	0.699	16	20	CZ	0.896	17
21	DL	0.689	3	21	SV	0.888	24
22	NZ	0.686	27	22	PR	0.862	36
23	QR	0.681	26	23	IB	0.854	20
24	AA	0.669	1	24	LA	0.853	23
25	AC	0.664	13	25	LX	0.849	22

(continued)

Table 4.11 (continued)

EC rank	Airline	Mean	Output rank	EE rank	Airline	Mean	Output rank
26	TK	0.659	25	26	SU	0.831	29
27	AY	0.658	35	27	TK	0.825	25
28	IB	0.651	20	28	GA	0.790	33
29	OS	0.644	34	29	AZ	0.790	21
30	AI	0.641	31	30	SK	0.775	28
31	SK	0.616	28	31	JJ	0.770	30
32	SU	0.613	29	32	US	0.768	18
33	CZ	0.611	17	33	AY	0.767	35
34	EI	0.610	38	34	OS	0.764	34
35	US	0.601	18	35	TP	0.761	37
36	TP	0.599	37	36	LY	0.757	32
37	JJ	0.591	30	37	AV	0.711	39
38	AZ	0.565	21	38	QR	0.710	26
39	AV	0.543	39	39	EI	0.673	38

Airways) and LH (Lufthansa)—are among the top 10 airlines ranked by the level of their efficiency. No American carrier was ranked among the top 10. In the case of the EE model, the ten highest ranked airlines include three European and 7 Asian carriers. Carriers that ranked low in efficiency are mostly small in size, measured in terms of RPK. This implies that economies of scale are at work in airline service production. Airlines such as KE, CX, and SQ show high levels of efficiency in both the EC and the EE models. The result of the EE model is consistent with the result of Barbot et al. (2008), suggesting that larger carriers measured with RPK are more efficient due to a better utilization of the potential of economies of scale. The top ranked airlines in terms of output such as AA, DL, and UA showed a medium range of efficiency. However, airlines such as LY (ElAl Israel Airlines) and PR (Philippine Airlines) had a higher rank in the EC model despite a relatively lower rank in terms of the output size, which indicates that output size is not always a prerequisite condition for high production efficiency.

Again, it is to be noted that these are averages for the airlines' technical production efficiency performance over time. Each airline's efficiency can vary greatly over time. The temporal patterns of efficiency for individual airlines are shown in Fig. 4.3. The EC trends indicate that airlines' efficiency is gradually improving over time. OS, CX, KE, and SQ showed a steady performance at a high level of efficiency throughout the sample period. In the context of the EE model, which incorporated inefficiency variables into the estimation, three Chinese airlines—CA, CZ, and MU—show a steady growth in their production efficiency. This probably reflects the fast-growing demand for air travel in China and airlines' cost effectiveness in expanding in the international market. In 2008 and 2009, almost all

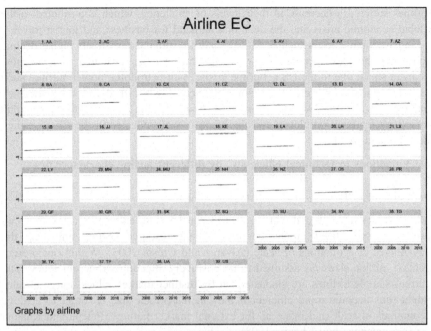

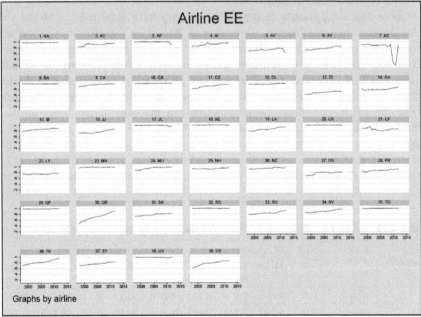

Fig. 4.3 Development of individual airlines' service production efficiency over time

airlines suffered a decrease in their levels of efficiency, which is attributed to the global economic crisis and the declining demand for business and tourist travel.

In particular, carriers such as AF, AV and AZ suffered a relatively higher decline following the global economic crisis, and this can be attributed to a negative demand shock due to the US subprime crisis. With petrodollar power, airlines such as QR acquired a high growth rate over the period, while JL declined its efficiency rate rapidly. In 2009, JAL asked for a relief loan from the Japanese government due to serious financial problems, and this trend is well reflected in the EE efficiency development trend.

D. **Variations in technical efficiency by different airline characteristics**

D.1. **Size of airlines**

Many studies have argued that large firms can be more efficient because they can use more specialized inputs, coordinate their resources better, and reap the advantages of economies of scale (Alvarez and Crespi 2003). Within our present context, airline size was assumed to be positively affecting airline efficiency. The current sample airlines are characterized by distinct market values. Large airlines might thus become more efficient if they increase their size on order to achieve economies of scale and make up for external market failures (Palepu and Khanna 2000; Ghemawat and Khanna 1998).

Given that many studies on the airline industry have indicated that airline size contributes to higher efficiency (Pitfield et al. 2010), we assumed that airline size would positively impact the efficiency of airlines. The mean technical efficiency score between airlines of different sizes measured by the number of aircrafts (categorized into six size classes) is reported in Table 4.12. According to the EC model, the efficiency variation between airlines of different sizes is relatively small, while the EE model shows higher efficiency in the case of the larger airlines. The EE model clearly demonstrates that the mean efficiency of the airlines with a large number of aircrafts achieved a high level of efficiency, which implies the effect of economies of scale—this is consistent with the findings of the study by Barros et al. (2013). Airlines with many aircrafts can flexibly decide the capacity

Table 4.12 Production efficiency by airlines' size (measured by the number of aircrafts)

Size category	Number of AC	NBR	EC model				EE model			
			Mean	Std. dev.	Min	Max	Mean	Std. dev.	Min	Max
1	≤ 100	199	0.685	0.074	0.532	0.810	0.811	0.110	0.465	0.994
2	100–200	204	0.740	0.141	0.553	0.975	0.890	0.109	0.180	1.000
3	200–300	77	0.733	0.053	0.622	0.807	0.942	0.041	0.828	0.994
4	300–400	60	0.679	0.047	0.590	0.722	0.925	0.100	0.609	0.993
5	400–500	31	0.683	0.073	0.601	0.764	0.946	0.059	0.816	0.995
6	≥ 500	14	0.670	0.006	0.661	0.679	0.979	0.003	0.973	0.983

Table 4.13 Production efficiency by airline size (measured by the number of employees)

Size category	Employment	NBR	EC model				EE model			
			Mean	Std. dev.	Min	Max	Mean	Std. dev.	Min	Max
1	≤ 5000	51	0.656	0.078	0.532	0.760	0.718	0.063	0.541	0.911
2	5000–10,000	113	0.667	0.068	0.545	0.927	0.788	0.076	0.465	0.982
3	10,000–20,000	205	0.749	0.133	0.553	0.975	0.909	0.100	0.180	1.000
4	20,000–30,000	100	0.708	0.081	0.558	0.922	0.909	0.078	0.724	0.994
5	30,000–40,000	33	0.688	0.080	0.590	0.798	0.919	0.092	0.609	0.995
6	40,000–50,000	17	0.721	0.059	0.591	0.780	0.940	0.109	0.636	0.991
7	50,000–60,000	24	0.721	0.026	0.686	0.770	0.981	0.022	0.892	0.994
8	60,000–70,000	11	0.691	0.017	0.675	0.716	0.977	0.011	0.961	0.992
9	70,000–80,000	11	0.679	0.012	0.667	0.698	0.979	0.013	0.953	0.992
10	80,000–90,000	4	0.699	0.027	0.660	0.721	0.983	0.008	0.974	0.992
11	90,000–100,000	10	0.709	0.044	0.661	0.759	0.985	0.008	0.973	0.994
12	>100,000	6	0.753	0.023	0.706	0.764	0.991	0.004	0.984	0.993

supply according to passenger demand; thus they can accommodate the market demands more efficiently.

The same trend is shown in the efficiency of airlines analyzed by size, measured in terms of size of employment, which is summarized in Table 4.13. Airlines with more workers show a higher score of mean efficiency in the case of both the EC and the EE models. Among airlines with 50,000 or more workers, there is no significant difference in the level of technical efficiency between airlines of different sizes. This means that reaching a certain scale is a necessary condition for increasing production efficiency but not a sufficient condition. A majority of airlines employ around 20,000 people and these airlines do not vary significantly in the level of technical production efficiency in the EC model. The dispersion of the EE results is also limited (Fig. 4.4).

D.2.   **Regional location and alliance memberships**

Barbot et al. (2008) showed that "Regional differences among the airlines' by efficiency levels might be expected. Legislation and de-regulation processes are specific to each region, giving different levels of competitive pressure on carriers, with sizable implications for productivity and efficiency" (Barbot et al. 2008). Our estimation results, which show different efficiency levels in different regions, confirm this conjecture. More specifically, our results indicate that airlines based in the Asia Pacific region achieved a higher efficiency level than those with operation headquarters in other regions. European airlines achieved the lowest efficiency, and this result is similar to that of several studies that compared airline efficiency across different regions.

Airline alliance membership results are broadly similar in the EE model and the EC model and suggest that airlines that do not join any alliance are far less efficient

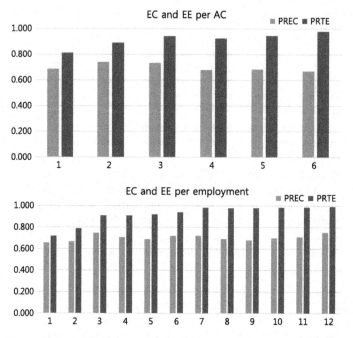

Fig. 4.4 Mean production efficiency by size of airlines (measured by AC and employment)

than airlines that are alliance members. Airline alliance memberships, including mergers and cross-investments, have been part of airline management strategies since the 1980s. Inter-airline alliance agreements can vary from a simple marketing alliance, such as a joint frequent flyer program and code-sharing agreements to a fully strategic alliance that culminates in a merger of two airlines. By 2011, the three global alliances, One World, Star Alliance and Sky Team, which were grouped and represented by dummy variables in this study, covered two-thirds of all international air traffic. The positive impact of alliance membership on the member airlines is in terms of not only cost savings but also direct benefits to consumers through the reduction of fares in some markets, increased frequencies and route offerings.

Although many studies have proved that alliances provide positive consumer benefits through cost reduction and additional route offerings, some also argue that alliances can adversely affect competition by reducing or eliminating competition on specific routes or relevant markets, which in turn negatively affects consumer welfare by limiting the available choices. This occurs when two carriers previously competing on a route on which there is no third carrier decide that only one of the alliances should operate the route (Table 4.14).

Our result estimated with both the EC and the EE model shows that Star Alliance is the least efficient in terms of service production, while One World is the most efficient airline alliance group. The difference in production efficiency between the

Table 4.14 Production efficiency of regional location and alliance membership

Region and alliance	Observation	EC				EE			
		Mean	Std. dev.	Min	Max	Mean	Std. dev.	Min	Max
Europe	240	0.672	0.062	0.553	0.780	0.826	0.120	0.180	0.995
Asia	225	0.782	0.111	0.601	0.975	0.941	0.062	0.749	1.000
America	120	0.648	0.059	0.532	0.725	0.866	0.109	0.603	0.992
One World	150	0.750	0.100	0.631	0.927	0.929	0.081	0.700	0.995
Star	240	0.694	0.101	0.532	0.955	0.868	0.104	0.603	0.995
Sky Team	120	0.699	0.118	0.553	0.975	0.912	0.110	0.180	1.000
No Alliance	75	0.707	0.100	0.553	0.975	0.881	0.105	0.609	0.994

different alliances is not so significant. For example, the mean efficiency of One World's member airlines is 0.929, followed by that of Sky Team at 0.912 and Star Alliance at 0.868. The similar efficiency scores across different airline alliances is probably due to the similar scope of services and the extent of cooperation among the member carriers such as sharing of network information and bilateral agreements on ground service handling between airlines.

As was shown in Fig. 4.5, each alliance effect within a region has a distinct result. In the case of the EC model, Star Alliance members are the most effective in

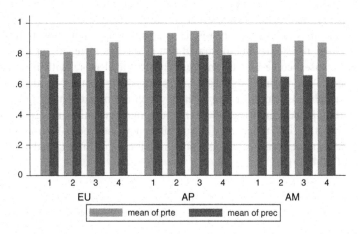

Fig. 4.5 Regional location and alliance membership's comparison of service production efficiency. *1*—One World, *2*—Star Alliance, *3*—Sky Team, *4*—No alliance

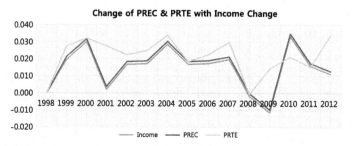

Fig. 4.6 Development of changes in average per capita income and production efficiency of airlines

every region, while the EE model reveals that the Sky Team alliance is the most effective group of airlines in every region. In the case of Asia and Europe, three alliances showed a more or less similar trend, indicating how competitive alliances in these regions are as a result of which the scope of services provided by the different alliances would be similar. Customers in these regions would not have a specific preference among the alliances when choosing one.

D.3. **Per capita income of the base country**

Since the interaction between air transportation and economic development is dynamic, in Fig. 4.6, we compared the yearly growth rates of efficiency and real GDP per capita growth based on the data for the period from 1998 to 2012. IATA and the previous studies have shown that air travel demand increases with growth in per capita incomes. Through a historical analysis of transportation trends across many countries, the studies demonstrated that as income increases, airlines' output increases because people and businesses tend to travel more with increased disposable income and business expansion, thus improving airlines' productivity. Our estimation results also confirm that airlines which are based in the higher income and purchasing power countries showed higher efficiency both in the EE and the EC models, and the difference in mean efficiency between high-income and low-income countries reaches almost 20 % in the case of the EC and 26 % in the EE model (Table 4.15).

Table 4.15 Technical efficiency of airlines by per capita average levels of income

GDP (USD)	Number of OBS	EC				EE			
		Mean	Std. dev.	Min	Max	Mean	Std. dev.	Min	Max
≥ 15,000	123	0.670	0.068	0.533	0.803	0.866	0.085	0.683	0.985
15,000–25,000	63	0.684	0.081	0.532	0.810	0.842	0.139	0.465	0.987
25,000–35,000	62	0.701	0.094	0.589	0.974	0.855	0.077	0.702	0.994
35,000–45,000	135	0.773	0.108	0.571	0.975	0.902	0.096	0.673	1.000
>45,000	202	0.701	0.104	0.553	0.975	0.889	0.130	0.180	0.995

Table 4.16 Growth rates of technical efficiency and per capita income levels (units: USD and %)

Year	GPP		EC		EE	
	Mean	% change	Mean	% change	Mean	% change
1998	31,183	–	0.701	–	0.841	–
1999	31,795	0.02	0.702	0.002	0.846	0.006
2000	32,752	0.03	0.703	0.002	0.846	0
2001	32,823	0.002	0.705	0.002	0.866	0.024
2002	33,373	0.017	0.706	0.002	0.87	0.004
2003	33,947	0.017	0.707	0.002	0.875	0.006
2004	34,924	0.029	0.708	0.002	0.878	0.004
2005	35,514	0.017	0.709	0.002	0.878	0
2006	36,131	0.017	0.71	0.002	0.882	0.004
2007	36,841	0.02	0.712	0.002	0.889	0.009
2008	36,776	−0.002	0.713	0.002	0.889	0
2009	36,358	−0.011	0.714	0.002	0.91	0.024
2010	37,568	0.033	0.715	0.002	0.898	−0.014
2011	38,161	0.016	0.716	0.002	0.896	−0.002
2012	38,586	0.011	0.717	0.002	0.915	0.021

Source www.worldbank.org

Although there was an income decrease in certain years such as 2001 and 2009, both the EC and the EE models showed a steady growth of airlines' services production and efficiency levels. This is consistent with the reports from IATA that airlines' demand resilience in the face of economic fluctuations has been faster than other industries—this trend is also confirmed by our estimation, described in Table 4.16.

4.6   Summary and Conclusion

In this chapter, we performed the stochastic frontier production function analysis based on data from 39 major airlines during the period 1998–2012. Our results from using two well-known parametric frontier production function models showed that the international airlines have made significant progress in terms of production efficiency. The results for the input variables in the error component model and technical efficiency effects model were largely consistent with our assumptions and expectations, which, in turn, were derived from the findings of previous studies on airline productivity and efficiency. The log likelihood values for the models confirmed the existence of significant technical inefficiency in the production of airline services, thus suggesting that the technical efficiency effect model is more appropriate for our analysis compared with the average production function that ignores inefficiency in production. Out of the seven hypotheses that we tested, the results of five were consistent with our prior expectations, while two were not supported by our prior assumptions.

The signs of the coefficients of the production function and inefficiency determinant variables were mostly consistent with our theory-based assumptions, but there were also a few exceptions. The size of airlines, measured by the number of aircrafts and the number of total employment, did have a marked effect on the airline efficiency level based on the EE model, while the case of the EC model shows a larger variation in technical efficiency among the airlines of different sizes.

Among the variables determining inefficiency, the market share effect resulted in a highly significant effect on airlines' efficiency level. This result supports Porter's hypothesis that a firm's productivity is the most important factor in achieving global competitiveness, which is represented by the market share in a global market.

The per capita income of countries where airlines have their headquarters is the most important factor of airlines' efficiency, and it showed a similar growth pattern as efficiency improvement over time. According to the EC model, the efficiency variation among airlines of different sizes is relatively small, while the EE model shows a higher efficiency level in the case of the larger airlines. The EE model clearly shows that the mean technical efficiency of airlines with a large number of aircrafts achieved a higher level of efficiency, which implies positive economies of scale effect. Airlines with many aircrafts can more flexibly decide the capacity supply according to the passenger demand.

The regional market effect was statistically significant, with Asian carriers showing a higher technical efficiency level than their EU or North American carrier counterparts. Alliance formation resulted in a statistically insignificant effect, but a comparison of the sample airlines' efficiency confirms that airline alliance members performed better than their non-member counterparts. However, there were only limited performance variances among different airline alliances.

In this chapter, we have analyzed airlines' production efficiency and tested several hypotheses through the production inefficiency estimation. Although this model can identify various aspects in terms of the production efficiency of airlines, its results might not be able to fully incorporate the airlines' sustainable competitiveness because achieving production efficiency alone cannot explain why many airlines that achieved high production efficiency went bankrupt in the course of financial crises (e.g., AA and JL). Other studies such as Oum and Yu (1998) found that Northwest[11] and Continental airlines showed a higher efficiency among the US carriers, and these airlines were eventually merged by DL and UA in 2008 and 2012, respectively. In order to have a sustainable competitiveness, firms need to generate a sound profit from their operation, which can be realized through maximizing output, minimizing cost or a combination of the two alternatives.

Looking at one side of the facts might not capture the reality of firms' competitiveness and might not fully reflect airlines' continuous entry into and exit from local and global markets. Taking into account the maximum output effect can only partially explain airlines' competitiveness. In the next chapter, we will review another important factor that affect airlines' competitiveness, namely, cost efficiency, to complement the analysis of production efficiency conducted in this chapter. The two approaches differ by the objectives of airlines, namely, output maximization in the case of production and cost minimization in the case of cost. For service productions, a cost minimization approach is usually more suitable as demand is given and the service provider is expected to provide services and maximize its profits by minimizing the cost of producing the demanded service. The disadvantage of a cost frontier approach is the difficulties in accessing data on input factor prices.

---

[11]"Prior to its merger with Delta in 2010, Northwest was the world's sixth largest airline in terms of domestic and international scheduled passenger miles flown and the US's sixth largest airline in terms of domestic passenger miles flown" (Wikipedia).

Appendix 4.1: Development of Different International Airline Production Efficiency, 1998–2012 (EC Model)

Airline	1998	1999	2000	2001	2002	2003	2004	2005	2006	2007	2008	2009	2010	2011	2012	AVG
AA	0.66	0.661	0.662	0.664	0.665	0.666	0.668	0.669	0.671	0.672	0.673	0.675	0.676	0.677	0.678	0.669
AC	0.654	0.656	0.657	0.658	0.66	0.661	0.663	0.664	0.665	0.667	0.668	0.669	0.671	0.672	0.673	0.664
AF	0.705	0.707	0.708	0.709	0.71	0.712	0.713	0.714	0.715	0.716	0.718	0.719	0.72	0.721	0.722	0.714
AI	0.631	0.633	0.634	0.636	0.637	0.639	0.64	0.641	0.643	0.644	0.646	0.647	0.648	0.65	0.651	0.641
AV	0.532	0.533	0.535	0.537	0.538	0.54	0.542	0.543	0.545	0.546	0.548	0.55	0.551	0.553	0.555	0.543
AY	0.648	0.65	0.651	0.652	0.654	0.655	0.657	0.658	0.659	0.661	0.662	0.663	0.665	0.666	0.668	0.658
AZ	0.553	0.555	0.557	0.558	0.56	0.561	0.563	0.565	0.566	0.568	0.57	0.571	0.573	0.574	0.576	0.565
BA	0.766	0.767	0.768	0.769	0.77	0.771	0.772	0.773	0.774	0.775	0.776	0.777	0.778	0.779	0.78	0.773
CA	0.736	0.737	0.738	0.739	0.74	0.741	0.742	0.743	0.744	0.746	0.747	0.748	0.749	0.75	0.751	0.743
CX	0.917	0.917	0.918	0.918	0.919	0.919	0.919	0.92	0.92	0.92	0.921	0.921	0.922	0.922	0.922	0.92
CZ	0.601	0.602	0.604	0.606	0.607	0.609	0.61	0.612	0.613	0.615	0.616	0.618	0.619	0.62	0.622	0.612
DL	0.68	0.681	0.682	0.684	0.685	0.686	0.687	0.689	0.69	0.691	0.693	0.694	0.695	0.696	0.698	0.689
EI	0.599	0.601	0.602	0.604	0.605	0.607	0.608	0.61	0.611	0.613	0.614	0.616	0.617	0.619	0.62	0.61
GA	0.71	0.711	0.713	0.714	0.715	0.716	0.717	0.719	0.72	0.721	0.722	0.723	0.724	0.726	0.727	0.719
IB	0.642	0.643	0.645	0.646	0.647	0.649	0.65	0.652	0.653	0.654	0.656	0.657	0.658	0.66	0.661	0.651
JJ	0.58	0.581	0.583	0.584	0.586	0.587	0.589	0.591	0.592	0.594	0.595	0.597	0.598	0.6	0.601	0.591
JL	0.922	0.922	0.922	0.923	0.923	0.923	0.924	0.924	0.924	0.925	0.925	0.926	0.926	0.926	0.927	0.924
KE	0.973	0.974	0.974	0.974	0.974	0.974	0.974	0.974	0.974	0.975	0.975	0.975	0.975	0.975	0.975	0.974
LA	0.708	0.709	0.711	0.712	0.713	0.714	0.715	0.717	0.718	0.719	0.72	0.721	0.723	0.724	0.725	0.717
LH	0.749	0.75	0.751	0.752	0.753	0.754	0.756	0.757	0.758	0.759	0.76	0.761	0.762	0.763	0.764	0.757
LX	0.724	0.725	0.726	0.727	0.728	0.729	0.731	0.732	0.733	0.734	0.735	0.736	0.737	0.738	0.74	0.732
LY	0.745	0.746	0.747	0.748	0.75	0.751	0.752	0.753	0.754	0.755	0.756	0.757	0.758	0.759	0.76	0.753

(continued)

(continued)

Airline	1998	1999	2000	2001	2002	2003	2004	2005	2006	2007	2008	2009	2010	2011	2012	AVG
MH	0.749	0.75	0.751	0.752	0.753	0.755	0.756	0.757	0.758	0.759	0.76	0.761	0.762	0.763	0.764	0.757
MU	0.69	0.691	0.692	0.694	0.695	0.696	0.697	0.699	0.7	0.701	0.702	0.704	0.705	0.706	0.707	0.699
NH	0.795	0.795	0.796	0.797	0.798	0.799	0.8	0.801	0.802	0.803	0.803	0.804	0.805	0.806	0.807	0.801
NZ	0.677	0.679	0.68	0.681	0.683	0.684	0.685	0.686	0.688	0.689	0.69	0.692	0.693	0.694	0.695	0.686
OS	0.634	0.636	0.637	0.638	0.64	0.641	0.643	0.644	0.645	0.647	0.648	0.65	0.651	0.652	0.654	0.644
PR	0.697	0.699	0.7	0.701	0.702	0.704	0.705	0.706	0.707	0.709	0.71	0.711	0.712	0.713	0.715	0.706
QF	0.785	0.786	0.787	0.788	0.789	0.789	0.79	0.791	0.792	0.793	0.794	0.795	0.796	0.797	0.798	0.791
QR	0.672	0.673	0.674	0.676	0.677	0.678	0.68	0.681	0.682	0.684	0.685	0.686	0.688	0.689	0.69	0.681
SK	0.605	0.607	0.609	0.61	0.612	0.613	0.615	0.616	0.617	0.619	0.62	0.622	0.623	0.625	0.626	0.616
SQ	0.952	0.952	0.952	0.952	0.953	0.953	0.953	0.953	0.954	0.954	0.954	0.954	0.954	0.955	0.955	0.953
SU	0.602	0.604	0.605	0.607	0.608	0.61	0.611	0.613	0.614	0.616	0.617	0.619	0.62	0.622	0.623	0.613
SV	0.716	0.717	0.719	0.72	0.721	0.722	0.723	0.724	0.726	0.727	0.728	0.729	0.73	0.731	0.732	0.724
TG	0.797	0.798	0.799	0.8	0.801	0.802	0.803	0.803	0.804	0.805	0.806	0.807	0.808	0.809	0.809	0.803
TK	0.649	0.65	0.652	0.653	0.655	0.656	0.657	0.659	0.66	0.661	0.663	0.664	0.666	0.667	0.668	0.659
TP	0.589	0.59	0.592	0.593	0.595	0.596	0.598	0.599	0.601	0.603	0.604	0.606	0.607	0.609	0.61	0.599
UA	0.704	0.705	0.706	0.708	0.709	0.71	0.711	0.712	0.714	0.715	0.716	0.717	0.718	0.72	0.721	0.712
US	0.59	0.591	0.593	0.594	0.596	0.598	0.599	0.601	0.602	0.604	0.605	0.607	0.608	0.61	0.611	0.601
AVG	0.701	0.702	0.703	0.705	0.706	0.707	0.708	0.709	0.71	0.712	0.713	0.714	0.715	0.716	0.717	0.709

Appendix 4.2: Development of Different International Airline Production Efficiency, 1998–2012 (EE Model)

Airline	1998	1999	2000	2001	2002	2003	2004	2005	2006	2007	2008	2009	2010	2011	2012	AVG
AA	0.974	0.976	0.973	0.982	0.977	0.979	0.981	0.982	0.983	0.980	0.978	0.982	0.981	0.980	0.979	0.979
AC	0.828	0.829	0.833	0.929	0.937	0.917	0.910	0.907	0.905	0.907	0.902	0.936	0.939	0.939	0.948	0.904
AF	0.991	0.992	0.991	0.993	0.993	0.993	0.992	0.992	0.992	0.992	0.991	0.992	0.990	0.990	0.892	0.985
AI	0.843	0.850	0.843	0.864	0.873	0.890	0.967	0.913	0.913	0.912	0.914	0.947	0.952	0.947	0.947	0.905
AV	0.673	0.686	0.683	0.697	0.710	0.733	0.703	0.708	0.715	0.733	0.732	0.768	0.768	0.760	0.603	0.711
AY	0.706	0.719	0.700	0.724	0.736	0.744	0.750	0.750	0.757	0.773	0.783	0.833	0.842	0.838	0.851	0.767
AZ	0.886	0.893	0.901	0.898	0.865	0.865	0.865	0.873	0.876	0.889	0.820	0.888	0.268	0.179	0.879	0.790
BA	0.994	0.993	0.993	0.991	0.991	0.991	0.990	0.989	0.988	0.987	0.988	0.989	0.986	0.988	0.989	0.990
CA	0.872	0.906	0.903	0.924	0.938	0.949	0.956	0.956	0.965	0.970	0.965	0.978	0.982	0.979	0.980	0.948
CX	0.989	0.989	0.989	0.990	0.992	0.992	0.992	0.993	0.994	0.994	0.994	0.994	0.995	0.994	0.994	0.992
CZ	0.816	0.819	0.818	0.860	0.876	0.905	0.903	0.898	0.901	0.913	0.933	0.957	0.953	0.947	0.945	0.896
DL	0.960	0.958	0.953	0.963	0.961	0.951	0.955	0.958	0.957	0.971	0.976	0.982	0.992	0.991	0.991	0.968
EI	0.604	0.609	0.610	0.666	0.656	0.667	0.670	0.678	0.684	0.693	0.697	0.721	0.712	0.711	0.721	0.673
GA	0.800	0.749	0.758	0.770	0.777	0.767	0.773	0.768	0.774	0.778	0.780	0.815	0.831	0.847	0.860	0.790
IB	0.790	0.801	0.810	0.840	0.842	0.852	0.852	0.855	0.866	0.874	0.865	0.898	0.900	0.887	0.883	0.854
JJ	0.724	0.731	0.730	0.732	0.716	0.716	0.731	0.762	0.747	0.780	0.796	0.831	0.832	0.858	0.869	0.770
JL	0.993	0.993	0.993	0.993	0.993	0.992	0.992	0.992	0.991	0.990	0.988	0.988	0.982	0.950	0.955	0.986
KE	0.993	0.994	0.994	0.993	0.994	0.995	1.000	1.000	0.995	1.000	0.994	1.000	1.000	0.994	0.994	0.996
LA	0.789	0.780	0.782	0.816	0.832	0.845	0.839	0.836	0.847	0.864	0.870	0.915	0.923	0.921	0.931	0.853
LH	0.994	0.994	0.994	0.995	0.994	0.994	0.994	0.993	0.993	0.993	0.992	0.993	0.992	0.992	0.992	0.993
LX	0.881	0.880	0.885	0.946	0.829	0.854	0.801	0.795	0.792	0.823	0.819	0.854	0.859	0.853	0.867	0.849

(continued)

(continued)

Airline	1998	1999	2000	2001	2002	2003	2004	2005	2006	2007	2008	2009	2010	2011	2012	AVG
LY	0.758	0.755	0.734	0.746	0.754	0.757	0.755	0.746	0.747	0.752	0.738	0.777	0.779	0.774	0.778	0.757
MH	0.957	0.971	0.976	0.979	0.983	0.984	0.986	0.985	0.985	0.983	0.981	0.984	0.984	0.981	0.982	0.980
MU	0.871	0.882	0.874	0.917	0.931	0.935	0.959	0.967	0.967	0.972	0.967	0.976	0.979	0.982	0.983	0.944
NH	0.919	0.925	0.913	0.916	0.924	0.920	0.909	0.905	0.909	0.929	0.928	0.945	0.945	0.941	0.959	0.926
NZ	0.902	0.914	0.899	0.928	0.915	0.930	0.937	0.936	0.940	0.941	0.982	0.952	0.952	0.947	0.953	0.935
OS	0.673	0.684	0.691	0.699	0.785	0.789	0.796	0.796	0.797	0.778	0.765	0.792	0.800	0.802	0.807	0.764
PR	0.846	0.809	0.801	0.843	0.852	0.860	0.859	0.864	0.862	0.866	0.867	0.898	0.890	0.903	0.911	0.862
QF	0.984	0.984	0.994	0.988	0.987	0.985	0.986	0.987	0.987	0.987	0.986	0.990	0.991	0.991	0.991	0.988
QR	0.465	0.541	0.565	0.620	0.644	0.671	0.697	0.716	0.723	0.755	0.773	0.825	0.858	0.877	0.913	0.710
SK	0.724	0.732	0.728	0.754	0.752	0.751	0.756	0.770	0.809	0.803	0.798	0.806	0.811	0.807	0.825	0.775
SQ	0.988	0.990	0.990	0.991	0.992	0.991	0.991	0.991	0.991	0.990	0.989	0.989	0.988	0.987	0.987	0.990
SU	0.773	0.786	0.783	0.802	0.807	0.817	0.831	0.826	0.831	0.822	0.822	0.855	0.889	0.896	0.925	0.831
SV	0.840	0.843	0.834	0.848	0.862	0.869	0.878	0.874	0.880	0.899	0.906	0.932	0.943	0.950	0.963	0.888
TG	0.974	0.977	0.976	0.982	0.985	0.985	0.985	0.983	0.984	0.986	0.984	0.987	0.987	0.986	0.987	0.983
TK	0.715	0.737	0.751	0.776	0.793	0.802	0.805	0.806	0.821	0.830	0.837	0.894	0.907	0.934	0.961	0.825
TP	0.702	0.702	0.711	0.731	0.741	0.746	0.751	0.748	0.761	0.774	0.779	0.809	0.816	0.819	0.832	0.761
UA	0.987	0.985	0.984	0.984	0.981	0.981	0.981	0.976	0.973	0.981	0.968	0.974	0.961	0.967	0.992	0.978
US	0.609	0.636	0.669	0.721	0.755	0.770	0.776	0.776	0.781	0.811	0.812	0.849	0.852	0.848	0.857	0.768
AVG	0.841	0.846	0.846	0.866	0.870	0.875	0.878	0.878	0.882	0.889	0.889	0.910	0.898	0.896	0.915	0.879

Appendix 4.3: Alliance Memberships and Market Data

Market data	One World	Star Alliance	Sky Team
Founded	1999	1997	2000
Passenger per year	506.98 million	637.62 million	612.00 million
Countries	152	193	177
Destinations	992	1269	1052
Fleet size	3324	4338	4634
Revenue billion US	142.571	173.12	186.331
Market share (%)	17.20	21.60	19.90
Members	15	27	20
	Air Berlin	Adria Airways	Aeroflot
	American Airlines	Aegean Airlines	Aerolíneas Argentinas
	British Airways	Air Canada	Aeromexico
	Cathay Pacific	Air China	Air Europa
	Finnair	Air India	Air France
	Iberia	Air New Zealand	Alitalia
	Japan Airlines	ANA	China Airlines
	LAN	Asiana Airlines	China Eastern
	Malaysia Airlines	Austrian	China Southern
	Qantas	Avianca	Czech Airlines
	Qatar Airways	Brussels Airlines	Delta Airlines
	Royal Jordanian	Copa Airlines	Garuda Indonesia
	SriLankan airlines	Croatia Airlines	Kenya Airways
	S7 Airlines	EGYPTAIR	KLM
	TAM Airline	Ethiopian Airlines	Korean Air
		EVA air	Middle East Airlines
		LOT Polish Airlines	Saudia
		Lufthansa	TAROM
		Scandinavian Airlines	Vietnam Airlines
		Shenzhen Airlines	Xiamen
		Singapore Airlines	
		South African Airways	
		SWISS	
		TAP Portugal	
		THAI	
		Turkish Airlines	
		United Airlines	

Source Each alliance's home page

Appendix 4.4: Correlation Matrix of Production Frontier Model Variables

Variables	EMP	AC	ENERGY	LF_INT	LF_DOM
EMP	1				
(*p*-value)					
AC	0.758	1			
(*p*-value)	0				
Energy	0.626	0.565	1		
(*p*-value)	0	0			
LF_INT	0.26	0.064	0.609	1	
(*p*-value)	0	−0.124	0		
LF_DOM	0.39	0.335	0.299	0.049	1
(*p*-value)	0	0	0	−0.235	

References

Aigner DJ, Lovell CAK, Schmidt P (1977) Formulation and estimation of stochastic frontier production function models. J Econom 6:21–37

Alvarez R, Crespi G (2003) Determinants of technical efficiency in small firms. Small Bus Econ 20(3):233–244

Assaf A (2009) Are US airlines really in crisis? Tour Manage 30:916–921

Assaf A, George JA (2009) The operational performance of UK airlines: 2002–2007. J Econ Stud 38(1):5–16

Barbot G, Costa A, Sochirca E (2008) Airlines performance in the new market context: a comparative productivity and efficiency analysis. J Air Transp Manage 14:270–274

Barros CP, Liang B, Peypoch N (2013) The technical efficiency of US Airlines. Transp Res Part A 50:139–148

Battese GE, Coelli TJ (1988) Prediction of firm-level technical efficiencies with a generalized frontier production function and panel data. J Econom 38:387–399

Battese G, Coelli T (1992) frontier Production functions, technical efficiency and panel data: with application to paddy farmers in India. J Prod Anal 3:153–169

Battese G, Coelli TJ (1995) A model for technical in efficiency effects in a stochastic frontier production function for panel data. Empir Econ 20:325–332

Battese GE, Corra GS (1977) Estimation of a production frontier model: with application to the pastoral zone of Eastern Australia. Aust J Agric Econ 21:169–179

Battese GE, Coelli TJ, Colby TC (1989) Estimation of frontier production functions and the efficiencies of Indian farms using panel data from ICRISAT's village level studies. J Quant Econ 5:327–348

Bauer PW (1990) Recent developments in the econometric estimation of frontier function. J Econom 46:39–56

Berry S, Jia P (2008) Tracing the woes: an empirical analysis of the airline industry. NBER working paper series, working paper 14503

Bilotkach V, Hüschelrath K (2012) Airline alliances and antitrust policy: the role of efficiencies. J Air Transp Manage 21:76–84

Campbell HF, Lindner RK (1990) The production function of fishing effort and the economic performance of license limitation programs. Land Econ 66(1):56–66

Clougherty JA (2006) The international drivers of domestic airline mergers in twenty nations: integrating industrial organization and international business. Manage Decis Econ 27(1):75–93

Clougherty JA (2009) Domestic rivalry and export performance: theory and evidence from international airline markets, Canadian Economics Association. Can J Econ/Revue Canadienne d'Economique 42(2):440–468

Coelli T (1996) FRONTIER version 4.1: a computer program for stochastic frontier production and cost function estimation, working paper 96/7, CEPA, Department of Econometrics, University of New England, Armidale, Australia

Cosmas A, Love R, Rajiwade S, Linz M (2013) Market clustering and performance of U.S. OD markets. J Air Transp Manage 28:20–25

Cristina M, Gramani N (2012) Efficiency decomposition approach: a cross-country airline analysis. Expert Syst Appl 39:5815–5819

Demydyuk G (2012) Optimal financial key performance indicators: evidence from the airline industry. Account Tax 4(1):39–51

Fana T, Vigeant L, Geissler C, Bosler B, Wilmking J (2001) Evolution of global airline strategic alliance and consolidation in the twenty-first century. J Air Transp Manage 7:349–360

Ferguson BR, Hong D (2007) Airline revenue optimization problem: a multiple linear regression model. J Concr Appl Math 5(2):153–167

Ghemawat P, Khanna T (1998) The nature of diversified business groups: a research design and two case studies. J Ind Econ 46:35–61

Gorin T, Belobaba P (2004) Impacts of entry in airline markets: effects of revenue management on traditional measures of airline performance. J Air Transp Manage 10:259–270

Graham DR, Kaplan DP, Sibley DS (1983) Efficiency and competition in the airline industry. Bell J Econ 14(1):118–138

Greene W (1993) The econometric approach to efficiency analysis. In: Fried HO, Lovell CAK, Schmidt SS (eds) The measurement of productive efficiency. Oxford University Press, New York, pp 68–119

Greer M (2009) Is it the labor unions' fault? Dissecting the causes of the impaired technical efficiencies of the legacy carriers in the United States. Transp Res Part A 43:779–789

Gudmundsson SV, Lechner C (2006) Multilateral, airline alliances: balancing strategic constraints and opportunities. J Air Transp Manage 12:153–158

Hannesson R (1983) Bioeconomic production function in fisheries: theoretical and Empirical analysis. Can J Fish Aquat Sci 13(3):367–375

Heshmati A (2003) Productivity growth, efficiency and outsourcing in manufacturing and services. J Econ Surv 17(1):79–112

Heshmati A (2013) Efficiency and productivity impacts of restructuring the Korean electricity generation. Korea World Econ 14(1):57–89

Johnston A, Ozment J (2011) Concentration in the airline industry: evidence of economies of scale? J Transp Manage Fall/Winter 2011:59–74

Kumbhakar SC (1991) Estimation of technical inefficiency in panel data models with firm-and time-specific effects. Econ Lett 41:11–16

Kumbhakar SC (1996) Efficiency measurement with multiple outputs and multiple inputs. J Prod Anal 7:225–255

Kumbhakar SC (1997) Modeling allocative inefficiency in a translog cost function and cost share equations: an exact relationship. J Econom 76(1/2):351–356

Kumbhakar SC, Lovell CAK (2000) Stochastic frontier analysis. Cambridge University Press, Cambridge

Kumbhakar SC, Wan H, Horncastle A (2015) A practitioner's guide to stochastic frontier analysis using stata. Academic Press, Cambridge

Lee CY, Johnson AL (2011) Two-dimensional efficiency decomposition to measure he demand effect in productivity, analysis. Eur J Oper Res 216:584–593

Liang J (2013) An econometric analysis on pricing and market structure in the U.S. airline industry. Adv Econom 3(2):1–28 (Article 2)

Meeusen, W, van den Broeck J (1977). Efficiency estimation from Cobb-Douglas production function with composed errors. Int Econ Rev 18(2):435–444

Merkert R, Hensher DA (2011) The impact of strategic management and fleet planning on airline efficiency—a random effects Tobit model based on DEA efficiency scores. Transp Res Part A 45:686–695

Merkert R, Williams G (2013) Determinants of European PSO airline efficiency: evidence from a semi-parametric approach. J Air Transp Manage 29:11–16

Obermeyer A, Evangelinos C, Püsche R (2012) Price dispersion and competition in European airline markets. J Air Transp Manage 26:31–34

Oum TH, Yu C (1998) Cost competitiveness of major airlines: an international comparison. Transp Res Part A Policy Pract 32(6):407–422

Oum TH, Fu X, Yu C (2005) New evidences on airline efficiency and yields: a comparative analysis of major North American air carriers and its implications. Transp Policy 12:153–164

Oum TH, Zhang A, Fu X (2009) Air transport liberalization and its impacts on airline competition and air passenger traffic. Transp J 49(4):24–41

Palepu K, Khanna T (2000) Is group affiliation profitable in emerging markets? An analysis of diversified Indian business groups. J Finance 55(2):867–891

Parast MM, Fini EH (2010) The effect of productivity and quality on profitability in US airline industry: an empirical investigation. Manage Serv Quality 20(5):458–474

Pascoe S, Robinson C (1998) Input controls, input substitution and profit maximization in the English channel beam trawl fishery. J Agric Econ 49(1):16–33

Pearson J, Merkert R (2014) Airlines-within-airlines: a business model moving East. J Air Transp Manage 38:21–26

Pitfield DE, Caves RE, Quddus MA (2010) Airline strategies for aircraft size and airline frequency with changing demand and competition: a simultaneous equations approach for traffic on the North Atlantic. J Air Transp Manage 16(3):151–158

Pitt MM, Lee LF (1981) The measurement and sources of technical inefficiency in the Indonesian weaving industry. J Dev Econ 9:43–64

Porter ME (1990) The competitive advantage of nations. Harv Bus Rev

Powell II, Robert A (2010) Productivity performance of US passenger airlines since deregulation. Master thesis MIT

Reifschneider D, Stevenson R (1991) Systematic departures from the frontier: a framework for the analysis of firm inefficiency. Int Econ Rev 32(3):715–723

Schmidt P (1986) Frontier production functions. Econom Rev 4:289–328

Sjogren S, Soderberg M (2011) Productivity of airline carriers and its relation to deregulation, privatization and membership in strategic alliances. Transp Res Part E Logistics Transp Rev 47:228–237

Tsekeris T (2009) Dynamic analysis of air travel demand in competitive island markets. J Air Transp Manage 15:267–273

Wang WK, Lu WM, Tsai CJ (2011) The relationship between airline performance and corporate governance amongst US listed companies. J Air Transp Manage 17:148–152

Whalen WT (2005) A panel data analysis of code sharing, antitrust immunity and open skies treaties in international aviation markets, U.S. Department of Justice - Antitrust Division, May 15, 2005

Chapter 5
Stochastic Frontier Cost Function Model Specification and Estimation Results

Abstract This chapter compares the cost efficiency of the world's 39 major airlines over the 1998–2012 period. We analyzed airlines' cost efficiency using the stochastic frontier function methodology and investigated which factors account for differences in the level of efficiency. The mean and dispersion of cost efficiency amongst airlines differ according to geographical areas of operation, which may be a result of different market structures and deregulation processes; so the differences can be attributed to specific competitive conditions such as resource availability and strategic cooperation with competitors. The results confirmed that airlines are less successful in achieving cost efficiency over the period studied. Airline size showed a positive correlation with the level of cost efficiency, while larger airlines were not more efficient than their smaller counterparts in the case of the cost model. Our main findings show that carriers based in the Asia region are in general more cost efficient than carriers based in Europe and North America.

Keywords Stochastic frontier functions · Cost efficiency · Panel data · Airlines

5.1 Introduction

In Chap. 4, we used a production function approach in which the objective of firms, in this case airlines, was to maximize output given the use of inputs of labor, capital (airplanes) and other input factors like energy available to the airlines. In this chapter, we employ an alternative approach in which the objective of firms is to minimize the cost of producing a given level of output with given factor input prices and technology. Based on the theory of duality, the cost and production function approaches—i.e., output maximization and cost minimization—should yield the same equilibrium conditions. See Varian (1984) for a detailed discussion of the duality between cost and production functions.

As reviewed in Chap. 3, most airlines have failed to recoup the cost of their capital over the airline business cycle of 8–10 years. This is despite investments undertaken by national governments in infrastructure like airports, security, and

© Springer Science+Business Media Singapore 2016

A. Heshmati and J. Kim, *Efficiency and Competitiveness of International Airlines*, DOI 10.1007/978-981-10-1017-0_5

transportation, which do not add to the airlines' operation costs. Several empirical studies and reports from the Airlines Industry Association have explained that the poor profitability of the airline industry is not due to a lack of efforts on the part of airlines. Instead, it is the specific market structure of the industry as well as national and international policy changes that take a heavy toll on airline profitability.

Airlines so far have made various attempts to streamline their operations in order to reduce their operational costs, including outsourcing of activities like maintenance and ground handling, cutting down on unnecessary services, and introducing much more sophisticated yield management systems. In addition, airlines have frequently attempted to improve their productivity by increasing aircraft utilization rates, adding extra revenue streams, introducing a wide range of customer loyalty programs, and establishing alliances or code-sharing systems. All these cost-saving and revenue-increasing efforts have contributed to lower operating costs and higher profitability, but the margin above the cost still lags far behind that of other industries competing for investment capital (IATA 2012).

In Chap. 4, we examined the airlines' production efficiency through the stochastic frontier production function model and confirmed that most airlines had successfully improved their production efficiency during the period 1998–2012. Having confirmed productivity improvement by the application of the stochastic cost frontier function estimation, this chapter will examine another key phenomenon—namely, the cost inefficiency that airlines face. In addition, we identify the factors that are responsible for the lower yield and poor profitability of the industry and, conversely, the factors that can enhance the cost efficiency of airlines. Considering that most features of the stochastic cost function are the same as those of the stochastic production model, we skip the details of the stochastic function and proceed to the estimation of the cost function model.

The differences between stochastic frontier production and cost functions can be summarized in terms of output maximization versus cost minimization, i.e., firms with maximum output and minimum cost serve as efficient firm references or benchmarks. Another difference lies in the change in the inefficiency components' sign from negative in the stochastic frontier production function to positive in the stochastic frontier cost function, indicating a shortfall of the reference maximum output and excess cost over the reference minimum cost, respectively.

The rest of this chapter is organized as follows. An overview of the stochastic frontier cost model is specified in Sect. 5.2. This is followed by a description of the data in Sect. 5.3. The estimation and analysis of the results are discussed in Sect. 5.4. The final Sect. 5.5 summarizes the results.

5.2   Model Specification

A *cost frontier function* characterizes the minimum expenditure required to produce a given bundle of outputs, or airline services in this case, given the prices of the factor inputs used in its production and given the technology in place. The characteristics of the airlines and the market constitute the context of the model. Producers operating on their cost frontier are labeled as cost efficient. Considering the relationship between production and cost frontier inefficiency, given the differences in the structures of the cost and production functions, Coelli (1996) mentions that "It is a simple matter to change the sign of the inefficiency error component U and convert the stochastic production frontier model to a stochastic cost frontier model Cost $= c(y, w; \beta) \exp\{V + U\}$, where $Cost$ is expenditure, $[c(y, w; \beta) \exp\{V\}]$ is a stochastic cost frontier, and U is intended to capture the cost of technical and allocative inefficiency." One common element in all of the specifications described in the stochastic frontier function in Chap. 4 is that they have been expressed in terms of a production function, which contains technical inefficiency effects U_{it}, that cause the firm to operate inside the stochastic production frontier. On the other hand, when we need to specify a stochastic frontier cost function, we just change the error term specification from $(V_{it}{}^{1} - U_{it})$ to $(V_{it} + U_{it})$ by changing the sign of the inefficiency component. U reflects the shortfall of production or excess cost compared with the maximum output and minimum cost obtainable, respectively. For example, such a substitution will transform the production function defined by Eq. 4.3 $Y_i = X_i\beta + (V_i - U_i)$, $i = 1,\ldots,N$ into the cost function below (Coelli 1996).

$$\text{Cost}_{it} = X_{it}\beta + (V_{it} + U_{it}), \quad i = 1,\ldots,N, \quad t = 1, 2, \ldots, T \qquad (5.1)$$

where Cost_{it} is the cost of production of the ith firm in the tth time period; X_{it} is a $k \times 1$ vector of transformations of the input prices and output of the ith firm at tth time period; β is a vector of unknown parameters to be estimated; V_{it} are random error terms that are assumed to be i.i.d. $N(0, \sigma_v^2)$ and are independent of U_{it}, which are nonnegative random variables that account for the excess cost over minimum cost or cost inefficiency in production, which, in turn, are usually assumed to be i.i.d. $|N(0, \sigma_u^2)|$. In this cost function, U_{it} now defines the gap between the firm's actual costs and the minimum cost at the cost frontier. Under the assumption of allocative efficiency, U_{it} is tightly linked to the cost of technical inefficiency. Much like the production frontier, the cost inefficiency effects in the efficiency effects model, U_{it}, could be specified as

$$U_{it} = \delta Z_{it} + W_{it} \qquad (5.2)$$

The inefficiency effect is an extension of the traditional cost frontier function in which in addition to the estimation of inefficiency for each unit, one explains the degree of inefficiency by its possible determinants. Z_{it} is a vector representing the

---

[1]A number of strong assumptions are made prior to the estimation of a cost function. "In the stochastic frontier literature, the V_{it} are nothing but "statistical noise that is, the V_{it} are unexplainable error components which should not be systematically related with firms' input or output decisions". "Thus, a firm's input decisions X_{it} should be strictly exogenous to the V_{it}; all leads and lags of X_{it} are uncorrelated with V_{it}. That is, $X_{i,t-1}$ and X_{it} should be uncorrelated with it, since it simply equals V_{it}" (Coelli 1996).

possible inefficiency determinants and δ is a corresponding vector of unknown parameters to be estimated, representing the effects of the determinants on the cost inefficiency of firms. W_{it} is a random variable that is defined by the truncation of the normal distribution with mean zero and constant variance σ^2, such that the point of truncation is $-Z_{it}\delta$ (Coelli 1996). The cost efficiency of individual units is derived as

$$\text{CEFF}_{it} = \exp(\hat{u}_{it}) \tag{5.3}$$

The unobservable quantity U_{it} may be obtained from its conditional expectation, given the observable value of the $(V_{it} + U_{it})$ measure computed at the mean or mode.

This is because both technical and allocative inefficiencies are possibly involved. Therefore, it is better to refer to inefficiencies measured relative to a cost frontier as cost inefficiencies, as we do in the rest of the volume, without separating the technical and allocative inefficiency components. The specific application will determine the exact interpretation of the cost inefficiencies. The cost frontier Eq. (5.1) is exactly equivalent to the one proposed by Schmidt and Lovell (1979), who point out that the log-likelihood of the production frontier is the same as that of the cost frontier except for a few changes in the signs. It is also possible to obtain the log-likelihood functions for the cost function analogs of the Battese and Coelli (1992, 1995) models by just changing a few signs. The advantage of the frontier analysis compared with the average function is that it provides an overall, objectively determined, numerical efficiency value and ranking of production units, which is not otherwise available using non-frontier approaches.

The stochastic frontier approach allows observations to depart from the frontier due to both random error and inefficiency sources, whereas models using Data Envelopment Analysis (DEA) mistakenly measure the random error as part of inefficiency because they attribute any departure from the frontier as inefficiency. However, DEA has the advantage of avoiding strong assumptions of functional forms and distributions of the error components. The stochastic frontier cost function also postulates the existence of allocation inefficiency, which has been examined by various studies such as (Kumbhakar 1991) and reviewed in Kumbhakar and Lovell (2000), Heshmati (2003) and Kumbhakar et al. (2015). Two different variants of the stochastic frontier are used here to ensure robustness of our results. These are the efficiency effects (EE) and the error components (EC) models. The EC model estimates a cost function and efficiency level for each observation, while the EE model additionally explains the degree of inefficiency attributed to its possible determinants. The empirical analysis made here is based on the estimation of the stochastic frontier cost model of Eq. (5.1) and the inefficiency function of Eq. (5.2). To render the models, the following log-linear frontier cost function is chosen as the functional form

$$\log(\text{Cost}_{it}) = \beta_0 + \beta_1 \log(\text{ATK\_TTL}_{it}) + \beta_2 \text{LF}_{it} + \beta_3 \log(\text{WAGE}_{it}) + \beta_4 \log(\text{ENG\_INDX}_{it})$$
$$+ \beta_5 \text{Trend} + \beta_6 \text{Trend}^2 + V_{it} + U_{it}$$
$$(i = 39 \text{ Airlines}, \quad t = 1998-2012)$$

$$\tag{5.4}$$

The inefficiency term following Battese and Coelli (1995) is modeled as follows in terms of its possible determinants. The determinants are further explained below in the data section.[2]

$$U_{it} = \delta_0 + \delta_1(\text{INT\_PS}_{it}) + \delta_2 \log(\text{EMP}_{it}) + \delta_3 \log(\text{FHRS}_{it}) + \delta_4\text{PRICE}_{it} + \delta_5\text{MS}_{it}$$
$$+ \delta_6\text{A1} + \delta_7\text{A2} + \delta_8\text{A3} + \delta_9\text{EU} + \delta_{10}\text{ASIA} + \delta_{11}\text{YEAR} + W_{it}$$

$$(5.5)$$

$$\text{CEFF}_{it} = \exp(\hat{u}_{it}) \tag{5.6}$$

5.3 Data and Variables

For the empirical analysis, we employ the data of 39 airlines from 33 different countries during the time period 1998–2012. Airlines incur several types of expenses, and for this reason and due to the limited access to attaining disaggregate and service-specific expenses data, we consider airlines' total operating expenses for each year as representing total cost. This covers airline's total expenditures for the given year, and all business activities of individual airlines are insured by this account. Having employed aggregate expenses as a dependent variable, the output parameters should comprise both passenger and cargo outputs from international and domestic flights on scheduled and nonscheduled routes. Other criteria used for selecting variables and data are the same as those used in Chap. 4. Table 5.1 provides a summary description of the variables of the cost frontier function.

5.3.1 Operating Costs

The dependent variable (EXPN) for the annual cost model is the operating expenses of airlines. We obtained the data and information from the Korean government's official statistics site (www.airportal.go.kr) and from each airline's home page. Operating expenses include the costs for the handling of passengers, fuel, aircraft maintenance charges, catering, cargo, excess baggage, and other transport-related

---

[2]"The measures of cost efficiency relative to the cost frontier is defined as: $\text{EFF}_i = E(Y_i^*|U_i, X_i)/E$ $(Y_i^*|U_i = 0, X_i)$, where Y_i^* is the cost (or production) of the ith firm, which will be equal to Y_i when the dependent variable is in original units and will be equal to $\exp(Y_i)$ when the dependent variable is in logs" (Coelli 1996). In the case of a production frontier, EFF_i will take a value between zero and one—one indicating fully efficient, while it will take a value between one and higher than one in the cost function case, where values in excess of one indicate degree excess cost or cost inefficiency.

Table 5.1 Description of variables used in specification of the stochastic frontier cost function

Variable category		Code	Description
Dependent variable, cost	Total cost	EXPN	Airline operating expenses
Cost function explanatory variables, X	Cost function	ATK_TTL	Available ton kilometers, sum of passenger, cargo and mails ton kilometers of both International and domestic flights from scheduled and nonscheduled routes
		LF	Load factor (the percentage of total RTK[1] over total ATK)
		WAGE[a]	Wages for airline staff (GDP[2] per person employed)—constant 1990 PPP $
		ENG_INDX	Jet fuel price index (MOP)
		TREND	(Year 1998 = 1, 1992 = 2, ..., 2012 = 15)
		TREND^2	Square year (Year 1998 = 1, 1992 = 2, ..., 2012 = 15)
Inefficiency determinant variables, Z	Determinants of cost inefficiency	INT_PS	Percentage of international passenger ton kilometer
		EMP	Number of airline staffs
		FHRS	Flying hours airlines flown per year
		PRICE[a]	Price index
		MS	Airline output[b] share in international market
		A1	Alliance 1 (One World)
		A2	Alliance 2 (Star Alliance)
		A3	Alliance 3 (Sky Team)
		A4	Alliance 4 (no alliance)
		EU	Region 1 (Europe)
		ASIA	Region 2(Asia)
		NA	Region 3 (North America)
		TREND	(Year 1998 = 1, 1992 = 2, ..., 2012 = 15)

[a]Monetary variables was deflated by the individual countries' annual inflation. However we did not deflated energy index because each airline is applied by the uniform energy price index
[b]Output includes passenger, cargo and mail services
[1]RTK includes revenue ton kilometers passenger cargo and mail service
[2]GDP per person employed is gross domestic product (GDP) divided by total employment in the economy and the Purchasing power parity (PPP) was converted to 1990 constant international dollars using PPP rates (www.worldbank.org)

costs[3] of both scheduled and nonscheduled services. In order to resolve the data contamination problem of monetary variables from the effect of both temporal and spatial price variation, we transform the monetarily measured variables using the price index to adjust for the annual inflation[4] rate of each country.

---

[3]It includes airport fees, landing fees, and ground handling charges.
[4]Annual inflation data was obtained from www.imf.org.

5.3.2 Explanatory Variables

The SFA application of the cost function requires that the number of explanatory variables be kept at a reasonable level; here we consider six X-variables including the time trend. For the inefficiency measurement, we use 11 Z-variables, including regions, alliances and time trend. The trend and trend squared were incorporated in the cost function, while only the time trend is included in the inefficiency estimation model. The use of the time trend in the cost function represents a shift in the cost function or a technological change, while it represents a change in inefficiency over time in the cost inefficiency effects model.

Output (ATK_TTL): We employ the sum of 'Available ton kilometers of passenger' and 'Available ton kilometers of cargo'[5] (ATK_TTL) of both international and domestic flights as an aggregate output measure. The output aggregate used here refers exclusively to the final output. Similar to the production frontier model estimation, we need to have output measured with a uniform unit per different types of production; thus ton kilometers is the only measurement that represents all outputs of passenger, cargo, and mail services. Coelli et al. (1999) argue that the use of ton kilometers best reflects the ticketing and marketing aspects of airline, while Lee and Worthington (2014) used available ton kilometers as an aggregate measure of the output of airlines. Besides these, there are many other output measurements such as Revenue ton kilometers (RPK) and Revenue miles or distance flown. Lee and Johnson (2011) used both RPK and available seat kilometers (ASK) as an output measure of airlines' performance in a cost-based efficiency estimation study. Barbot et al. (2008), Greer (2009), Wang et al. (2011), Assaf and George (2009) and Merkert and Hensher (2011) used available seat kilometers (ASK) as one of the output measurements in efficiency or productivity studies.

Load factor (LF): The load factors of both international and domestic passenger flights are included here to measure productivity. "Airlines operating with a high load factor coefficient would expect to have a stronger demand, and thus consequently a higher production/efficiency" (Assaf and George 2009). At the same time, airlines' productivity is closely related to the revenues realized per supplied capacity. Studies such as Graham (1983), Assaf and George (2009), Parast et al. (2010) and Johnson and Ozment (2011) included the load factor in the modeling of airline productivity and efficiency analyses.

Employment Wage (WAGE): One of the main input costs is the labor cost including that of airline staff such as cockpit crew, cabin crew, maintenance staff, marketing personnel, and airport staff. It is widely known that airline staff wages are comparatively higher than the income of other occupation groups. This is especially so in the case of the cockpit crew that has a high demand. However, due to limited

---

[5]Cargo output includes mail services.

information and unavailability of data needed, we used the GDP[6] per capita workforce (in constant 1990 PPP $) of the airlines' respective home countries as a proxy for the wage of airline staff. In a study of US carriers' profitability, Parast et al. (2010) used the actual salary data on US carriers because US carriers disclose such information. However, most international carriers usually do not provide any salary information to the public due to the confidentiality of the data. Thus many studies that have used actual wage data are centered on the US airlines market.

Energy price (ENG_INDX): Airlines located in Asia use the MOP (Mean of Platt's Singapore) energy price index, while US carriers use LA West Coast Pipeline, New York Cargo or US Gulf Coast Pipeline. European carriers use the Platt's of Barge FOB Rotterdam energy price index. The price formulas used by these three index categories are not much different. Thus we have used the MOP price index here for all the airlines over the period of study. Previous studies estimating efficiency such as Parast et al. (2010), Oum et al. (2005) and Barbot et al. (2008) employed the energy price index as the cost of energy factor.

Time trend (TREND) and its square: In order to capture the shift in cost over time representing technological change, we include the time trend and its square as explanatory variables in the cost model specification. The trend captures the direction of the change, while the square trend captures the nonlinear shift in the cost function over time.

5.3.3 Airlines' Characteristics

The set of variables representing the airline and market characteristics can appear in the cost model relation as determinants of cost, inefficiency or both as determinants and conditioning variables. In this study, they are used to explain the patterns of airline-specific inefficiency. The set of characteristic variables are defined as follows.

International passenger output share (INT_PS): This variable has been chosen to assess whether the concentration of airlines' international passenger operations affects their cost efficiency. Clougherty et al. (2009) included the passenger output share to examine the effect of domestic rivalry on the international airline market and found that airlines that face substantial domestic rivalry tend to perform better —holding other things constant—in international or export markets. Depending on the share of sales in the domestic or international market, airlines may pursue different business strategies. Our study uses international passenger output share (INT_PS) to investigate whether airlines that have a higher concentration in the international market perform better in their operation cost management.

---

[6]GDP per person employed is gross domestic product (GDP) divided by total employment in the economy; the purchasing power parity (PPP) index was use to convert the variable to 1990 constant international dollars using PPP rates (www.worldbank.org).

Employment (EMP): This variable includes the employment figure for cockpit crew, cabin crew, maintenance staff, marketing personnel, airport staff, and the staff of other service departments of each airline from 1998 to 2012. Since airlines typically report only the aggregate number of workers, we were not able to segregate the number of staff in terms of passenger and cargo services. We therefore measured the total number of workforces in same way as many previous studies of airline productivity and efficiency had used (e.g. Oum and Yu 1998; Oum et al. 2005; Barbot et al. 2008; Greer 2009; and Wang et al. 2011). It is assumed that the allocation of labor to different categories of tasks due to internal operations and the high competitiveness of the market is about the same among the sample airlines.

Flying hours (FHRS): Since financial information such as current capital assets of airlines is not readily available for the research use, studies like Assaf (2009), Lee and Johnson (2011) and Merket and Hensher (2011) used the aircrafts number as a proxy for the capital input. Bhadra (2009) utilized the number of seats per aircraft and the aircraft utilization rate in hours as the input variables. In this study, we use the flying hours as the proxy of the airlines' capital assets and also airlines' size. Airlines have a series of aircrafts that differ in terms of seat numbers, engines, flying capability, cargo space in the belly, and fuel consumption; thus just adding up the total number of aircrafts cannot provide us with comparable information on airlines' size or capital asset. Given the data availability, we consider that flying hours can be one of the proxies for this input because in order to fly longer hours, airlines need to operate many destinations including long-distance destinations. Distance, frequency or airline destination can also be used as the proxy, and our result with FHRS produced the most significant and robust estimation.

Market share (MS): Passenger market share is one of the decisive indications for measuring the global competitiveness of a firm in any industry. Adding market share as the inefficiency variable enables us to see whether an airline's global competitiveness departs from the cost efficiency

Ticket price index (Price): Airline ticket price varies by routes, season, time of the reservation, group reservations, one way/round trip/multiple destinations, validity days of the return ticket, etc. Therefore, data on price information at the country level is readily unavailable. To estimate the country's relative price index, this chapter uses airlines' revenue per unit of the aggregate output. Table 5.1 shows detailed information on all the variables that were carefully selected with the reference to existing studies of airline efficiency. Table 5.2 reports the summary statistics of the airlines data. Liang (2013) included the price index to examine market power in his study of the performance of nine US carriers. Similarly, Oum et al. (1998), Demydyuk (2012), Obermeyer et al. (2012), Feurguson (2007), Gorin and Belobaba (2004) and Tsekeris (2009) included the price index in their efficiency estimation. These analyses showed evidence of mixed results, but the major conclusion is that price as expected has a negative effect on the travel demand, thus reducing the production/cost efficiency.

Alliance membership: Most airlines in our sample belong to major alliances such as One World, Star Alliance, and Sky Team. In order to assess the impact of joining

Table 5.2 Summary statistics of the data[a] used in the stochastic frontier cost function

Variable	Mean	Std. dev.	Min	Max
Cost frontier function variables				
COST (1000 USD)	5,796,000	6,269,000	0	34,900,000
ATK_TTL (1000)	11,200,000	9,726,120	91,943	47,000,000
WAGE (USD)	35,115	17,906	4097	68,374
ENG_INDX (USD)	64.92	37.10	16.44	125.71
Technical inefficiency effect variables				
INT_PS (%)	0.751	0.253	0.008	1[b]
EMP	22,729	21,345	1034	119,084
FHRS	572,289	534,403	18,914	2,848,633
PRICE INDX(USD)	0.826	0.544	0.019	5.808
MS (%)	0.016	0.014	0.000	0.062

[a]Number of observations is $39 \times 15 = 585$
[b]Airlines which operates only international routes such as cathay pacific airways and Singapore airlines

an alliance on cost efficiency—for example, by sharing a network and expanding the membership program—alliance dummies are included in the model.

Region: Airlines are grouped into three regions based on the home country of the airlines to see if there are significant differences across regions. (For details, see Tables 4.1 and 4.2 of Chap. 4.)

The variables listed in Table 5.2 are assumed to affect the cost function relation in the following way:

- The output variable, ATK_TTL, is obviously expected to have a positive effect in the form of an increase in the airlines' cost.
- Load factor is expected to be affected by technological progress; thus the co-efficient sign is expected to be negative in relation to the unit cost.
- The coefficients of wage of employees and energy price index are assumed to be positively related to cost. Because these are the main categories of airline expenses, their effects on the cost are assumed to be technologically regressive. Tsekeris (2009), Obermeyer et al. (2012), Oum and Yu (1998), Assaf (2009) and Cristina et al. (2012) all included wage cost in their airline efficiency studies. We expect that the higher the wage and energy price index, the higher the cost to the airlines.
- The airline cost is expected to increase over time due to continuous price increases of resources including fuel and other charges as well as the improved quality of services. Airlines have suffered low yield due to a rapid increase of input costs as well as various charges and fees associated with safety and environmental regulations.

The variables listed as determinants of cost inefficiency in the inefficiency effects model are assumed to have the following effects:

- INT_PS, which is defined as the international passenger share of each airline services, is expected to positively affect cost efficiency. In other words, it will have negative signs of the estimated coefficient as the determinant of efficiency. A higher percentage of international passenger output would require lesser expenses than being domestic-market-oriented by saving costs such as landing fees, airport handling fees, and crew management. Clougherty et al. (2009), Johnston and Ozment (2011), and a number of other studies included international passenger share as both an independent variable and as a determinant of efficiency. We use international passenger share here to investigate whether airlines with higher international passenger shares can achieve a greater cost efficiency through output maximization.
- EMP and FHRS, which measure airlines' size, are assumed to serve as technologically regressive to the cost due to their effects in form of increase in expenses. Especially after the entry and penetration of low-cost carriers on the medium and short haul routes, the bigger legacy airlines are facing increasing costs to maintain their market share due to the high rates of investment in their fleets, safety, marketing, and staff training. Maintaining a regular airline staff also involves higher costs than outsourcing these functions.
- MS is an important factor in the evaluation of airline efficiency. Market share is an important indicator of the global competitiveness of airlines, and it indirectly represents the airlines' market structure.[7] Airlines that have a higher share of the global market are able to use their resources more optimally with a long-term investment plan and strategy. The coefficient sign of the market share is therefore expected to be negative—i.e., it has a positive effect on an airline's efficiency.
- The sign of PRICE INDX is expected to be negative, i.e., an increasing effect on cost efficiency. Being able to charge a higher price in the market implies that the airline enjoys brand loyalty over its competitors and has a market power so that it can achieve a higher profit using resources more efficiently. On the other hand, follower airlines usually lower their prices to attract customers, and they need to spend more resources to promote their services and create brand value. Thus, the effect of cost inefficiency on the follower airlines is much stronger than the corresponding for the leading airlines.
- Alliance membership is expected to show a positive effect on cost efficiency due to the expanded networks and greater diversity of services, which will induce a higher cost efficiency of airlines. Alliance membership provides more choices in flight schedules and membership benefits to clients. At the same time, the member airlines can mutually share costly information and data and jointly promote their services. These factors will collectively increase the sales of the

---

[7]Various studies used the HHI (Herfindahl-Hirschman Index) to proxy the market structure and competition. See also Chap. 2 for more details.

alliance members at a lower cost. The variance of efficiency between the different alliances is assumed to be limited because most alliances have a similar scope of services, and the degree of cooperation among members is similar.

• Regional location has been included in the specification to investigate if there is a regional difference between airline efficiency levels, which can be expected to vary due to the different extent of market deregulation and the level of competition in the different regions. Due to price-level differences across regions, the size of the coefficient is assumed to vary by region.

Our major hypothesis with the estimation of the cost function and measurement of cost efficiency of international airlines and explanation of cost efficiency differences by its possible determinants can be summarized as follows[8]:

H1	International share of passenger service will positively affect the airlines' cost efficiency
H2	Airline size (measured as flying hours) will have a negative effect on cost efficiency
H3	Airline size (number of employees) will have a negative effect on cost efficiency
H4	Airlines cost efficiency improves with the expansion of services or market share
H5	Airlines that charge a higher price will have a higher cost efficiency
H6	Airline alliance has a positive effect on the improvement of cost efficiency
H7	Asian carriers operate more cost efficiently than carriers based in other regions

5.4 Estimation and Analysis of Results

The maximum likelihood estimation of both EC and EE models specified above led to the estimation results presented in Table 5.3.

5.4.1 Analysis of the Estimation Results

Model specification tests

In order to identify the final specification of the stochastic cost frontier model, we tested the parameters validation through the log-likelihood ratio test and the null hypothesis that variables, both individually and jointly, are statistically insignificant. Following the test, statistically insignificant variables were rejected and later withdrawn from the final model specification. The following are the results of the specification test. The first and second null hypothesis in Table 5.4 specifies that the

---

[8]These hypotheses are aimed to be tested on the basis of estimation results obtained from the Efficiency Effect model (EE).

Table 5.3 Maximum likelihood estimation results of stochastic frontier cost function

Variables	Parameters	EC model			EE model		
		Coefficient	Std err	Z	Coefficient	Std err	Z
Frontier cost frontier:							
Constant	β_0	2.782***	0.27	10.291	2.971***	0.469	6.339
ATK_TTL	β_1	0.522***	0.035	15.122	0.578***	0.066	8.778
LF	β_2	0.185*	0.089	2.092	0.22	0.142	1.544
WAGE	β_3	0.523***	0.055	9.448	0.448***	0.048	9.357
ENG_INDX	β_4	0.127	0.068	1.871	0.076	0.104	0.734
YEAR	β_5	−0.029***	0.009	−3.164	−0.006	0.015	−0.393
YEAR2	β_6	0.001	0	1.425	0.001	0.001	0.595
Determinants of cost inefficiency (U_{it}):							
Constant	δ_0				−2.348***	0.443	−5.296
INT_PS	δ_1				−0.175*	0.088	−1.99
EMP	δ_2				0.224***	0.068	3.286
FHRS	δ_3				0.268***	0.09	2.963
PRICE	δ_4				0.096***	0.008	12.284
MS	δ_5				0.202	1.186	0.17
A1	δ_6				0.201**	0.077	2.606
A2	δ_7				0.201***	0.072	2.802
A3	δ_8				0.153*	0.074	2.085
EU	δ_9				0.081*	0.038	2.121
ASIA	δ_{10}				0.201***	0.039	5.116
YEAR	δ_{11}				−0.007	0.006	−1.122
Log-likelihood		234.89			47.37		
σ^2		0.167***	0.029	5.811	0.050***	0.003	17.174
$\gamma = \sigma_u^2/(\sigma_v^2 + \sigma_u^2)$					0.049***	0.015	3.145
μ		0.764***	0.167	4.584			
η		−0.030***	0.004	−7.838			

EC Error component model and *EE* Efficiency effects model
*$p < 0.05$; **$p < 0.01$; ***$p < 0.001$
Number of cross-sections 39 airlines, number of time periods 15 years, total Number of observation 585

coefficients of all the explanatory variables in the cost model are simultaneously equal and jointly equal to zero, and these variables are thus not relevant to cost. The two null hypotheses have been rejected since the χ^2 test results with 6 and 5 degrees of freedom exceed the critical value of 16.81 and 15.09, respectively, which specifies that the explanatory variables in the cost model are relevant and statistically significantly different from zero at the 1 % level of significance.

The log-likelihood values and likelihood ratio (LR) test statistics at the bottom of Table 5.4 allow us to test for the presence of technical inefficiency. The LR statistics in the table present the test statistics for the null hypothesis of no technical

Table 5.4 Generalized likelihood ratio tests results based on stochastic frontier cost function

Null hypothesis, H_0	Test statistic[a]	Critical value
H_0: $\beta_i = 1$, $i \leq 1, 2, ..., 6$	$\chi^2(6) = 345.98$	16.81
H_0: $\beta_1 = \beta_2 = \cdots = \beta_6$	$\chi^2(5) = 300.49$	15.09
H_0^2: $\gamma = \delta_0 = \delta_1 \cdots = \delta_{11} = 0$	$\chi^2(10) = 264.28$	23.21

[a]The test statistics has been conducted by STATA 'sfpanel' command using model BC92 and BC95. The test statistics from the programs Frontier 4.1 and STATA result in almost same results
Notes Hypothesis tests for significance of the cost function parameters and inefficiency effects model

Table 5.5 Model specification test results from estimation of the stochastic frontier cost model

Cost model	LL value	K	N	AIC	BIC
Error components model (EC)	639.32	7	585	−1266.44	−1240.41
Inefficiency effects model (EE)	264.28	12	585	−506.56	−458.4723

inefficiencies in the cost modeling of airline services. LR = −2[ln L_R − ln L_u] ~ χ^2 (J), where ln L_R and ln L_u are log the likelihood of the restricted and unrestricted cost models, respectively, and J is the number of restrictions imposed on the model. The test statistics follow the χ^2 distribution. If the null hypothesis is rejected, it implies that when estimating the cost efficiency of airlines, a model that includes the allocation inefficiency variables is more appropriate than an average cost model without these inefficiency determinant factors.

Table 5.5 reports the results of model test, and it indicates that a cost model with the inefficiency variables is less complex and fits better for the performance analysis purpose. Since our criterion for choosing the inefficiency model is to capture the individual airlines' efficiency index together with the estimation result that we could not attain otherwise, we present the results from both the EC and the EE cost models.

Lastly, multi-collinearity among the variables is a potential concern regarding confounded effects. Appendix 5.3 presents the correlation coefficients and means of variables used in the frontier cost function. Among the variables, ATK_TTL, EMP, FHRS, and MS have a correlation coefficient above 0.5, the benchmark level indicating the presence of serious collinearity. The levels of correlation between ATK_TTL, EMP, and FHRS are relatively mild and also rather obvious because EMP and FHRS measure the airline size, which will naturally increase ATK_TTL, and a higher market share will lead to higher costs. This explains the presence of the relatively high correlation between ATK_TTL and MS (market share). While there are multi-collinearity concerns, collinearity does not produce biased estimates, although it does cause difficulties in obtaining significant coefficient estimates due to confounded effects. We thus decided not to drop any of the explanatory variables from the model specification.

Output and input price elasticities

The β coefficient's sign and significance are consistent with our assumptions, while the size of the coefficients shows a little variation between the EC and the EE models due to the different model specifications. The maximum likelihood estimates, expressed in equation form, with estimated standard errors in parentheses are as follows (where the superscripts a, b, c indicate significant probabilities $p < 0.001$, $p < 0.01$, $p < 0.05$ respectively).

The EC Model:

$$\log \text{COST} = \underset{(0.270)}{2.782^{a}} + \underset{(0.035)}{0.522^{a}} \log \text{ATK\_TTL} + \underset{(0.089)}{0.185^{c}} \text{LF} + \underset{(0.055)}{0.523^{a}} \log \text{WAGE}$$
$$+ \underset{(0.068)}{0.127} \log \text{ENG\_INDX} - \underset{(0.009)}{0.029^{a}} \text{TREND} + \underset{(0.000)}{0.001} \text{TREND}^{2}$$

$$(5.7)$$

The EE Model:

$$\log \text{COST} = \underset{(0.469)}{2.971^{a}} + \underset{(0.066)}{0.578^{a}} \log \text{ATK\_TTL} + \underset{(0.142)}{0.220} \text{LF} + \underset{(0.048)}{0.448^{a}} \log \text{WAGE}$$
$$+ \underset{(0.104)}{0.076} \log \text{ENG\_INDX} - \underset{(0.015)}{0.006} \text{TREND} + \underset{(0.001)}{0.000} \text{TREND}^{2}$$

$$(5.8)$$

- The coefficients of output variable ATK_TTL in both the EC and the EE models are statistically significant. This suggests that the operating costs of airlines surge when aggregate passenger and cargo outputs increase. Because these constitute the main production in the airline business, the cost elasticity with respect to changes in ATK_TTL will be high.
- The coefficient sign of LF (Load Factor) in the EC model is positive and statistically significant at the 5 % level. The positive sign of LF indicates that the higher occupancy rate of flights induces an increase in the cost. The result represents that the increase in cost is higher than the increase in passenger occupancy rate; thus airlines in our analysis demonstrated the diseconomies of scale. Due to the extreme competition in the airline industry, especially after the emergence of low-cost carriers in the short haul, this result is not surprising.
- The cost elasticity of WAGE is found to be positive in both the EC and the EE models, which is consistent with our expectation. This result implies that higher wage increases the airline cost. According to a study by Parast et al. (2010), the effect of airline employees' salaries on airline profit was positive, while other studies such as Assaf (2009) and Oum and Yu (1998) found that higher salary as expected increases the cost.
- The positive signs of the energy price index in both the EC and the EE models indicate a positive effect on the cost but these are statistically insignificant. The coefficient sign of energy is, however, consistent with previous studies such as

that of Parast et al. (2010). As explained in Chap. 3, fuel makes up around 25–35 % of the total operating costs of an airline (IATA 2012). Any political, social, or economic instability in the oil-producing nations leads to a higher energy price, which significantly affects the cost increase of airlines. For example, jet fuel prices, which were approximately USD 83 per barrel in August 2010, escalated to USD 129 per barrel in March 2011, a surge of 55.4 % in only 8 months.

- The sign of the time trend is negative and statistically significant, while that of the square of time trend is positive and statistically insignificant in the EC model. The result demonstrates the time trend effects of the cost indicating technological progress. Our study, however, could not capture the direction over the sample period. According to IATA (2011), airlines reduced almost 50–60 % of their operating costs, including workforce cost and energy cost, through use of better technology and improved productivity.

Determinants of cost inefficiency

In the context of the variables in the technical inefficiency effect model, most of the signs of δ coefficients are consistent with the assumption in this study and the findings from the previous studies.

$$
\begin{aligned}
\hat{U} = &-2.348^a - 0.175\,\text{INT\_PS}^c + 0.224^a\log\text{EMP} + 0.268^a\log\text{FHRS} + 0.096^a\,\text{PRICE} \\
&\;\;{\scriptstyle(0.443)}\quad\;\;{\scriptstyle(0.088)}\qquad\qquad{\scriptstyle(0.068)}\qquad\qquad\quad{\scriptstyle(0.090)}\qquad\qquad\;{\scriptstyle(0.008)} \\
&+ 0.202\,\text{MS} + 0.201^b\,\text{A1} + 0.201^a\,\text{A2} + 0.153^c\,\text{A3} + 0.081^a\,\text{EU} + 0.201^a\,\text{ASIA} \\
&\;\;{\scriptstyle(1.186)}\qquad{\scriptstyle(0.077)}\qquad\;\;{\scriptstyle(0.072)}\qquad\;\;{\scriptstyle(0.074)}\qquad\;\;{\scriptstyle(0.038)}\qquad\;{\scriptstyle(0.039)} \\
&- 0.007^a\,\text{YEAR} \\
&\;\;{\scriptstyle(0.006)}
\end{aligned}
$$

$$(5.9)$$

a, b, c indicates $p < 0.001$, $p < 0.01$, $p < 0.05$, respectively, and estimated standard errors are in parentheses.

Many of the estimated coefficients are bigger than their standard errors, which is coherent with the test result that favors rejection of the null hypothesis that all the parameters of the inefficiency models are equal to zero. This result with the rejected null hypothesis suggests that inclusion of the technical inefficiency effect variables better captures the effects on airline cost than the restricted model without the inefficiency determinant variables. Table 5.6 provides a complete description of the consistency of the results for determinants of both cost and cost inefficiency effects models.

- The sign of δ coefficient for INT_PS is negative and statistically significant at the 5 % level, which implies that airlines with a higher share of international passenger output are more efficient in cost management. This probably merits further investigation and analysis. One possible explanation for this is that airlines with a higher percentage of international passenger flights such as Singapore Airlines and Cathay Pacific Airways perform better in cost efficiency by hedging the risks from the domestic/within regions demand fluctuation of passenger service where high elasticity prevails.

Table 5.6 Summary of the consistency of the result based on EE cost model

Variables	Effect to cost	Assumption	Result	Statistically significant	Result
ATK_TTL	↑ → ↑	+	+	Yes	Consistent
LF	↑ → ↑	+	+	Yes	Consistent
WAGE	↑ → ↑	+	+	Yes	Consistent
ENG_INDX	↑ → ↑	+	+	No	Consistent
TREND	↑ → ↓	−	−	Yes	Consistent
TREND^2		−	+	No	N/A[a]

Variables	Hypothesis		Assumption	Result	Statistically significant	Result
INT_PS	H1	↑ → ↑	−	−	Yes	Consistent
EMP	H2	↑ → ↓	+	+	Yes	Consistent
FHRS	H3	↑ → ↓	+	+	Yes	Consistent
MS	H4	↑ → ↑	−	+	No	N/A[a]
PRICE	H5	↑ → ↑	−	+	Yes	Inconsistent
A1	H6	Progressive	−	+	Yes	Inconsistent
A2			−	+	Yes	
A3			−	+	Yes	
ASIA	H7	Progressive	−	+	Yes	Inconsistent

[a]Not applicable

- EMP and FHRS measure the airline size effects. Maintaining large numbers of employees and operating longer distances involve higher investment and expenses. The coefficient signs of these two variables are thus assumed to be positive—in other words, they have a negative impact on airline cost efficiency. In the US airlines market analysis of Ciliberto and Tamer (2009), larger airlines were found to be less cost efficient. On the other hand, Chin and Tay (2001) found that airline growth, measured by the growth of the number of aircrafts, indicated that airline profitability is positively related with size because most profitable airlines expand primarily by procuring more aircrafts. Because of this possible endogeneity problem, we used flying hours instead of aircraft numbers as a measure of size. Both the coefficients of EMP and FHRS show positive signs, with statistically significant coefficients at the 1 % level. According to IATA (2011), airlines typically have a low yield in long-distance flights. This supports the positive sign of FHRS, which implies a positive correlation with cost inefficiency and is consistent with the findings of Ciliberto and Tamer (2009). On the other hand, in an airline operation, output expansion does not proportionally increase cost. In light of large fixed costs such as aircrafts, an airline can make long-term investment plans if it foresees that the market have a stable growth. In particular, when airlines purchase aircrafts or hedge fuel prices, the largest global airlines tend to receive more favorable terms of payment and delivery, and they can enjoy the volume discount as well. These advantages will eventually improve the airline's cost efficiency. In this sense, our estimation results can be used as the starting point for further studies to shed light on any irregularities in the expected results.

- Airfare (PRICE) shows an increasing effect on cost inefficiency, with a statistically significant estimate at the 1 % level. The result indicates that a 1 % increase in price leads to a more than 9.6 % increase in cost inefficiency. We expected PRICE to have a positive effect on cost efficiency. Being able to charge a higher price means that an airline enjoys a high market power and as such the airline faces less cost burdens than its competitors—e.g., promotion and marketing or service upgrading. Liang (2013), using data from the nine largest US domestic airlines in the third quarter of 1987 for 5428 routes, found that an airline's share of passengers on a route is positively associated with its ability to charge prices above costs. However, our result is inconsistent with our expectation, and it demonstrates that when price increases, the demand decreases, thus showing an increasing effect on unit cost inefficiency.
- The coefficient of market share (MS) is statistically insignificant. We hoped to confirm Porter's hypothesis that firms' global competitiveness, measured by market share, ultimately comes from firms' cost competitiveness. On the other hand, a higher market share will lead to a more efficient use of inputs, which will help reduce the cost. We could not prove this hypothesis because of the insufficient cost data; thus further analysis in this regard is required.
- The positive coefficients sign of the airline alliance dummy reveals that alliance members' cost inefficiency is higher than airlines that did not join any alliance membership. The result does not confirm our assumption, and we presume this inconsistency is due to the insufficient cost data. Whalen (2005) showed that alliances are associated with large increases in passenger volumes, and Oum et al. (2009) and Fana et al. (2001) found similar evidence. Our result is similar to Gudmundsson and Lechner (2006) that joining an alliance could result in airlines losing some control over their passengers, which is the most important asset of airlines, by allowing other members to access their customer base. At the same time, joining an alliance can create some cost burdens for member airlines in order to cope with the services agreed upon among the members such as reservation system, in-flight services, and language services. Alliance members can share costs related to check-in counters, ground handling, airport lounges, and other facilities. Through such cooperation, airlines can economize on resources such as manpower and on expenses. We will examine airline alliance memberships and regional comparison effects on the cost efficiency in greater depth.
- The coefficients of the Europe dummy (EU) and Asia dummy (ASIA) are 0.081 and 0.201 and statistically significant at the 5 and 1 % levels, respectively. This result implies that EU and Asian airlines are less efficient than their North American counterparts. The result is especially interesting when compared with findings from previous studies such as Oum and Yu (1998), who found that Asian carriers, except Japan Airlines and All Nippon Airways, were generally more competitive than the major US carriers, mostly due to their substantially lower input prices. Among European carriers, British Airways and Scandinavian

Airlines Systems were 7 and 42 % less competitive, respectively than American Airlines, due to higher input prices and lower cost efficiency. A detailed summary of the results that are captured with alliance membership and region variables is reviewed at the end of the chapter.

- The time trend coefficient is −0.007 and statistically insignificant; so we could not confirm our hypothesis of overall improvement in the cost efficiency of airlines over time. While airlines have made great strides in cutting costs and improving their productivity, these efforts may be insufficient to offset the continuous price increase of key inputs such as energy, fees, and charges. In any case, a more detailed analysis will be performed at a later stage.

5.4.2   Airline Efficiency

A. Frequency distribution of cost efficiency

The measures of cost efficiency relative to the cost frontier is defined as: $EFF_i = E(COST_i^*|U_i, X_i)/E(COST_i^*|U_i = 0, X_i)$, where $COST_i^*$ is the cost of the ith firm, which will be equal to $COST_i$ when the dependent variable is in original units and will be equal to $\exp(COST_i)$ when the dependent variable is in logs. In the case of a production frontier, EFF_i will take a value between zero and one in the production case, where a value of one indicates full production efficiency, while it will take a value of one or more in the cost function case, where 1 indicates minimum cost or highest cost efficiency. The distance from value one measures the cost inefficiency of airlines or excess cost over the best cost-effective technology. In order to compare airlines' cost efficiency with production efficiency, we then invert the efficiency value to percentage cost effectiveness, with values in the interval zero and one compared with the airline with the lowest cost. Summary statistics of the cost efficiencies from the EC and EE model specifications are presented in Table 5.7. The frequency of cost efficiency obtained from the two models is reported in Table 5.8 and Fig. 5.1. Appendices 5.1 and 5.2 report the full cost efficiency results for each airline and model specification over the study period.

B. Cost efficiency time variation

We estimate a cost model using the panel data of airlines. The estimation allows for time-variant efficiency for the individual sample airlines. The mean average cost efficiency of the EE model also shows a steady but small improvement from 0.747 in 1998 to 0.751 in 2012. The mean efficiency of the EC model shows a rather

Table 5.7 Descriptive statistics of airlines' cost efficiencies

Cost model	Mean	Std. dev.	Min	Max
EC	0.541	0.152	0.265	0.980
EE	0.756	0.150	0.119	0.994

Table 5.8 Frequency of airlines' cost efficiencies

Range	EC model		EE model	
	Freq.	%	Freq.	%
0.0–0.3	10	2	2	0
0.3–0.4	85	15	0	0
0.4–0.5	160	27	0	0
0.5–0.6	165	28	106	18
0.6–07	93	16	109	19
0.7–0.8	34	6	156	27
0.8–0.9	8	1	71	12
0.9–1	30	5	141	24

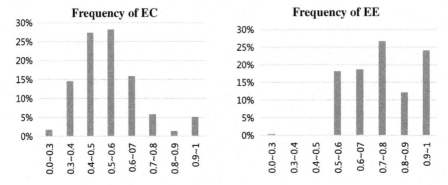

Fig. 5.1 Cost efficiency frequency distribution (%)

different pattern—a decreasing trend from 0.606 in 1998 to 0.474 in 2012. Both the EE and the EC models effectively capture the negative shocks to cost efficiency caused by the Asian financial crisis of 1997–1998, the 9/11 terror attack, and the global financial crisis in 2008. The full summary statistics of airlines' efficiency for each year are presented in Table 5.9. The development of cost efficiency is shown in Fig. 5.2. In general, the yearly trend of EE shows that airlines have successfully improved their cost efficiency over time as reported by IATA. When comparing the gap or range between the value of minimum and maximum efficiencies, we can see that the difference in efficiency across airlines narrows noticeably, especially in the EE model. Due to broader and deeper cooperation among airlines, through closer information sharing, bilateral agreements such as code sharing, as well as more formal and systematic airline alliances, the efficiency gap among different airlines becomes smaller over the period studied.

C. **Airlines' cost efficiency ranks**

In the case of the EC model, five carriers, including four European carriers (TK, SU, EI, LY) and one Asian carrier (GA) ranked among the top five airlines in terms of cost efficiency. In the EE model, the five highest-ranked airlines included three

Table 5.9 Development of airlines mean and summary statistics of cost efficiencies over time

Year	EC model				EE model			
	Mean	Std. dev.	Min	Max	Mean	Std. dev.	Min	Max
1998	0.606	0.131	0.419	0.980	0.747	0.143	0.505	0.991
1999	0.597	0.134	0.408	0.980	0.757	0.150	0.504	0.991
2000	0.588	0.136	0.397	0.980	0.760	0.151	0.503	0.991
2001	0.579	0.138	0.386	0.980	0.764	0.148	0.509	0.994
2002	0.570	0.141	0.375	0.980	0.761	0.146	0.504	0.994
2003	0.560	0.143	0.364	0.980	0.765	0.147	0.534	0.993
2004	0.551	0.145	0.353	0.980	0.756	0.151	0.543	0.992
2005	0.542	0.148	0.342	0.980	0.762	0.152	0.537	0.992
2006	0.532	0.150	0.331	0.980	0.762	0.148	0.530	0.992
2007	0.523	0.152	0.320	0.980	0.754	0.148	0.524	0.992
2008	0.513	0.154	0.309	0.980	0.752	0.145	0.523	0.991
2009	0.503	0.157	0.298	0.980	0.765	0.144	0.530	0.992
2010	0.493	0.159	0.287	0.980	0.748	0.170	0.230	0.992
2011	0.484	0.161	0.276	0.980	0.742	0.177	0.119	0.992
2012	0.474	0.163	0.265	0.980	0.751	0.151	0.510	0.992

Note Each year, 39 observation

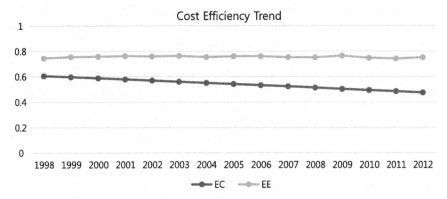

Fig. 5.2 Development of airlines mean cost efficiency

European (LY, EI, QR) and two Asian carriers (GA, PR). Carriers that ranked low in cost efficiency are mostly carriers that suffer from high operation costs and tend to be relatively larger in size. On the other hand, airlines that ranked high are carriers from countries where the cost of labor and other key inputs is competitive, for example, South Asian countries and China. But costs were by no means the only determinants of the level of cost efficiency. Airlines such as KE and CX ranked high in cost efficiency even though their cost ranks are high, especially in the EE model. In contrast, airlines such as QR, NZ, and LY showed the opposite pattern; they ranked low in cost efficiency even though their cost ranks are low. In general, the results show that cost efficiency is highly dependent on the airlines' cost structure, but some airlines overcome the cost burden through the employment of sound business strategies and efficient cost management approaches. The mean cost efficiency of individual airlines and their characteristics are reported in Table 5.10.

The EC and the EE ranks are based on our frontier cost function estimation results. Due to limited data availability on important aspects of airlines' operation such as the breakdown of total cost into different airline activities, the above rank represents at best a very rough estimate of the cost efficiency of airlines. We can, however, detect some interesting trends in the result. For example, airlines that spent or invested more were less cost efficient in general, but some airlines such as EI, NZ, BA, and KE were more efficient than their cost rank. Most American and Japanese carriers performed poorly in terms of cost efficiency, and this is consistent with previous studies such as Oum and Yu (1998) and Assaf (2009). Development of individual airlines' efficiency obtained from the EC model over time is reported in Fig. 5.3a.

As described above, airlines show a gradual deterioration in their efficiency performance over time based on the EC cost model specification. SU, TK, and GA performed well over the sample period. Four US-based carriers, namely, AA, DL, UA, and US, showed a similar trend as well as a steadily decreasing rate of cost efficiency over time.

The level of cost efficiency obtained from the EE cost model is fluctuating over time and across airlines compared with the trend in the EC cost model. In the EE model specification case, which incorporates inefficiency variables into the estimation, two Chinese airlines (CA and MU) show a rapid decrease in their cost efficiency. This deterioration may reflect the inability of Chinese airlines to cope with the explosive growth of demand due to rapid economic growth in the region. In 2008 and 2009, most airlines experienced a decrease in their efficiency scores. In particular, European carriers such as AF, AZ, and AV and two USA carriers, UA and US, suffered a relatively higher decline in efficiency. This result can be attributed to a negative demand shock due to the global economic crisis, which had a disproportionately larger effect on the American and European airlines. The crisis originated in the USA, and many European countries were hit hard due to the heavy exposure of their financial institutions to US subprime assets. Development of individual airlines' efficiency obtained from the EE cost model over time is reported in Fig. 5.3b.

D. **Variations in cost efficiency by different airlines' characteristics**

Airlines' size

The cost efficiency analysis by airlines' size, measured by the number of flying hours (proxy for the number of aircrafts adjusted for their flying hours) and number of employees, shows a positive correlation between size and cost inefficiency. This result suggests that larger airlines performed less efficiently in managing their costs. Distribution of cost efficiency by airline size measured by flying hours is reported in Table 5.11 and Fig. 5.5 for the two specified EC and EE model specifications. In an

Table 5.10 Mean cost efficiency of individual airlines and their rank (1998–2012)

Airline	Code	Country	Region	Alliance	AC	AC year	Cost rank	Cost rank	EC rank	Mean	EE rank	Mean
American Airlines	AA	United States	America	One World	896	14.9	TK	1	TK	0.980	LY	0.992
Air Canada	AC	Canada	America	Star	205	12.2	GA	2	SU	0.941	EI	0.989
Air France	AF	France	Europe	Sky Team	377	9.5	SU	3	GA	0.799	PR	0.978
Air India	AI	India	Asia	One World	88	7.3	PR	4	EI	0.744	GA	0.971
Avianca	AV	Colombia	America	Star	71	6.9	EI	5	LY	0.716	QR	0.967
Finn Air	AY	Finland	Europe	One World	68	8.4	QR	6	QR	0.652	AV	0.942
Alitalia	AZ	Italy	Europe	Sky Team	160	9.4	LY	7	AV	0.649	SU	0.909
British Airways	BA	U.K	Europe	One World	240	–	JJ	8	NZ	0.637	TP	0.905
Air China	CA	China	Asia	Star	275	6.5	AI	9	JJ	0.627	LA	0.904
Cathay Pacific Airways	CX	Hong Kong	Asia	One World	134	10.3	AV	10	AY	0.612	AY	0.900
China Southern	CZ	China	Asia	Sky Team	259	6.2	TP	11	LA	0.583	TK	0.898
DELTA Airline	DL	United States	America	Sky Team	722	16.7	NZ	12	PR	0.578	OS	0.889
Air Lingus	EI	Ireland	Europe	None	44	6.7	AY	13	MH	0.574	LX	0.851
Garuda Airways	GA	Indonesia	Asia	None	81	6.5	OS	14	OS	0.569	JJ	0.842
Iberia	IB	Spain	Europe	One World	112	9.3	LA	15	TP	0.569	SV	0.784

(continued)

Table 5.10 (continued)

Airline	Code	Country	Region	Alliance	AC	AC year	Cost rank	Cost rank	EC rank	Mean	EE rank	Mean
Tam Linhas Aereas	JJ	Brazil	America	Star	146	–	MH	16	KE	0.561	NZ	0.762
Korean Air	JL	Korea	Asia	Sky Team	130	9.4	TG	17	CX	0.561	AI	0.757
Japan Airlines	KE	Japan	Asia	One World	180	9.5	LX	18	SQ	0.545	KE	0.741
Lan Airlines	LA	Chile	America	One World	107	5.1	SV	19	LX	0.529	AC	0.732
Lufthansa,	LH	Germany	Europe	Star	427	12.3	MU	20	QF	0.514	CX	0.723
Swiss Air	LX	Switzerland	Europe	Star	91	–	AZ	21	IB	0.505	SQ	0.72
El Al	LY	Israel	Europe	None	40	13.4	IB	22	SV	0.496	MH	0.718
Malaysia Airlines	MH	Malaysia	Asia	One World	108	10.3	CA	23	TG	0.489	IB	0.713
China Eastern	MU	China	Asia	Sky Team	413	6.6	CZ	24	AC	0.483	TG	0.707
All Nippon Airways	NH	Japan	Asia	Star	151	12.1	KE	25	AI	0.467	SK	0.706
Air New Zealand	NZ	New Zealand	Asia	Star	98	9.4	SK	26	AZ	0.456	AZ	0.680
Austrian	OS	Austria	Europe	Star	80	14.3	SQ	27	BA	0.447	MU	0.673
Philippine Airlines	PR	Philippines	Asia	None	40	9.8	CX	28	US	0.444	US	0.644
Qantas Airways	QF	Australia	Asia	One World	141	10.8	AC	29	SK	0.443	BA	0.636
Qatar Airways	QR	Qatar	Europe	None	111	5.1	QF	30	UA	0.439	CA	0.634
SAS Scandinavian Airlines	SK	Sweden	Europe	Star	143	12.9	US	31	DL	0.437	QF	0.615

(continued)

Table 5.10 (continued)

Airline	Code	Country	Region	Alliance	AC	AC year	Cost rank	Cost rank	EC rank	Mean	EE rank	Mean
Singapore Airlines	SQ	Singapore	Asia	Star	128	6.4	NH	32	AA	0.436	AF	0.601
Aeroflot Russian Airlines	SU	Russian Federation	Europe	Sky Team	123	5.5	BA	33	MU	0.405	JL	0.601
Saudi Arabian Airlines	SV	Saudi Arabia	Europe	Sky Team	163	10.3	JL	34	CA	0.397	DL	0.583
Thai Airways	TG	Thailand	Asia	Star	98	10.7	DL	35	NH	0.376	CZ	0.577
Turkish Airlines	TK	Turkey	Europe	Star	189	6.4	UA	36	AF	0.37	UA	0.575
Tap Portugal	TP	Portugal	Europe	Star	71	11.5	AA	37	CZ	0.367	LH	0.566
UNITED Airline	UA	United States	America	Star	704	13.3	AF	38	JL	0.355	NH	0.563
Us Air	US	United States	America	Star	339	12.6	LH	39	LH	0.342	AA	0.547

Note Cost is ordered in ascending order, low number indicates airline with low cost

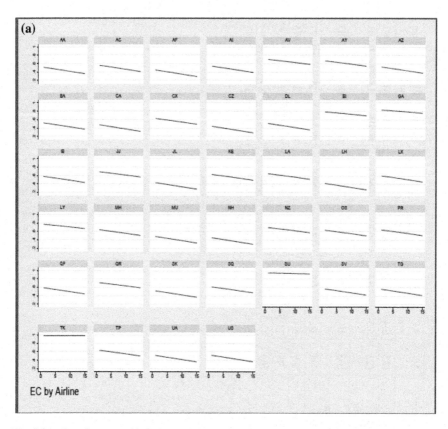

Fig. 5.3 a Development of individual airlines' cost efficiency over time, 1998–2012, EC model.
b Development of individual airlines' cost efficiency over time, 1998–2012, EE model

investigation of 856 US manufacturing firms between 1970 and 1980, Mills and
Schumann (1985) found that "small firms were able to compete successfully with
larger, more efficient (in a static sense) producers by absorbing a disproportionate
share of industry-wide fluctuations in output" (Mills and Schuman 1985). "Smaller
firms seemed to respond better to cyclical swings in demand while large firms have the
comparative advantage of lower minimum average costs, due largely to scale
economies" (Mills and Schumann 1985). Although size is related to greater profitability, the relationship is nonetheless indirect. Efficiency difference accounts for the
differences in the profitability of firms in the industry (Mills and Schumann 1985).

On the other hand, Merkert and Hensher (2011) evaluated the key determinants
of the efficiency of 58 passenger airlines by applying a two-stage data envelopment
analysis (DEA). Their research found that airline size and key fleet mix characteristics, such as aircraft size and the number of different aircraft families in the
fleet, were more relevant for the successful cost management of airlines since they
had significant impacts on airline efficiency.

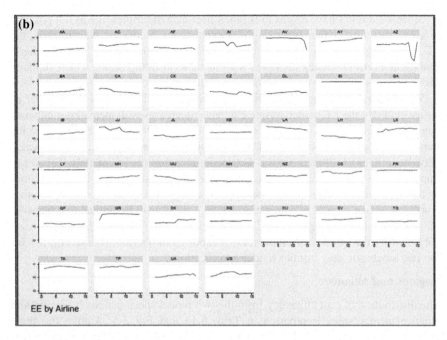

Fig. 5.3 (continued)

Table 5.11 Distribution of cost efficiency by airline size measured by flying hours

Category	Flying hours	OBS	EC model				EE model			
			Mean	Std. dev.	Min	Max	Mean	Std. dev.	Min	Max
1	<100,000	15	0.513	0.161	0.342	0.980	0.821	0.276	0.119	0.994
2	100,000–200,000	102	0.513	0.140	0.293	0.980	0.944	0.065	0.720	0.993
3	200,000–300,000	92	0.524	0.162	0.265	0.980	0.830	0.112	0.535	0.987
4	300,000–400,000	92	0.527	0.124	0.278	0.948	0.775	0.095	0.575	0.983
5	400,000–500,000	59	0.564	0.161	0.289	0.980	0.726	0.095	0.522	0.976
6	500,000–600,000	65	0.549	0.150	0.320	0.980	0.685	0.079	0.556	0.963
7	600,000–1,000,000	67	0.560	0.151	0.299	0.980	0.668	0.103	0.523	0.975
8	1,000,000–2,000,000	70	0.563	0.150	0.321	0.980	0.595	0.034	0.510	0.702
9	2,000,000–3,000,000	23	0.599	0.214	0.287	0.980	0.539	0.028	0.503	0.586

Since we did not have access to detailed fleet data of airlines, it was not possible to assess the effect of fleet types on the cost efficiency of airlines. Nevertheless, the EC score segregated by flying hours is consistent with Merkert and Hensher's finding that cost efficiency improves with increase in flying hours, which supports the economies of scale effects of the airline market structures.

We obtained the same result when we measured airline size by the number of airline staff. By the EE model, airline efficiency decreases with increased number of employees, but the EC model shows that airline's cost efficiency increases when the number of employees increases. At the same time, the variation of mean efficiency between airlines of different sizes is not so significant in the EC models. This result implies that in airline industry, we cannot conclude that a large size is always better or the opposite, namely, small is beautiful, as suggested in the literature. In other words, an airline's profit maximization strategy should not be limited to expansion of size and scales of operation. Distribution of cost efficiency by airline size, measured by the number of employees, is reported in Table 5.12 and Fig. 5.4 for the two stochastic cost frontier model specifications.

Regions and alliances

The distribution of cost efficiency from the two model specifications by region and alliance memberships is reported in Table 5.13 and Fig. 5.5. Among the three regions—Asia, Europe and North America—the mean cost efficiency of airlines is highest in Asia in the EC model but the lowest in the EE model. This result confirms our conjecture that cost efficiency levels differ across different regions due to differences in the regulatory and competitive environments. In the maximum likelihood estimation, the coefficients of the Europe dummy (EU) and Asia dummy (ASIA) are 0.081 and 0.201 and statistically significant at the 1 % level. The result from the EC model implies that European and Asian airlines are more cost efficient than their North American counterparts, while the EE model demonstrates the very

Table 5.12 Cost efficiency by airlines size measured by the number of employee

Category	Employment	FREQ	EC model				EE model			
			Mean	Std. dev.	Min	Max	Mean	Std. dev.	Min	Max
1	≤ 5000	51	0.440	0.069	0.293	0.556	0.980	0.022	0.898	0.994
2	5000–10,000	113	0.554	0.156	0.265	0.980	0.902	0.087	0.601	0.990
3	10,000–20,000	205	0.547	0.149	0.278	0.980	0.744	0.124	0.119	0.982
4	20,000–30,000	100	0.526	0.141	0.309	0.980	0.696	0.059	0.550	0.839
5	30,000–40,000	33	0.582	0.155	0.364	0.950	0.618	0.054	0.510	0.704
6	40,000–50,000	17	0.574	0.176	0.323	0.980	0.622	0.031	0.560	0.702
7	50,000–60,000	24	0.537	0.138	0.299	0.980	0.601	0.018	0.551	0.636
8	60,000–70,000	11	0.577	0.210	0.321	0.980	0.578	0.016	0.542	0.597
9	70,000–80,000	11	0.602	0.227	0.430	0.980	0.559	0.019	0.534	0.586
10	80,000–90,000	4	0.661	0.277	0.422	0.980	0.538	0.025	0.505	0.563
11	90,000–100,000	10	0.599	0.165	0.287	0.795	0.525	0.023	0.503	0.558
12	100,000–120,000	6	0.504	0.085	0.395	0.627	0.527	0.008	0.514	0.536

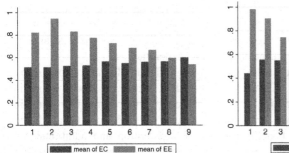

Fig. 5.4 Cost efficiency by airlines size (flying hours). Cost efficiency (number of employee). *Note* The categories in horizontal axes are is in accordance with the table

Table 5.13 Cost efficiency of regions and alliances memberships

Regions and alliances	Frequency	EC				EE			
		Mean	Std. dev.	Min	Max	Mean	Std. dev.	Min	Max
Europe	240	0.542	0.159	0.265	0.980	0.812	0.151	0.119	0.994
Asia	225	0.548	0.139	0.309	0.980	0.716	0.124	0.510	0.986
North America	120	0.524	0.160	0.276	0.980	0.721	0.160	0.503	0.989
One World	150	0.561	0.155	0.299	0.980	0.711	0.120	0.503	0.973
Star	240	0.532	0.150	0.265	0.980	0.746	0.135	0.511	0.989
Sky Team	120	0.548	0.156	0.278	0.980	0.694	0.133	0.119	0.930
No alliance	75	0.517	0.140	0.315	0.980	0.979	0.029	0.745	0.994

Fig. 5.5 Regional and alliance memberships comparison of cost efficiency. *1*—One World, *2*—Star Alliance, *3*—Sky Team, and *4*—No alliance

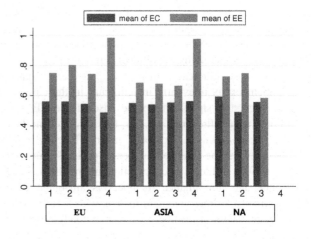

opposite result. The cost efficiency score of each individual airline is consistent with the regression result. In line with the cost frontier function, one reason for the differences across regions may be variations in the input costs such as labor and other services such as in-flight meals and other amenities.

The differences in mean cost efficiency among different alliance memberships is broadly similar in both the EC and the EE models. In the EE model estimation, non-alliance airlines had the highest mean efficiency, while in the EC estimation, they had the lowest efficiency level. Although many studies found that alliances provide positive consumer benefits through cost reduction and additional route offerings, others point out that they can adversely affect competition by reducing or eliminating competition on specific routes or markets which, in turn, can adversely affect consumer welfare and consumer choice. This occurs when two carriers previously competing on a route on which there is no third carrier decide that only one alliance should operate the route. Our EE results, which show that non-alliance member airlines' mean efficiency is higher than that of member airlines, support this line of reasoning.

The EC cost model results suggest that airlines that do not join any alliance are less efficient than airline members of an alliance. Airline alliances, including mergers and cross-investments, have been part of airline management strategy since the 1980s. Inter-airlines alliance agreements can vary from a simple marketing alliance, such as a joint frequent flyer program and code-share agreements, to a fully strategic alliance that gradually culminates in a merger of two airlines. By 2015, the three global alliances, One World, Star Alliance and Sky Team, the effects of which are captured by dummy variables in this study, covered two-thirds of all international air traffic.

The positive impact of alliances on member airlines' operation and performance is not only limited to cost savings. Alliances also provide direct benefits to consumers through the reduction of fares in some markets, as well as increased frequencies and route offerings. The different result between the EC and the EE frontier cost models is probably due to the inclusion of inefficient variables such as airline characteristics in the EE estimation. The EC model simply informs us about the cost minimization effects of alliance membership, given the output, input prices and services technology available to the airlines.

The cost efficiency difference between alliance members and alliance non-members is relevantly insignificant in the case of the EC model, while it is quite high and significant in the case of the EE model. Star Alliance member airlines' mean efficiency is 0.746, followed by One World at 0.711 and Sky Team at 0.694; non-alliance members' mean efficiency is 0.979. The similar efficiency score between the alliance members is probably due to the similarity in the scope of their service and level of cooperation among them. The high difference between the alliance and non-alliance members is attributed to the fact that many of the non-alliance airlines are small in size, with less diversified services and destination coverage. The non-members might be already efficient and not in need of alliance memberships to attain their efficiency goal. The test results show that the smaller airlines performed better in their cost managements, suggesting the size effects dominate the alliance effects.

The other possible explanation for the results discussed above is that airlines belonging to an alliance do not concentrate on reducing expenses and saving costs but are instead focusing their efforts on expanding their passenger volume through network sharing and membership mileage programs, which also increase their operation costs. Although this kind of cooperation can indeed help airlines to achieve a higher volume, it seems that it somehow did not enable airlines to improve their cost efficiency. In fact, our EE model results support these arguments.

Income of the country

Since the interaction between air transportation and economic development is dynamic, in Fig. 5.6, we additionally compare the yearly growth rates of efficiency and per capita growth rate in real GDP based on the data between 1998 and 2012. IATA and other existing studies have shown that air travel demand increases with the level of per capita income.

Through historical analysis of transportation trends across a large number of countries, some studies show that when economies grow and income levels increase, airline output increases because businesses and people tend to travel more as their revenues and disposable incomes increase, thus pushing airlines' productivity to a higher level. Since cost efficiency improves with output level, we compared the GDP growth and the cost efficiency growth rates. Summary statistics of cost efficiency by level of income is reported in Table 5.14.

Our estimation result shows that the difference in cost efficiency between high- and low-income countries is not so significant. This is plausible because higher income is likely to raise the travel demand, but at the same time, it will cause escalation of labor costs and other input prices. According to our results from both the EC and the EE models, an increase in the income and output of a country does not lead to a corresponding proportionate improvement in the cost efficiency.

As for the growth trend, although there were income declines in certain years such as 2001 and 2009, the EC model shows a steady growth in airline efficiency,

Table 5.14 Summary statistics of cost efficiency by level of incomes

GPP (USD)	NBR of OBS	EC				EE			
		Mean	Std. dev.	Min	Max	Mean	Std. dev.	Min	Max
≥ 10,000	71	0.552	0.154	0.321	0.980	0.743	0.152	0.230	0.994
10,000–20,000	102	0.525	0.151	0.289	0.980	0.749	0.142	0.504	0.993
20,000–30,000	49	0.558	0.139	0.364	0.980	0.699	0.153	0.503	0.994
30,000–40,000	73	0.508	0.159	0.265	0.980	0.770	0.143	0.510	0.991
40,000–50,000	185	0.550	0.146	0.287	0.980	0.783	0.157	0.119	0.992
50,000–60,000	56	0.552	0.144	0.299	0.980	0.761	0.138	0.527	0.992
60,000–70,000	49	0.544	0.179	0.293	0.980	0.722	0.141	0.534	0.992

while the EE model moves in the same direction as GDP-level development. The models capture the trend changes in efficiency, but they are unable to capture the year-to-year changes adequately. The EE model, however, performs better due to the incorporation of inefficiency determinants in addition to a time trend. The relationship between the growth rate in cost efficiency and income is reported in Table 5.15 and Fig. 5.6.

Table 5.15   Cost efficiency growth rate by income growth rate

Year	Income[a]		EC model		EE model	
	Mean	% change	Mean	% change	Mean	% change
1998	31,183	0.00	0.61	0.00	0.747	0.00
1999	31,795	0.02	0.60	−0.01	0.757	0.01
2000	32,752	0.03	0.59	−0.01	0.76	0.00
2001	32,823	0.00	0.58	−0.02	0.764	0.01
2002	33,373	0.02	0.57	−0.02	0.761	0.00
2003	33,947	0.02	0.56	−0.02	0.765	0.01
2004	34,924	0.03	0.55	−0.02	0.756	−0.01
2005	35,514	0.02	0.54	−0.02	0.762	0.01
2006	36,131	0.02	0.53	−0.02	0.762	0.00
2007	36,841	0.02	0.52	−0.02	0.754	−0.01
2008	36,776	0.00	0.51	−0.02	0.752	0.00
2009	36,358	−0.01	0.50	−0.02	0.765	0.02
2010	37,568	0.03	0.49	−0.02	0.748	−0.02
2011	38,161	0.02	0.48	−0.02	0.742	−0.01
2012	38,586	0.01	0.47	−0.02	0.751	0.01

[a]As a measure of income we have used the GDP per person employed (in constant 1990 PPP $)
Source www.wordbank.org

Fig. 5.6   The association between cost efficiency growth and per capita income growth

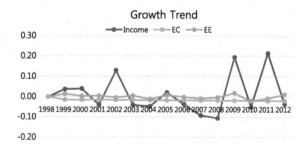

5.5 Summary and Conclusion

In this chapter, we performed a stochastic frontier cost function analysis on data from 39 airlines for the 1998–2012 period. Two well-known and frequently' used models in empirical performance analysis were estimated. The two stochastic frontier cost models estimated are the error components and efficiency effects models. The first model estimates a cost model and obtains time-variant individual airline efficiency for each year, while the second model also explains variations in cost inefficiency levels by its possible and identified determinants.

Our estimation results show that airline cost efficiency decreases over the observed period of study, and this result is consistent with the results of previous studies as well as the industry report that the airline industry has failed to recoup the cost of its capital over the airline business cycle of 8–10 years. The period of study covers the aftermath of the Asian financial crisis of 1997 and the period before and after the 2008 global economic crisis. The emergence of crises and recoveries has a strong influence on the temporal patterns of airline industry's development, growth, efficiency and dynamics.

The results for the variables used as inputs in the error components model and the efficiency effects model were largely consistent with our assumptions and expectations, which, in turn, were derived from cost theory and the findings of previous studies on airline cost efficiency. The estimated value of the log-likelihood function confirmed the existence of cost inefficiency, thus suggesting that the stochastic frontier cost model is more appropriate for our analysis. The model is suitable for the analysis of performance of the services industry. In such a case, the demand is given. The firms' objective is to minimize cost, given demand, market prices for production factors and technology, and is conditioned by the characteristics of firms and the market.

Several important hypotheses were tested in relation with the estimation of the two stochastic frontier cost models. Out of the seven hypotheses that we tested, three are found to be consistent, one is statistically insignificant and three are found to be inconsistent with our expectations at statistical significance levels of 1 or 5 %. The signs of the coefficients of variables in the cost frontier function were consistent with our assumptions, while there were a few exceptions in the EE model. The model specification is quite general, is consistent with the theory and is based on output and input factors prices. It is conditioned by technology and airline and market characteristics.

Among the variables treated as determinants of inefficiency, ticket price and airline size, the latter measured in terms of flying hours and number of employees had significant impacts on the cost efficiency of airlines. The per capita income of the operation regions of airlines has only a limited effect on the airlines' cost efficiency, as shown in the descriptive analysis reported in Table 5.15 and Fig. 5.6. This suggests that increased travel demand from increased income and booming businesses does not guarantee cost efficiency since costs and expenses also tend to rise when the income level increases.

The mean cost efficiency in the EC and the EE models are estimated to be 0.541 and 0.756 respectively. These figures imply that with the given output level and input prices, airlines are spending 1.85 and 1.32 times the optimal cost or minimum level of cost by using the best-practiced production technology. Measured in a different way, given expenses, airlines produce only 54.1 and 75.6 % respectively of the full capacity output based on the best-practiced technology in the airline industry.

Both the EC and the EE models results show that the mean efficiency level varies between different sizes of airlines, and cost efficiency is negatively correlated with airline size in the case of the EE model specification. In the case of the airline industry, large size is not always better—as is empirically evident, many mega-size airlines such as JL, AZ and AA faced financial difficulties and were either bankrupt or nearly bankrupt during the period of study. Expansion to a larger size requires massive investment in infrastructure, exposing the airline industry to significant financial dependency and difficulties and the high risk of bankruptcy.

The regional effect on cost inefficiency was statistically significant, with North American carriers showing a higher cost efficiency level than EU or Asian carriers. However, when comparing the individual airlines' efficiency score, the small carriers in the European region showed a much higher cost efficiency. Alliance effects were also statistically significant, but in contrast to our assumption, cost efficiency is negatively related to alliance membership, suggesting that non-member airlines show a more superior efficiency performance. This result suggests that alliance member airlines are not focusing on reducing costs through alliance cooperation. Instead they may be more concerned about expanding their volumes through network sharing and membership mileage programs. Although this kind of cooperation can help individual airlines to achieve higher sales, it somehow failed to generate cost efficiency gains. What is more surprising is that the EC model results suggest the opposite—namely, alliance membership is conductive to cost efficiency.

Appendix 5.1: Development of Airline Cost Efficiency Over Time Based on the EC Model Specification

Airline	1998	1999	2000	2001	2002	2003	2004	2005	2006	2007	2008	2009	2010	2011	2012	AVG
AA	0.512	0.501	0.491	0.480	0.469	0.459	0.448	0.437	0.426	0.415	0.404	0.393	0.382	0.371	0.360	0.436
AC	0.556	0.546	0.536	0.526	0.516	0.505	0.495	0.484	0.473	0.463	0.452	0.441	0.430	0.419	0.408	0.483
AF	0.447	0.436	0.426	0.415	0.404	0.392	0.381	0.370	0.359	0.348	0.337	0.326	0.315	0.304	0.293	0.370
AI	0.540	0.530	0.520	0.510	0.499	0.489	0.478	0.468	0.457	0.446	0.435	0.424	0.413	0.402	0.391	0.467
AV	0.706	0.698	0.691	0.683	0.675	0.667	0.658	0.650	0.641	0.633	0.624	0.615	0.606	0.597	0.587	0.649
AY	0.673	0.665	0.657	0.649	0.640	0.631	0.622	0.613	0.604	0.595	0.585	0.576	0.566	0.556	0.547	0.612
AZ	0.531	0.520	0.510	0.500	0.489	0.478	0.468	0.457	0.446	0.435	0.424	0.413	0.402	0.391	0.380	0.456
BA	0.522	0.511	0.501	0.490	0.480	0.469	0.458	0.447	0.436	0.426	0.415	0.404	0.392	0.381	0.370	0.447
CA	0.473	0.462	0.452	0.441	0.430	0.419	0.408	0.397	0.386	0.375	0.364	0.352	0.341	0.330	0.319	0.397
CX	0.627	0.618	0.609	0.600	0.590	0.581	0.571	0.562	0.552	0.542	0.532	0.522	0.511	0.501	0.490	0.561
CZ	0.444	0.433	0.422	0.411	0.400	0.389	0.378	0.367	0.356	0.345	0.334	0.323	0.312	0.301	0.290	0.367
DL	0.512	0.502	0.491	0.481	0.470	0.459	0.448	0.438	0.427	0.416	0.405	0.394	0.382	0.371	0.360	0.437
EI	0.788	0.782	0.776	0.770	0.765	0.758	0.752	0.745	0.739	0.732	0.725	0.717	0.710	0.703	0.695	0.744
GA	0.835	0.831	0.826	0.821	0.816	0.811	0.806	0.800	0.795	0.789	0.784	0.778	0.772	0.766	0.759	0.799
IB	0.576	0.566	0.556	0.547	0.537	0.527	0.516	0.506	0.496	0.485	0.474	0.464	0.453	0.442	0.431	0.505
JJ	0.686	0.678	0.670	0.662	0.654	0.646	0.637	0.628	0.619	0.610	0.601	0.592	0.582	0.573	0.563	0.627
JL	0.432	0.421	0.410	0.399	0.388	0.377	0.366	0.355	0.344	0.332	0.321	0.310	0.299	0.289	0.278	0.355
KE	0.627	0.618	0.609	0.600	0.591	0.581	0.571	0.562	0.552	0.542	0.532	0.522	0.512	0.501	0.490	0.561
LA	0.647	0.638	0.629	0.621	0.612	0.602	0.593	0.584	0.574	0.565	0.555	0.545	0.535	0.525	0.514	0.583
LH	0.419	0.408	0.397	0.386	0.375	0.364	0.353	0.342	0.331	0.320	0.309	0.298	0.287	0.276	0.265	0.342
LX	0.598	0.589	0.579	0.569	0.560	0.550	0.540	0.530	0.519	0.509	0.499	0.488	0.478	0.467	0.456	0.529

(continued)

(continued)

Airline	1998	1999	2000	2001	2002	2003	2004	2005	2006	2007	2008	2009	2010	2011	2012	AVG
LY	0.765	0.758	0.752	0.745	0.739	0.732	0.725	0.717	0.710	0.703	0.695	0.688	0.680	0.672	0.664	0.716
MH	0.639	0.630	0.621	0.612	0.603	0.594	0.584	0.575	0.565	0.556	0.546	0.535	0.525	0.515	0.505	0.574
MU	0.482	0.471	0.460	0.449	0.439	0.428	0.417	0.406	0.395	0.384	0.372	0.361	0.350	0.339	0.328	0.405
NH	0.453	0.442	0.431	0.420	0.409	0.398	0.387	0.376	0.365	0.354	0.343	0.332	0.321	0.310	0.299	0.376
NZ	0.695	0.688	0.680	0.672	0.664	0.655	0.647	0.639	0.630	0.621	0.612	0.603	0.593	0.584	0.574	0.637
OS	0.635	0.626	0.617	0.608	0.599	0.590	0.580	0.571	0.561	0.551	0.541	0.531	0.521	0.510	0.500	0.569
PR	0.643	0.634	0.625	0.616	0.607	0.598	0.589	0.579	0.569	0.560	0.550	0.540	0.530	0.519	0.509	0.578
QF	0.585	0.575	0.566	0.556	0.546	0.536	0.526	0.515	0.505	0.495	0.484	0.473	0.463	0.452	0.441	0.514
QR	0.708	0.701	0.693	0.685	0.678	0.669	0.661	0.653	0.644	0.636	0.627	0.618	0.609	0.600	0.591	0.652
SK	0.518	0.507	0.497	0.486	0.476	0.465	0.454	0.443	0.433	0.422	0.411	0.399	0.388	0.377	0.366	0.443
SQ	0.613	0.604	0.594	0.585	0.575	0.566	0.556	0.546	0.536	0.526	0.515	0.505	0.495	0.484	0.473	0.545
SU	0.952	0.951	0.950	0.948	0.946	0.944	0.943	0.942	0.940	0.938	0.935	0.934	0.932	0.930	0.928	0.941
SV	0.568	0.558	0.548	0.538	0.528	0.517	0.507	0.497	0.486	0.476	0.465	0.454	0.443	0.432	0.421	0.496
TG	0.561	0.552	0.542	0.532	0.521	0.511	0.501	0.490	0.480	0.469	0.458	0.447	0.436	0.425	0.414	0.489
TK	0.980	0.980	0.980	0.980	0.980	0.980	0.980	0.980	0.980	0.980	0.980	0.980	0.980	0.980	0.980	0.980
TP	0.635	0.626	0.617	0.608	0.599	0.589	0.580	0.570	0.561	0.551	0.541	0.531	0.521	0.510	0.500	0.569
UA	0.514	0.503	0.493	0.482	0.471	0.461	0.450	0.439	0.428	0.417	0.406	0.395	0.384	0.373	0.362	0.439
US	0.519	0.509	0.499	0.488	0.477	0.467	0.456	0.445	0.434	0.423	0.412	0.401	0.390	0.379	0.368	0.444
AVG	0.606	0.597	0.588	0.579	0.570	0.560	0.551	0.542	0.532	0.523	0.513	0.503	0.493	0.484	0.474	0.541

Appendix 5.2: Development of Airline Cost Efficiency Over Time Based on the EE Model Specification

Airline	1998	1999	2000	2001	2002	2003	2004	2005	2006	2007	2008	2009	2010	2011	2012	AVG
AA	0.505	0.504	0.503	0.509	0.504	0.534	0.543	0.551	0.558	0.563	0.568	0.585	0.589	0.591	0.597	0.547
AC	0.715	0.720	0.699	0.676	0.698	0.713	0.729	0.747	0.751	0.747	0.766	0.774	0.744	0.751	0.755	0.732
AF	0.631	0.632	0.618	0.614	0.620	0.612	0.590	0.587	0.585	0.580	0.587	0.598	0.607	0.608	0.551	0.601
AI	0.792	0.814	0.818	0.822	0.828	0.821	0.682	0.803	0.809	0.655	0.669	0.692	0.702	0.712	0.730	0.757
AV	0.976	0.982	0.982	0.983	0.985	0.989	0.987	0.986	0.976	0.974	0.972	0.972	0.964	0.887	0.522	0.942
AY	0.831	0.850	0.858	0.866	0.880	0.882	0.886	0.891	0.894	0.904	0.915	0.941	0.959	0.970	0.973	0.900
AZ	0.729	0.729	0.751	0.738	0.734	0.753	0.765	0.746	0.756	0.760	0.742	0.818	0.230	0.119	0.833	0.680
BA	0.588	0.594	0.597	0.604	0.611	0.615	0.620	0.620	0.629	0.636	0.664	0.676	0.686	0.704	0.702	0.636
CA	0.719	0.744	0.735	0.728	0.704	0.631	0.615	0.609	0.600	0.592	0.590	0.575	0.574	0.550	0.552	0.634
CX	0.744	0.752	0.734	0.741	0.739	0.747	0.731	0.725	0.720	0.718	0.688	0.710	0.700	0.693	0.695	0.723
CZ	0.626	0.615	0.607	0.614	0.616	0.584	0.556	0.537	0.530	0.524	0.601	0.602	0.574	0.558	0.510	0.577
DL	0.541	0.541	0.540	0.561	0.570	0.582	0.582	0.599	0.606	0.615	0.623	0.636	0.580	0.582	0.587	0.583
EI	0.980	0.982	0.984	0.988	0.990	0.991	0.991	0.992	0.991	0.991	0.991	0.991	0.991	0.991	0.992	0.989
GA	0.955	0.965	0.970	0.970	0.968	0.972	0.967	0.976	0.978	0.978	0.978	0.980	0.978	0.970	0.963	0.971
IB	0.672	0.674	0.687	0.690	0.697	0.702	0.691	0.702	0.712	0.717	0.725	0.756	0.758	0.750	0.765	0.713
JJ	0.941	0.949	0.953	0.879	0.826	0.877	0.886	0.945	0.803	0.764	0.766	0.769	0.755	0.751	0.762	0.842
JL	0.613	0.613	0.630	0.642	0.595	0.587	0.563	0.570	0.576	0.581	0.580	0.598	0.617	0.615	0.631	0.601
KE	0.738	0.740	0.728	0.737	0.734	0.742	0.742	0.745	0.740	0.735	0.738	0.750	0.749	0.751	0.750	0.741
LA	0.972	0.948	0.954	0.938	0.937	0.940	0.921	0.904	0.898	0.887	0.867	0.878	0.861	0.839	0.818	0.904
LH	0.625	0.602	0.605	0.599	0.601	0.600	0.558	0.552	0.554	0.543	0.523	0.530	0.533	0.527	0.536	0.566
LX	0.763	0.755	0.773	0.868	0.815	0.841	0.863	0.887	0.883	0.899	0.871	0.892	0.892	0.876	0.882	0.851

(continued)

(continued)

Airline	1998	1999	2000	2001	2002	2003	2004	2005	2006	2007	2008	2009	2010	2011	2012	AVG
LY	0.991	0.991	0.991	0.992	0.992	0.992	0.992	0.991	0.992	0.992	0.991	0.992	0.992	0.992	0.992	0.992
MH	0.658	0.693	0.693	0.697	0.702	0.703	0.693	0.702	0.712	0.730	0.736	0.762	0.755	0.754	0.781	0.718
MU	0.781	0.745	0.745	0.735	0.721	0.723	0.689	0.664	0.629	0.625	0.623	0.617	0.596	0.597	0.603	0.673
NH	0.575	0.565	0.565	0.574	0.575	0.567	0.558	0.558	0.558	0.562	0.556	0.559	0.561	0.552	0.564	0.563
NZ	0.765	0.765	0.758	0.762	0.750	0.754	0.756	0.751	0.766	0.754	0.738	0.760	0.780	0.785	0.786	0.762
OS	0.898	0.922	0.927	0.924	0.864	0.865	0.855	0.857	0.855	0.852	0.847	0.883	0.917	0.929	0.939	0.889
PR	0.952	0.978	0.978	0.981	0.980	0.981	0.982	0.980	0.979	0.980	0.979	0.977	0.978	0.981	0.986	0.978
QF	0.630	0.632	0.632	0.631	0.619	0.613	0.615	0.622	0.627	0.624	0.576	0.597	0.599	0.595	0.622	0.615
QR	0.745	0.971	0.976	0.994	0.994	0.993	0.992	0.990	0.987	0.985	0.983	0.982	0.976	0.969	0.963	0.967
SK	0.638	0.644	0.654	0.664	0.646	0.660	0.651	0.654	0.776	0.767	0.768	0.749	0.774	0.766	0.775	0.706
SQ	0.716	0.714	0.711	0.720	0.713	0.728	0.722	0.714	0.712	0.711	0.706	0.735	0.734	0.730	0.733	0.720
SU	0.871	0.894	0.907	0.900	0.920	0.925	0.923	0.921	0.919	0.910	0.900	0.930	0.923	0.907	0.889	0.909
SV	0.770	0.769	0.763	0.760	0.767	0.773	0.767	0.768	0.778	0.786	0.794	0.802	0.812	0.819	0.828	0.784
TG	0.697	0.699	0.696	0.699	0.706	0.709	0.704	0.708	0.707	0.699	0.699	0.717	0.723	0.719	0.728	0.707
TK	0.845	0.871	0.897	0.907	0.927	0.938	0.935	0.927	0.919	0.915	0.901	0.892	0.877	0.865	0.856	0.898
TP	0.876	0.881	0.904	0.906	0.908	0.908	0.904	0.932	0.929	0.899	0.879	0.897	0.912	0.916	0.923	0.905
UA	0.512	0.511	0.514	0.534	0.549	0.581	0.581	0.595	0.595	0.603	0.611	0.635	0.596	0.643	0.563	0.575
US	0.535	0.560	0.587	0.633	0.676	0.697	0.705	0.719	0.713	0.662	0.614	0.635	0.640	0.640	0.644	0.644
AVG	0.747	0.757	0.760	0.764	0.761	0.765	0.756	0.762	0.762	0.754	0.752	0.765	0.748	0.742	0.751	0.756

Appendix 5.3: Correlation Matrix of the Determinants of Cost Efficiency Effects

Parameters	ATK_TTL	LF	WAGE	ENG_INDX	INT_CS	EMP	FREQ	PRICE	MS
ATK_TTL	1.000								
LF	0.147	1.000							
(sig)	(0.000)								
WAGE	0.401	0.218	1.000						
(sig)	(0.000)	(0.000)							
ENG_INDX	0.215	0.221	0.129	1.000					
(sig)	(0.000)	(0.000)	(0.002)						
INT_CS	−0.272	0.357	0.192	−0.004	1.000				
(sig)	(0.000)	(0.000)	(0.000)	(0.921)					
EMP	0.795	0.143	0.269	0.040	−0.326	1.000			
(sig)	(0.000)	(0.001)	(0.000)	(0.331)	(0.000)				
FHRS	0.880	0.130	0.426	0.228	−0.429	0.795	1.000		
(sig)	(0.000)	(0.002)	(0.000)	(0.000)	(0.000)	(0.000)			
PRICE	−0.198	0.019	0.172	0.058	0.006	0.041	−0.128	1.000	
(sig)	(0.000)	(0.646)	(0.000)	(0.161)	(0.880)	(0.318)	(0.002)		
MS	0.745	0.355	0.423	−0.066	0.228	0.610	0.588	−0.064	1.000
(sig)	(0.000)	(0.000)	(0.000)	(0.111)	(0.000)	(0.000)	(0.000)	(0.123)	

References

Assaf A (2009) Are US airlines really in crisis? Tour Manage 30:916–921

Assaf A, George JA (2009) The operational performance of UK airlines: 2002–2007. J Econ Stud 38(1):5–16

Barbot G, Costa A, Sochirca E (2008) Airlines performance in the new market context: a comparative productivity and efficiency analysis. J Air Transp Manage 14:270–274

Battese G, Coelli TJ (1992) Frontier production functions, technical efficiency and panel data: with application to paddy farmers in India. J Prod Anal 3:153–169

Battese G, Coelli TJ (1995) A model for technical in efficiency effects in a stochastic frontier production function for panel data. Empirical Econ 20:325–332

Bhadra D (2009) Race to the bottom or swimming upstream: performance analysis of US airlines. J Air Transp Manage 15(5):227–235

Chin ATH, Tay JH (2001) Developments in air transport: implications on investment decisions, profitability and survival of Asian airlines. J Air Transp Manage 7:319–330

Ciliberto F, Tamer E (2009) Market structure and multiple equilibria in airline markets. Econometrica 77(6): 1791–1828

Clougherty JA (2009) Domestic rivalry and export performance: theory and evidence from international airline markets, Canadian Economics Association. Canadian J Econ/Revue Canadienne d'Economique 42(2):440–468

Coelli TJ (1996). FRONTIER version 4.1: a computer program for stochastic frontier production and cost function estimation. Working paper 96/7, CEPA, Department of Econometrics, University of New England, Armidale, Australia

Coelli T, Perelman S, Romano E (1999) Accounting for environmental influences in stochastic frontier models: with application to international airlines. J Prod Anal 11:251–273

Cristina M, Gramani N (2012) Efficiency decomposition approach: a cross-country airline analysis. Expert Syst Appl 39:5815–5819

Demydyuk G (2012) Optimal financial key performance indicators: evidence from the airline industry. Acc Tax 4(1):39–51

Fana T, Vigeant L, Geissler C, Bosler B, Wilmking J (2001) Evolution of global airline strategic alliance and consolidation in the twenty-first century. J Air Transp Manage 7:349–360

Ferguson BR, Hong D (2007) Airline revenue optimization problem: a multiple linear regression model. J Concr Appl Math 5(2):53–167

Gorin T, Belobaba P (2004) Impacts of entry in airline markets: effects of revenue management on traditional measures of airline performance. J Air Transp Manag 10:259–270

Graham DR, Kaplan DP, Sibley DS (1983) Efficiency and competition in the airline industry. Bell J Econ 14(1):118–138

Greer M (2009) Is it the labor unions' fault? Dissecting the causes of the impaired technical efficiencies of the legacy carriers in the United States. Transp Res Part A 43:779–789

Gudmundsson SV, Lechner C (2006) Multilateral, airline alliances: balancing strategic constraints and opportunities. J Air Transp Manage 12:153–158

Heshmati A (2003) Productivity growth, efficiency and outsourcing in manufacturing and services. J Econ Surveys 17(1):79–112

IATA (International Air Transport Association). Annual report 2011, Annual report 2012, Annual report 2013. www.IATA.org

Johnston A, Ozment J (2011) Concentration in the airline industry: evidence of economies of scale? J Transp Manage Fall/Winter 2011:59–74

Kumbhakar SC (1991) The measurement and decomposition of cost-inefficiency: the translog cost system. Oxf Econ Pap 43:667–683

Kumbhakar SC, Lovell CAK (2000) Stochastic frontier analysis. Cambridge University Press, Cambridge

Kumbhakar SC, Wan H, Horncastle A (2015) A practitioner's guide to stochastic frontier analysis using stata. Academic Press, Cambridge

Lee CY, Johnson AL (2011) Two-dimensional efficiency decomposition to measure he demand effect in productivity, analysis. Eur J Oper Res 216:584–593

Lee BL, Worthington AC (2014) Technical efficiency of mainstream airlines and low-cost carriers: new evidence using bootstrap data envelopment analysis truncated regression. J Air Transp Manage 38:15–20

Liang J (2013) An econometric analysis on pricing and market structure in the U.S. airline industry. Adv Econ 3(2):1–28 (Article 2)

Merkert R, Hensher DA (2011) The impact of strategic management and fleet planning on airline efficiency—a random effects Tobit model based on DEA efficiency scores. Transp Res Part A 45:686–695

Mills DE, Schumann L (1985) Industry structure with fluctuating demand. Am Econ Rev 75(4):758–767

Obermeyer A, Evangelinos C, Püsche R (2012) Price dispersion and competition in European airline markets. J Air Transp Manage 26:31–34

Oum TH, Yu C (1998) Cost competitiveness of major airlines: an international comparison. Elsevier Sci 32(6):407–422

Oum TH, Fu X, Yu C (2005) New evidences on airline efficiency and yields: a comparative analysis of major North American air carriers and its implications. Transp Policy 12:153–164

Oum TH, Zhang A, Fu X (2009) Air transport liberalization and its impacts on airline competition and air passenger traffic. Transp J 49(4):24–41

Parast MM, Fini EH (2010) The effect of productivity and quality on profitability in US airline industry: an empirical investigation. Managing Serv Qual 20(5):458–474

Schmidt P, Lovell CAK (1979) Estimating technical and allocative inefficiency relative to stochastic production and cost frontiers. J Econ 9:343–366

Tsekeris T (2009) Dynamic analysis of air travel demand in competitive island markets. J Air Transp Manage 15:267–273

Varian H (1984) Microeconomic analysis (Chaps. 1 and 4). Norton Publishing Company, New York

Wang WK, Lu WM, Tsai CJ (2011) The relationship between airline performance and corporate governance amongst US Listed companies. J Air Transp Manage 17:148–152

Whalen WT (2005) A panel data analysis of code sharing, antitrust immunity and open skies treaties in international aviation markets, U.S. Department of Justice - Antitrust Division, May 15, 2005

World Bank: http://www.worldbank.org

Chapter 6
Summary, Conclusion, and Policy Recommendations

Abstract This chapter summarizes the findings of the previous chapters on production and cost function analyses and proposes the policy implications based on
the key findings. The results confirmed that the airlines are successful in achieving
production efficiency over the period studied but are less successful in cost efficiency. Airline size showed a progressive effect on the level of output efficiency,
but larger airlines were not more competent than their smaller counterparts with
respect to cost efficiency. Our main findings show that carriers based in the Asia
region in general are more capable of achieving production efficiency than carriers
based in Europe and North America, while the cost model reveals the opposite
result. Airlines need to be more strategic about the utilization of their resources
when making operating decisions such as planning flying frequencies, stage length,
and destinations. Market share is important in achieving higher production efficiency, and alliances are also progressive for production efficiency. Airline market
liberalization also helps airlines to attain production efficiency, but the airlines
based in the less liberalized markets show better performance in their cost management. Domestic competition and price strategy are important elements and their
implications differ again in the production and cost function perspectives.

Keywords Airlines · Performance analysis · Efficiency analysis · Policy implication · Air liberalization index

6.1 Summary of Analysis

So far, we have reviewed the literature on performance analysis in general and
production and cost efficiency in particular. The focus has been on airlines and the
estimation of the airlines' efficiency throughout the chapters. In our view, we have
arrived at certain credible findings in line with the objectives of this volume.

As the first objective of this study, we aimed to estimate the level of efficiency
and look at how the efficiency of international airlines relates to their determinant
(allocation) factors both in production and cost function perspectives. Airlines that

© Springer Science+Business Media Singapore 2016
A. Heshmati and J. Kim, *Efficiency and Competitiveness
of International Airlines*, DOI 10.1007/978-981-10-1017-0_6

perform with higher efficiency in production maximization and cost minimization realized higher levels of profits. However, there were a few exceptional instances in which the unit profit was not correlated with the airline's efficiency level. In general, airlines' efficiency contributed to attaining maximum profit. In light of our empirical results, we found that the sample airlines displayed a reasonable level of production efficiency during 1998–2012, but they were much less successful in achieving cost efficiency. The difference is partially attributed to allocative efficiency. Cost or economic efficiency is a product of allocative and technical efficiency components, while production efficiency consists of only technical efficiency.

Asian airlines showed a higher efficiency in the production function analysis, but in the event of cost efficiency, we could not establish the transcendence of the Asian carriers. Some airlines attained a remarkable gain in efficiency over time. Such high achievers include Chinese carriers—CA (Air China), CZ (China Southern Airlines), and MU (China Eastern Airlines)—in case of production efficiency and GA (Garuda Airlines) and SU (Aeroflot Russian Airlines) in the case of cost efficiency. Our estimation results suggest that the approach we used by looking at both sides of airlines' efficiency, in terms of production and cost functions, seems to be superior compared to a single production- or cost-based performance analysis. This mixed approach provides information on the sensitivity of the results with respect to the estimation approaches. The difference in the level of technical and economic efficiencies is expected as the two approaches used different sets of information. In addition, in our view, our approach captures well the factors affecting efficiency and more accurately reflects the reality of the ongoing process of airlines' mergers and exits from the market.[1]

The second objective of this volume was to investigate the components or determinant factors that affect the airlines' efficiency. The determinants include several characteristics such as airline size, market share, geographical location, and alliance memberships. Our finding on the production function analysis is consistent with Oum and Yu (1998), who concluded that Asian carriers were generally more cost competitive than the major US carriers. The underlying reasons are substantially lower input costs and increased productivity (Chan 2000). On the other hand, our finding through the cost function analysis is similar to Barboot et al. (2008), who revealed that the majority of European and American carriers have a higher efficiency than ones based in the Asia-Pacific and China/North Asia region. Our evidence also differs from Demydyuk (2012), who did not find a much significant correlation between efficiency and the regional location of airlines. Our production efficiency model results are consistent with those of Lee and Johnson (2011), who showed that airline productivity declined in 2007 and 2008 due to the demand fluctuation attributed to the global economic crisis.

In case of production efficiency, out of the seven hypotheses that we tested, five are found to be consistent with our a priori expectations, while two of them were

---

[1] See Appendix 1.1 US carriers' exit and entry.

inconsistent (see Fig. 4.6). The results derived from the cost efficiency model are mixed in nature since only three hypotheses are consistent with our assumptions, while another three provide inconsistent results with our expectation and the one based on the market share shows a statistically insignificant result. The signs of the estimated coefficients of the explanatory variables of both the production and the cost functions were mostly consistent with the theory-based assumptions except in the case of domestic load factor in the production model, which had the opposite sign. Such differing and unexpected results can be attributed to various reasons. In general, depending on the sample size of airlines and period of time considered, the estimated results can show substantial variations. In sum, our major empirical evidence is found to be similar to the findings from previous studies.

As we have shown with descriptive analysis of the data and estimation results both in Chaps. 4 and 5, the income level of a country showed a similar growth pattern with airline efficiency improvement over time. Airline size, measured by the number of employees, number of aircrafts , and the flying hours in the case of the cost model, showed a positive correlation with the level of production efficiency. However, in case of the cost model, the larger airlines were not more efficient than their smaller counterparts. The variables used in the inefficiency model represent each airline's core business strategies such as resource allocation, route selection, and strategic cooperation with competitors. It is worth noting that one should take into account differences in resource availability across the home countries of the sampled airlines. In other words, the availability of resources and airlines' capabilities differ substantially amongst airlines. "These resources and capabilities may not be perfectly mobile across the industry, giving a competitive advantage to the best-performing airline companies" (Porter 1986). However, we tried to look at the most common options that airlines have at their disposal to improve their production and cost efficiencies.

The estimated values of the log likelihood function for the MLE (Maximum Likelihood Estimation) method confirmed the existence of technical inefficiency in both the production and cost functions. This suggests that average production and cost functions are not suitable functional forms for airlines' performance analysis. Estimation of two commonly used stochastic frontier functions—error components and efficiency effects model—showed that the technical inefficiency model is more appropriate than error components or an average production or cost function for our analysis (Coelli 1996). Kumbhakar and Lovell (2000), Heshmati (2003) and Kumbhakar et al. (2015) provide comprehensive reviews of the efficiency literature. Due to space constraints and our specific interest in the empirical estimation of production and cost models, we focused on the estimation of Battese and Coelli's (1992, 1995) error component and efficiency effects models.

Finally, our third objective was to investigate how airlines' efficiency affects competitiveness in the global market. Among the inefficiency determinant variables, the market share effect was especially significant in production efficiency, but in the case of the cost model, we were unsuccessful in showing its robustness. However, we are fully confident that our result supports Porter's hypothesis, which we adopted as the main theoretical framework of our analysis. The hypothesis posits that the firm's productivity is the most important factor in achieving global competitiveness, which can be captured by the individual airlines' market shares in the overall global market in a given year. In order to expand the market share, the policy of accommodating market access to foreign countries is recommended with careful examinations of other countries' experience in liberalization process in order to maximize the efficiency gain from liberalization and minimize the cost of severe competition simultaneously.

6.2 Policy Implications

We analyzed airline efficiency in services provision through the stochastic frontier functions and reviewed the result in terms of various common and time-invariant characteristics of the airlines. Based on the findings from the estimation of production and cost functions, here we present implications that can be applicable to airlines or national governments that are considering the formulation of policies to promote airline performance. For both the production and cost models, the results for several of the seven hypotheses we tested were in accordance with our expectations. Since the variables accounting for opposite signs used to explain the degree of inefficiency—which also served to test the stated hypothesis for the production and cost models—are more or less the same as our underlying assumptions, we present the implication of each result in a general context without distinguishing between the two models.

6.2.1 Airlines Strategy

By airlines strategy, we refer to strategies related to flying hours, frequency of flights, and alliance membership. First, the flying hours and frequency of flights showed a positive relationship with the production efficiency of airlines. This means that airlines should minimize the time that their aircrafts stay idle on the ground. Airways, by being aware of this fact, have tried hard to minimize the connecting time at airports, thereby maximize the use of aircrafts. In most cases, however, the increase in ground time is usually due to airport congestion, especially at busy hub airports such as Heathrow in London and Charles De Gaulle in Paris.

After the 9/11 terrorist attacks, security inspection in many airports, especially in the USA and flights heading for the USA, has been intensified, and it takes a significantly longer time, resulting in substantial delays for passenger boarding. In order to mitigate this constraint and in order to expand passenger volume handling capacity, governments need to improve airport facilities or increase the investment for building new airports. Some countries such as Korea, Japan, and Hong Kong have already built new airports with high reserve capacity. Furthermore, many countries, including Korea, have introduced electronic visa and passport systems to expedite immigration procedures. Airlines have also widely introduced electronic check-in facilities such as automatic seat assignments, electronic boarding passes and baggage handling at the airports. Such efforts will enhance an airline's production efficiency by reducing the ground handling time.

The alliance membership effect from code sharing and worldwide networks of routes and destinations should in principle improve efficiency since it increases the market share of the participating airlines and enhances their resource and capacity utilization. Our estimation result confirmed the positive effect of airline alliance on production efficiency but found the opposite in the cost efficiency estimation. The result revealed that contrary to conventional wisdom, alliances focusing on network expansion do not contribute to the cost saving of airlines. This is because almost all carriers are now members of alliances and the services provided by the different alliances do not vary significantly. The various mileage programs that alliance members provide to their customers become a cost burden for them because airlines need to allocate a certain percentage of their sales to provide free trips to their customers.

As shown in Chap. 3, the prices of key inputs are escalating rapidly and the free trips due to mileage programs impose an additional cost burden on airlines. To maximize the efficiency from joining an alliance, airlines should focus more on saving operation costs through the sharing of resources between members such as airport lounges and check-in facilities. Some alliance member airlines also share the training facilities of both cockpit and cabin crews. Such activities help airlines not only to save costs but also improve the customer services quality by upgrading their employee standard. Sharing information on customer preferences and market characteristics also benefit airlines in reducing the expenses related to marketing and promotions.

6.2.2 Market Share

The global market share of airlines, which we included as a proxy to measure the market competition level and the market structure, partly affects both the production and cost efficiency of airlines. It induces airlines to optimally utilize their resources and thus achieve economies of scale. Our estimation with the production frontier function model confirmed the positive correlation between market share and degree of efficiency. In particular, an airline's capacity to access foreign markets can be one of the crucial factors in enhancing its market share in the global market. In the case of the airline industry, the degree of market access can be measured either by the number of airlines operating to and from a country or by regulatory restrictions such as the degree of "freedom of the skies", a concept we explained in Chap. 3. Countries with fully liberalized markets allow cabotage[2] rights that enable airlines

---

[2]According to the WTO, it is the exclusive right of a country to operate air traffic within its territory.

to operate within the home-based states of other alliance members with positive effects on their market shares.

The WTO (World Trade Organization) measures air transportation openness by the Air Liberalization Index (ALI), which obtains information from each country's bilateral air services agreements (ASAs) and uses the information to provide a synthetic measure of the openness of each ASA.[3] ALI[4] has been constructed by attributing weights to the different variants or indicators of the key market access features of Air Services Agreements (e.g., freedoms of the skies, capacity).

Figure 6.1 depicts the growth trend of airlines' average efficiency in the production and cost approaches, along with ALI growth, for the period 1998–2012. Except for 2009 and 2010, when there were huge demand disruptions in the air transportation industry caused by the global economic crisis, the growth pattern of both the production and the cost efficiency follows the same pattern as the ALI index changes over time (see Table 6.1).

Since we could not include ALI into our estimation model because it is not a firm-specific factor, it is not possible to measure the direct effect of ALI on the efficiency of individual airlines. However, studies such as Clougherty (2009), Kontsas and Mylonakis (2008), Oum et al. (2010) and Sjoren and Soderberg (2011) showed that airline market liberalization contributes to airline productivity enhancement and improvement of consumer welfare.

The country-level ALI data shows that airlines based in relatively open countries achieved high scores in production efficiency but lower scores in cost efficiency (see Appendix 6.1). This suggests that greater competition in the domestic market forces airlines to lower their prices. The airlines that show high efficiency in the cost model, such as LY (El Al), GA (GARUDA), SU (Aeroflot Russian Airlines), and PR (Philippine Airlines), are mostly located in countries where the Air

---

[3]The Air Services Agreements Projector (ASAP) is an analytical tool that enables users to obtain information on a Signatory's network of bilateral Air Services Agreements (ASAs) and correlated traffic flows. It is based on the QUASAR methodology devised by the WTO Secretariat in 2006 to assess the openness of bilateral ASAs. A comprehensive account of the methodology can be found in document S/C/W/270/Add.1, dated 30 November 2006 (see in particular, pages II.644 to II.667). This version of ASAP is based on 2011 data. It builds on several information sources. On the regulatory side, it relies on bilateral ASAs that are included in the World Air Services Agreements (WASA) database of the International Civil Aviation Organization (ICAO) (last consulted on 31 August 2012). This data is complemented by ASAs that were submitted by Australia, Guatemala and New Zealand in 2007 in the context of the second GATS air transport Review, and information obtained from the WTO's Trade Policy Review Secretariat Reports of China (WT/TPR/S/264/Rev.1, dated 20 July 2012), Colombia (WT/TPR/S/265/Rev.2, dated 1 August 2012), Guyana (WT/TPR/S/218/Rev.1, dated 10 August 2009), Japan (forthcoming), and Norway (WT/TPR/S/205/Rev.1, dated 16 January 2009), as all these reports contain comprehensive ASA data (see below, for the calculation of the ALI). On the traffic side, it makes use of 2011 scheduled passenger traffic statistics kindly provided by the International Air Transport Association (IATA). In view of its commercial value and confidentiality, IATA statistics are presented as ranges, rather than exact figures.

[4]The WTO Secretariat in consultation with a panel of professionals, academics, and air transport negotiators devised ALI.

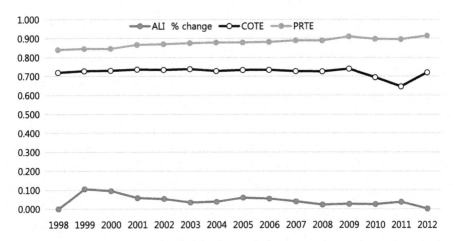

Fig. 6.1 ALI and average efficiency growth development, 1998–2012. *Note* COTE—Cost efficiency and PRTE—Production efficiency

Year	ASA	% change	COEC	COTE	PREC	PRTE
1998	1846.92	0.00	0.58	0.72	0.70	0.84
1999	2042.23	0.11	0.57	0.73	0.70	0.85
2000	2237.19	0.10	0.56	0.73	0.70	0.85
2001	2367.96	0.06	0.55	0.74	0.70	0.87
2002	2494.50	0.05	0.54	0.73	0.71	0.87
2003	2580.12	0.03	0.53	0.74	0.71	0.88
2004	2677.81	0.04	0.52	0.73	0.71	0.88
2005	2838.00	0.06	0.51	0.73	0.71	0.88
2006	2992.15	0.05	0.50	0.73	0.71	0.88
2007	3109.18	0.04	0.49	0.73	0.71	0.89
2008	3177.78	0.02	0.48	0.73	0.71	0.89
2009	3260.35	0.03	0.46	0.74	0.71	0.91
2010	3341.99	0.03	0.45	0.69	0.72	0.90
2011	3465.18	0.04	0.44	0.65	0.72	0.90
2012	3470.69	0.00	0.43	0.72	0.72	0.91

Table 6.1 Air Liberalization Index (ALI) and average efficiency over the period 1998–2012

Source www.wto.org/asap/index.html

Liberalization Index is lower. Inferring from the current trends in global trade liberalization, those countries where the services sector is still highly protected from competition will face significant challenges when the country opens up its services sector market to foreign producers. When this happens, the airline industry will not be an exception. The findings from previous literature reveal direct and indirect effects of opening up markets on airlines' efficiency. With respect to the effect of liberalization on airlines' efficiency, most studies have focused on the US and European markets, probably because airline liberalization in Asia began only after

2000. The market liberalization in general and open skies policies in particular was previously met with a degree of success in both the US and Europe. Since Asia is a relative latecomer in the market liberalization trend, it is worthwhile to investigate the progress it has made so far.

In order to attain a sustainable competitive position in the global market, airlines need to maximize their efforts to expand their market share by improving their technological efficiency and by offering favorable fares and better services to customers with the help of an efficient cost management system. At the same time, policymakers need to carefully examine the experiences of other countries that have fully opened up their air transportation markets. These experiences can then be used in fine-tuning the aviation-related policies. The US is a classic example of a highly liberalized and deregulated airline market. In the case of the US, as laid out in Appendix 1.1, a large number of carriers went bankrupt due to financial difficulties or got merged with other carriers. On the other hand, although Hong Kong and the UK opened up their air transportation markets, CX and BA performed well, both in production and cost efficiency.

6.2.3 Airline Prices

According to our estimation, the impact of price on production efficiency was negative due to the high demand sensitivity in the airline market, but price showed a positive impact on cost efficiency. In general, the airline pricing system is quite complex since airfare varies, depending on the season, ticket agent management system, and the level of competition in each market. Airline price plays an important role in increasing profit by generating revenues, but, at the same time, a higher price reduces demand. In order to attract more passengers, airlines have to cut costs and deliver services at a lower fare. Otherwise, passengers will turn to competitors who offer a more competitive price. To achieve this, the complex system of pricing needs to be simplified and one of the alternatives that airlines can consider is the E-ticket system. In fact, many airlines have already implemented the E-ticket system on a wide scale, which can minimize the intermediate handling costs and make a positive contribution to both airline profit and consumer welfare.

In addition to introducing an E-ticketing system, airlines have simultaneously been outsourcing some of their functions such as ground handling and maintenance. Since the wages of airline staff, including fringe benefits, are higher than those of other industries, limiting employment to core activities will contribute positively to the cost minimization objectives of airlines. While airlines try to keep their price competitiveness high by optimizing expenses, governments need to foster fair competition policies and reduce the inefficiency incurred from imperfect competition in the market. Our result confirms the findings of Liang (2013) and Oum et al. (2010) that less competition in the domestic market will eventually lead to less competition among airlines in the international market; thus a positive sign of price will eventually result in less total output.

6.2.4   Domestic Competition

Porter (1990) indicates that severe domestic rivalry forces firms to upgrade their product quality while nurturing positive static and dynamic externalities in the local business environment—e.g., supplier availability, easier access to technology and market information, and specialized human resources growth. Intensified domestic competition gives rise to positive externalities, but it creates robust competitive incentives along with resilient pressures to upgrade productivity, as domestic competition neutralizes advantages due to the input costs and other local business conditions (Sakakibara and Porter 2001).

We tested the domestic competition effect in the production model using load factor and international market shares. The result showed that airlines' domestic load factor was positively related to production inefficiency. Based on an analysis of around 670 UK companies, Nickell (1996) found evidence that competition, using proxies of the amplified numbers of competitors or the level of rents, is highly linked with a greater degree of total factor productivity growth (Nickell 1996). Applying data from 732 medium-sized manufacturing firms in the US, France, Germany and the UK, Bloom and Van Reenen (2006) found that inadequate management practices are more widespread when product market competition is fragile and that a higher degree of market competition reduces poor managerial practices. Better managerial practices are, in turn, significantly associated with higher productivity and profitability.

Contrary to findings from previous studies, our estimation result showed a different effect of domestic competition on airline efficiency. A possible explanation for this phenomenon is the emergence of low-cost carriers. Recently, several countries have allowed low-cost carriers to operate in their domestic markets. As such, legacy airlines have to compete with these new entrants, which reduces airline yield in the domestic market to very low levels. Some airlines such as Lufthansa, Air France, and Korean Air introduced multiple management systems for hiring airline staff to overcome the low yield of domestic operations. In order to minimize operating costs, airlines have different labor contracts for domestic crew, including wages and fringe benefits. These airlines including Air India and Alitalia also own low-cost carriers within their organization, the so-called "airline within airline"[5] (see also Appendix 6.4), to compete with the prevalence of low-cost carriers in the short-haul sector.

In order to fully accommodate the new trends in the airline market, airlines should reorganize their structures and make a separate strategy for domestic and short-haul sector operations. Having a different management system for the domestic crew and ground handling staff is one of the alternatives that can help achieve a desirable level of efficiency and competitiveness. Flexible use of resources, including airport facilities, for domestic routes will enable airlines to have a better cost allocation so that they can have a parallel cost advantage when competing in the global market. According to the IATA analysis (Pearce 2012), rigid labor market regulations allow

---

[5]For the details, see Pearson and Merkert (2014), Airlines-within airlines: A business model moving East.

unions to create advantages for new entrants to the market, and such a strong labor power will make airlines lose their competitiveness in the global market due to the higher cost inefficiency. Keeping labor laws flexible would allow for a more efficient allocation of labor and generate savings in manpower cost (Pearce 2012).

6.2.5 Regional Operation Effect

As shown in our stochastic frontier estimation in both the production and cost function analysis cases, airlines in different regions achieved varying efficiency scores in their production and cost structures, depending on their strategic choices, which we analyzed through the inefficiency effect cost and production models. Strategic decisions on route management, resource allocation, and strategic coop-eration have enabled airlines to secure a profitable and sustainable position in the competitive airline industry. As Porter described, firm-level efficiency gives airlines a competitive advantage in the form of either lower costs or differentiated products that command premium prices. Although Asian carriers have achieved a relatively higher production and cost efficiency, the fundamental factors supporting such achievements are the lower cost of labor and other inputs in the region. The less liberalized market condition in Asia also showed to have a positive impact on airlines' cost efficiency.

Technological differences in the airline industry have narrowed down since there are only a limited number of suppliers in the industry—Boeing and Airbus—thus the facilities and service equipment available for airlines are very homogenous in nature. Therefore, in order to achieve a sustainable competitive position in the global market, Asian airlines should focus on expanding their market share by upgrading the quality of their services. Singapore Airlines, Cathay Pacific Airways, and Korean Airlines are good examples of airlines that have a strong brand loyalty and that command leading positions in the industry by delivering premium-quality services. The quality of human capital and the level of education are also relatively high among the service staff of the above-mentioned Asian airlines. Therefore, concentrating on enhancing software with the maximum utilization of skilled manpower will help airlines to attain a premium brand value while keeping prices at a reasonably low level.

6.3 Limitations and Recommendations for Future Research

Many countries and carriers are members of ICAO and IATA. The member carriers submit data and information on the basis of standardized instructions and defini-tions issued by ICAO and IATA either on a monthly or annual basis. The data includes operational, traffic, and capacity statistics for all types of services—i.e., passenger, freight, and mail services. However, access to such data, including the financial performance of airlines, for research purposes is very limited except for data on some US carriers. Given such constraints in accessing data and information, we could not include disaggregated data on airline expenses, employment activities, and airline fleet figures during the sample period. Therefore, our estimation results do not fully incorporate those variables that could have a major positive impact on airline performance analysis.

Apart from passenger and cargo operations, some airlines engage in non-airline activities such as catering, hotel businesses, and ground transportation services. Therefore, the employment and expenses attributed to these operations should be separated when analyzing the impacts of the explanatory variables on output and cost. Alternatively, this group of airlines should be identified and the difference be captured using a dummy variable in the estimation of frontier functions. Due to data unavailability, however, we failed to capture the detailed effects of such nonspecialized activities.

As for the model specification and estimation, if industry-level data on airlines were available, including input prices and output data of each country, the various alternatives of the second step or determinants of estimation of efficiency and industry-level variables would be more feasible. Such analyses will show ways to a better comparison of competitiveness within the airline industry at the country level. A comparison of the airline industry's competitiveness with related sectors such as tourism and transportation related to exports is a promising area for future research.

6.4 Conclusion and Policy Recommendations

International tourist arrivals increased to 1133 million in 2014 from only 25 million in 1995. The American region recorded the strongest growth, with an 8 % increase in international arrivals, followed by Asia-Pacific and the Middle East that experienced a 5 % growth (UNWTO 2015). This trend suggests that the industry will continue to expand its services across regions.

Despite continued economic volatility around the globe, the demand for international travel held up well throughout the recent years, and its future prospects for growth are promising.[6] The growth of tourism is set to be a main driver of the Asia region's airline industry. Except for a few cases, our estimation result strongly suggests that in order to achieve sustainable global competitiveness, which can be done through maximization of production and cost efficiency, airlines need to expand their market shares, optimally reallocate manpower and other costs between domestic and international operations, and intensify the cost saving efforts of airline alliances by sharing networks for check-in facilities, training centers, and other facilities.

---

[6]According to the prospects for 2015 by UNWTO, Asia and the Pacific and the Americas will have +4 to +5 % growth in 2015, followed by Europe (+3 to +4 %), the Middle East (+2 to +5 %) and Africa (+3 to +5 %).

Since wages in most parts of Asia-Pacific are increasing rapidly, airlines can no longer rely on business models based on cheap labor. Instead, Asian carriers should focus more on efficiency improvement through better reallocation of resources and maximum utilization of the high level of human resources in this region. At the same time, the growth of airlines is closely related to the growth of global trade. Rapid growth of trade will foster and facilitate the growth of airlines as well. Airlines, in return, will contribute to a country's economy by creating revenues and jobs, and expedite the globalization of the country by augmenting and improving the mobility of goods, services, and people. Achieving the global competitiveness of airlines by improving efficiency will therefore benefit both the industry itself and the economy at large, which, in turn, will benefit and mutually strengthen each other. This understanding of course ignores the environmental effects of expanding airline services.

Airline competitiveness analysis has a special resonance in Korea, which has a rapidly expanding airline industry. Furthermore, Incheon airport has emerged as a major air travel hub in East Asia, and air transportation is a key tool for Korea's dynamic export sector. At the same time, Asia, especially East Asia, now has a well-developed, globally competitive manufacturing sector, but its services sector still lags far behind the advanced economies. As such, a competitiveness analysis of the airline industry, one of the most important service industries, can help Asian policymakers to better prepare for the liberalization of the services sector, which is expected to attain momentum in the coming years.

Appendix 6.1: Mean of Air Liberalization Index (ALI) by Countries, 1998–2012

Code	Airline	Country	Mean ALI	Openness rank	Output rank	PRTE efficiency rank	CRTE efficiency rank
AA	American Airlines	United States	8776.633	1	1	11	39
AC	Air Canada	Canada	2160.6	16	12	19	19
AF	Air France	France	2780.4	12	6	8	32
AI	Air India	India	2200.4	15	29	18	17
AV	AVIANCA	Colombia	716.9	37	39	37	6
AY	Finn air	Finland	1313.4	31	34	33	10
AZ	Alitalia	Italy	1186.7	32	27	28	26
BA	British Airways	United Kingdom	4534.9	5	5	4	29
CA	Air China	China	1523.8	27	15	14	30
CX	Cathay Pacific Airways	Hong Kong SAR, China	2576.9	13	8	3	20

(continued)

(continued)

Code	Airline	Country	Mean ALI	Openness rank	Output rank	PRTE efficiency rank	CRTE efficiency rank
CZ	China Southern Airlines	China	1523.8	28	19	20	35
DL	Delta Air Lines	United States	8583.9	2	4	13	34
EI	Air Lingus	Ireland	630.1	39	38	39	2
GA	GARUDA	Indonesia	1054.8	33	32	29	4
IB	IBERIA	Spain	1891.2	23	17	23	23
JJ	TAM Linhas Aereas	Brazil	1869.8	25	31	31	14
JL	Japan Airlines	Japan	2017.8	17	10	7	33
KE	Korean Air	Korea	1717.1	26	9	1	18
LA	LAN Airlines	Chile	1887	24	23	24	9
LH	Lufthansa	Germany	3345.9	10	3	2	37
LX	SWISS Air	Switzerland	4281	6	21	25	13
LY	El Al	Israel	951	35	30	36	1
MH	Malaysia Airlines	Malaysia	1952.2	21	16	10	22
MU	China Eastern Airlines	China	1523.8	29	20	15	27
NH	ALL Nippon Airways	Japan	2017.8	18	14	17	38
NZ	Air New Zealand	New Zealand	3842.5	8	24	16	16
OS	Austrian	Austria	1904.8	22	33	34	12
PR	Philippine Airlines	Philippines	1483.7	30	35	22	3
QF	Qantas Airways	Australia	4198.2	7	11	6	31
QR	Qatar Airways	Qatar	995	34	36	38	5
SK	SAS Scandinavian Airlines	Sweden	2865.2	11	25	30	25
SQ	Singapore Airlines	Singapore	3701.5	9	7	5	21
SU	Aeroflot Russian Airlines	Russian Federation	2562.8	14	28	26	7
SV	Saudi Arabian Airlines	Saudi Arabia	710.6	38	22	21	15

(continued)

(continued)

Code	Airline	Country	Mean ALI	Openness rank	Output rank	PRTE efficiency rank	CRTE efficiency rank
TG	Thai Airways	Thailand	1962	20	13	9	24
TK	Turkish Airlines	Turkey	1997.3	19	26	27	11
TP	TAP Portugal	Portugal	842.4	36	37	35	8
UA	United Airlines	United States	8583.9	3	2	12	36
US	US Airways	United States	8583.9	4	18	32	28

Source www.wto.org/asap/index.html
Note We accumulated the ALI index for each country over the period of 1998–2012 who signed the bilateral agreement with other countries and the 2011 year data was replicated for the 2012

Appendix 6.2: Types of Air Services Agreements (ASA)

Type	Freedoms	Designation	Withholding/ownership	Tariffs	Capacity
A	3rd and 4th	Single designation	Substantive ownership and effective control	Double approval	Predetermination
B	3rd and 4th	Multi designation	Substantive ownership and effective control	Double approval	Predetermination
C	3rd, 4th, 5th	Single designation	Substantive ownership and effective control	Double approval	Predetermination
D	3rd, 4th, 5th	Single designation	Substantive ownership and effective control	Double approval	Bermuda 1
E	3rd, 4th, 5th	Multi designation	Substantive ownership and effective control	Double approval	Predetermination
F	3rd, 4th, 5th	Multi designation	Substantive ownership and effective control	Double approval	Bermuda 1
G	3rd, 4th, 5th	Multi designation	Substantive ownership and effective control or community of interest or principal of business	Free pricing or Double approval	Free determination
I Incomplete ICAO coding	If either		"n/a"	"n/a"	"Other"
O All other combinations					

Source http://www.wto.org/asap/resource/data/html/methodology_e.htm

Appendix 6.3: Air Liberalization Index (ALI) Weighting Systems

Element	Air Liberalization Index			
	Standard	5th+	OWN+	DES+
Grant of rights				
Fifth freedom	6	12	5	
Seventh freedom	6	5	5	5.5
Cabotage	6	5	5	5.5
Capacity				
Predetermination	0	0	0	0
"Other restrictive"	2	1.5	1.5	1.5
Bermuda 1	4	3.5	3.5	3.5
"Other liberal"	6	5	5	5.5
Free determination	8	7	7	7.5
Tariffs				
Dual approval	0	0	0	0
Economy of origin	3	2.5	2.5	2.5
Dual disapproval				
Zone pricing	8 4 / 7	7 3.5 / 6	7 3.5 / 6	7.5 3.5 / 6
Free pricing	8	7	7	7.5
Withholding				
Substantial ownership and effective control	0	0	0	0
Community of interest	4	3.5	7	3.5
Principal place of business	8	7	14	7.5
Designation				
Single designation	0	0	0	0
Multiple designation	4	3.5	3.5	7.5
Statistics				
Exchange of statistics	0	0	0	0
No exchange of statistics	1	1	1	1
Cooperative arrangement				
Not allowed	0	0	0	0
Allowed	3	2.5	2.5	2.5
Total	50	50	50	50

Source http://www.wto.org/asap/resource/data/html/methodology_e.htm

Note Weighted Air Liberalization Index (WALI): The WALI is a synthetic measure of the openness of the air transport policy of a given Signatory. It is calculated as an average of the ALIs of all the ASAs concluded by that Signatory, weighted by the respective traffic they cover. WALIs are computed for all four ALI weighting systems

WASA: WASA refers to the World Air Services Agreements database produced by the International Civil Aviation Organization (ICAO)

ASAP traffic: The traffic covered by the ASAs concluded by the Signatory concerned, as captured in ASAP

ASAP traffic share: The traffic covered by the ASAs concluded by the Signatory concerned as a share of the total traffic covered by the ASAs included in ASAP

Appendix 6.4: Airlines with Within Airline Operating Status

Country	Airline within airline	Ownership	Start
Germany	Germanwings	100 % by Lufthansa	2002
Belgium	Jetairflya	100 % by TUI	2005
Netherlands	Transavia	100 % by KLM	2003
France	Transavia	60 % by Air France	2007
Czech Republic	SmartWings	100 % by Travel service	2004
Spain	Iberia Express	100 % by IAGD	2012
Spain	Vueling	46 % by Iberia	2004
Italy	Air One	100 % by Alitalia	2010
Italy	Blu-Express	100 % by Blue Panorama	2005
Turkey	AnadoluJet	100 % by Turkish	2008
South	Africa Kulula	90 % by Comair	2001
South	Africa Mango	100 % by South African	2006
India	Air India Express	100 % by Air India	2005
India	Jet Konnect	100 % by Jet Airways	2009
India	Kingfisher Redi	100 % by Kingfisher	2008
Thailand	Nok Air	49 % by Thai Airways	2006
Malaysia	Firefly	100 % by Malaysia Airlines	2007
Singapore	Jetstar Asia	49 % by Qantas	2004
Singapore	Tiger	100 % by Tiger Airways hold	2004
Singapore	Scoot	100 % by Singapore Airlines	2012
Vietnam	Jetstar Pacific	100 % by Vietnam Airlines	2008
Indonesia	Citilink	100 % by GARUDA	2008
Philippines	AirPhil Express	100 % by Philippine Airlines	2010
South Korea	Air Busan	46 % by Asiana	2008
South Korea	Jin	100 % by Korean Air	2006
Japan	Air Japan	100 % by All Nippon	2003
Japan	JAL express	100 % by Japan Airlines	1998
Japan	Peach	39 % by All Nippon	2012
Japan	Jetstar	42 % by All Nippon	2012
Australia/NZ	Jetstar	100 % by Qantas	2003

Source Pearson and Merkert (2014, Table 2 "Highlights of presently-operating AWAs")

References

Barbot G, Costa A, Sochirca E (2008) Airlines performance in the new market context: a comparative productivity and efficiency analysis. J Air Transp Manag 14:270–274

Battese G, Coelli TJ (1992) Frontier production functions, technical efficiency and panel data: with application to paddy farmers in India. J Prod Anal 3:153–169

Battese G, Coelli TJ (1995) A model for technical in efficiency effects in a stochastic frontier production function for panel data. Empirical Econ 20:325–332

Bloom N, Van Reenen J (2006). Measuring and Explaining Management Practices Across Firms and Countries. CEP Discussion Paper No. 716, Published by Centre for Economic Performance London School of Economics and Political Science

Chan D (2000) Air wars in Asia: competitive and collaborative strategies and tactics in action. J Manag Dev 19(6):473–488

Clougherty JA (2009) Domestic rivalry and export performance: theory and evidence from international airline markets, Canadian economics association. Can J Econ/Revue Canadienne d'Economique 42(2):440–468

Coelli T (1996) FRONTIER version 4.1: a computer program for stochastic frontier production and cost function estimation. Working paper 96/7, CEPA, Department of Econometrics, University of New England, Armidale

Demydyuk G (2012) Optimal financial key performance indicators: evidence from the airline industry. Acc Taxation 4(1):39–51

Heshmati A (2003) Productivity growth, efficiency and outsourcing in manufacturing and services. J Econ Surv 17(1):79–112

Kontsas S, Mylonakis J (2008) Pricing competition policy in the European airlines industry: a firm behavior model proposal. Innovative Mark 4(4):23–27

Kumbhakar SC, Lovell CAK (2000) Stochastic frontier analysis. Cambridge University Press, Cambridge

Kumbhakar SC, Wan H, Horncastle A (2015) A practitioner's guide to stochastic frontier analysis using stata. Academic

Lee CY, Johnson AL (2011) Two-dimensional efficiency decomposition to measure he demand effect in productivity, analysis. Eur J Oper Res 216:584–593

Liang J (2013) An econometric analysis on pricing and market structure in the U.S. airline industry. Adv Econometrics 3(2):1–28

Nickell SJ (1996) Competition and corporate performance. J Polit Econ 104(4):724–746

Oum TH, Yu C (1998) Cost competitiveness of major airlines: an international comparison. Elsevier Sci 32(6):407–422

Oum TH, Zhang A, Fu X (2010) Air transport liberalization and its impacts on airline competition and air passenger traffic. Transp J 49(4):24–41

Pearce B (2012) The state of air transport markets and the airline industry after the great recession. J Air Transp Manag 21:3–9

Pearson J, Merkert R (2014) Airlines-within-airlines: a business model moving East. J Air Transp Manag 38:21–26

Porter ME (1986) Competition in global industries. Harvard Business Press, Boston

Porter ME (1990) The competitive advantage of nations. Harvard Business Review, Boston

Sakakibara M, Porter ME (2001) Competing at home to win abroad: evidence from Japanese industry. Rev Econ Stat 83(2):310–322

Sjogren S, Soderberg M (2011) Productivity of airline carriers and its relation to deregulation, privatization and membership in strategic alliances. Transp Res Part E Logistics and Transp Rev 47:228–237

World tourism organization (UNWTO) (2015) UNWTO tourism highlights 2015 edition (press release) UNWTO, 25 June 2015. Retrieved 3 July 2015

World Trade Organization. www.wto.org/asap/index.html

Index of Authors

© Springer Science+Business Media Singapore 2016
A. Heshmati and J. Kim, *Efficiency and Competitiveness
of International Airlines*, DOI 10.1007/978-981-10-1017-0

Index of Subjects

A

Additive error term, 76
Aeroflot Russian airlines, 166, 170
Age of aircraft, 85, 89, 97
Airbus, 56, 174
Air Canada, 11, 81, 118, 145, 176
Air cargo services, 28
Air China, 12, 81, 118, 145, 166, 176
Aircraft, 2, 3, 19–24, 28, 37, 41, 44, 51, 53, 59,
    61, 64, 69, 71, 80, 84, 85, 88, 97, 106, 112,
    124, 127, 131, 139, 144, 167, 168
Aircraft fleet series, 23
Airfare, 67, 68, 97, 98, 140, 172
Air federation, 13
Air France, 12, 82, 118, 145, 173, 176, 180
Airfreight, 27
Air India, 12, 81
Air liberalization index, 170, 171
Airline competitiveness analysis, 5, 176
Airline designation, 67
Airline industry, 1, 3–8, 10, 16, 20, 22, 25–28,
    30, 32–34, 36, 51–53, 55, 59, 60, 64, 65,
    67, 87, 99, 106, 124, 137, 150, 155, 156,
    169, 171, 174–176
Airlines, 1–3, 5, 6, 8–10, 16, 18, 19, 21–25,
    27–29, 32, 34, 38, 52, 53, 56, 59–61, 63,
    65–68, 80, 83–85, 88, 90, 95–100, 104,
    106, 108, 111, 112, 124, 127, 129–133,
    136, 137, 139–142, 144, 148, 150, 152,
    153, 155, 156, 165–169, 172–175
Airlines' competitiveness, 4, 8, 113
Airline security, 59, 123
Airlines strategy, 168
Airlines sustainable competitiveness, 8, 113
Airlines within airlines, 173, 180
Air Lingus, 12, 82, 145, 177
Airmail, 56
Air New Zealand, 12, 81, 118, 146, 177
Airplanes, 61, 123

Airport, 2, 3, 32, 34, 53, 59, 65, 84, 123, 129,
    131, 133, 168, 173
Airport lounges, 140, 169
Airport presence, 32
Air services agreements, 170, 178
Air transport market, 27–29
Air travel demand, 36–38, 110, 153
Airways, 168
Alitalia, 12, 82, 118, 145, 173, 176, 180
Alliance, 6, 8, 29, 30, 39, 53, 84, 85, 88, 98,
    103, 107, 108, 112, 124, 129, 131, 133,
    140–142, 150, 152, 156, 166, 168, 169
All Nippon Airways, 12, 18, 81, 99, 140
Allocative efficiency, 7, 15, 19, 20, 79, 125,
    166
Amenities, 152
American airlines, 18, 99, 141
Antitrust immunity, 29, 30, 99
Arrivals, 175
Asia, 5, 16, 28, 31, 99, 110, 130, 140, 150,
    166, 172, 174
Asian carriers, 18, 89, 99, 103, 104, 112, 140,
    143, 156, 166, 174, 176
Austrian, 12, 82, 118, 146, 177
Available ton kilometers of cargo, 129
Available ton kilometers of passenger, 129
Aviation, 1, 2, 5, 38, 52, 65, 66, 85, 172
Aviation industry, 29, 61, 64

B

Bankruptcy, 156
Bayesian random stochastic frontier model, 19,
    41
Bermuda, 67, 179
Bilateral agreements, 10, 28, 31, 65, 109, 142
Bilateral air service agreements, 65, 67
Biofuel, 56
Biotechnology, 36
Boarding, 168

© Springer Science+Business Media Singapore 2016   187
A. Heshmati and J. Kim, *Efficiency and Competitiveness*
of International Airlines, DOI 10.1007/978-981-10-1017-0

Lightning Source UK Ltd.
Milton Keynes UK
UKOW01n2214080917
308851UK00010B/133/P

9 789811 010156